Android™ Database Best Practices

About the Android Deep Dive Series

Zigurd Mednieks, Series Editor

The Android Deep Dive Series is for intermediate and expert developers who use Android Studio and Java, but do not have comprehensive knowledge of Android system-level programming or deep knowledge of Android APIs. Readers of this series want to bolster their knowledge of fundamentally important topics.

Each book in the series stands alone and provides expertise, idioms, frameworks, and engineering approaches. They provide in-depth information, correct patterns and idioms, and ways of avoiding bugs and other problems. The books also take advantage of new Android releases, and avoid deprecated parts of the APIs.

About the Series Editor

Zigurd Mednieks is a consultant to leading OEMs, enterprises, and entrepreneurial ventures creating Android-based systems and software. Previously he was chief architect at D2 Technologies, a voice-over-IP (VoIP) technology provider, and a founder of OpenMobile, an Android-compatibility technology company. At D2 he led engineering and product definition work for products that blended communication and social media in purpose-built embedded systems and on the Android platform. He is lead author of *Programming Android* and *Enterprise Android*.

Android™ Database Best Practices

Adam Stroud

✦✦Addison-Wesley

Boston • Columbus • Indianapolis • New York • San Francisco • Amsterdam • Cape Town
Dubai • London • Madrid • Milan • Munich • Paris • Montreal • Toronto • Delhi • Mexico City
São Paulo • Sydney • Hong Kong • Seoul • Singapore • Taipei • Tokyo

Library of Congress Control Number: 2016941977

ISBN-13: 978-0-13-443799-6
ISBN-10: 0-13-443799-3

Text printed in the United States on recycled paper at RR Donnelley in Crawfordsville, Indiana.
1   16

Publisher
Mark L. Taub

Executive Editor
Laura Lewin

Development Editor
Michael Thurston

Managing Editor
Sandra Schroeder

Full-Service Production Manager
Julie B. Nahil

Project Editor
codeMantra

Copy Editor
Barbara Wood

Indexer
Cheryl Lenser

Proofreader
codeMantra

Editorial Assistant
Olivia Basegio

Cover Designer
Chuti Prasertsith

Compositor
codeMantra

To my wife, Sabrina, and my daughters, Elizabeth and Abigail.
You support, inspire, and motivate me in everything you do.

Contents in Brief

Contents

Preface

The explosion in the number of mobile devices in all parts of the word has led to an increase in both the number and complexity of mobile apps. What was once considered a platform for only simplistic applications now contains countless apps with considerable functionality. Because a mobile device is capable of receiving large amounts of data from multiple data sources, there is an increasing need to store and recall that data efficiently.

In traditional software systems, large sets of data are frequently stored in a database that can be optimized to both store the data as well as recall the data on demand. Android provides this same functionality and includes a database system, SQLite. SQLite provides enough power to support today's modern apps and also can perform well in the resource-constrained environment of most mobile devices. This book provides details on how to use the embedded Android database system. Additionally, the book contains advice inspired by problems encountered when writing "real-world" Android apps.

Who Should Read This Book

This book is written for developers who have at least some experience with writing Android apps. Specifically, an understanding of basic Android components (activities, fragments, intents, and the application manifest) is assumed, and familiarity with the Android threading model is helpful.

At least some knowledge of relational database systems is also helpful but is not necessarily a prerequisite for understanding the topics in this book.

How This Book Is Organized

This book begins with a discussion of the theory behind relational databases as well as some history of the relational model and how it came into existence. Next, the discussion moves to the Structured Query Language (SQL) and how to use SQL to build a database as well as manipulate and read a database. The discussion of SQL provides some details on Android specifics but generally discusses non-Android-specific SQL.

From there, the book moves on to provide information on SQLite and how it relates to Android. The book also covers the Android APIs that can be used to interact with a database as well as some best practices for database use.

With the basics of database, SQL, and SQLite covered, the book then moves into solving some of the problems app developers often face while using a database in Android. Topics such as threading, accessing remote data, and displaying data to the user are covered. Additionally, the book presents an example database access layer based on a content provider.

Following is an overview of each of the chapters:

- Chapter 1, "Relational Databases," provides an introduction to the relational database model as well as some information on why the relational model is more popular than older database models.
- Chapter 2, "An Introduction to SQL," provides details on SQL as it relates to databases in general. This chapter discusses the SQL language features for creating database structure as well as the features used to manipulate data in a database.
- Chapter 3, "An Introduction to SQLite," contains details of the SQLite database system, including how SQLite differs from other database systems.
- Chapter 4, "SQLite in Android," discusses the Android-specific SQLite details such as where a database resides for an app. It also discusses accessing a database from outside an app, which can be important for debugging.
- Chapter 5, "Working with Databases in Android," presents the Android API for working with databases and explains how to get data from an app to a database and back again.
- Chapter 6, "Content Providers," discusses the details around using a content provider as a data access mechanism in Android as well as some thoughts on when to use one.
- Chapter 7, "Databases and the UI," explains how to get data from the local database and display it to the user, taking into account some of the threading concerns that exist on Android.
- Chapter 8, "Sharing Data with Intents," discusses ways, other than using content providers, that data can be shared between apps, specifically by using intents.
- Chapter 9, "Communicating with Web APIs," discusses some of the methods and tools used to achieve two-way communication between an app and a remote Web API.
- Chapter 10, "Data Binding," discusses the data binding API and how it can be used to display data in the UI. In addition to providing an overview of the API, this chapter provides an example of how to view data from a database.

Example Code

This book includes a lot of source code examples, including an example app that is discussed in later chapters of the book. Readers are encouraged to download the example source code and manipulate it to gain a deeper understanding of the information presented in the text.

The example app is a Gradle-based Android project that should build and run. It was built with the latest libraries and build tools that were available at the time of this writing.

The source code for the example can be found on GitHub at https://github.com/android-database-best-practices/device-database. It is made available under the Apache 2 open-source license and can be used according to that license.

Conventions Used in This Book

The following typographical conventions are used in this book:

- `Constant width` is used for program listings, as well as within paragraphs to refer to program elements such as variable and function names, databases, data types, environment variables, statements, and keywords.
- **`Constant width bold`** is used to highlight sections of code.

Note
A Note signifies a tip, suggestion, or general note.

Register your copy of *Android™ Database Best Practices* at informit.com for convenient access to downloads, updates, and corrections as they become available. To start the registration process, go to informit.com/register and log in or create an account. Enter the product ISBN (9780134437996) and click Submit. Once the process is complete, you will find any available bonus content under "Registered Products."

Acknowledgments

I have often believed that software development is a team sport. Well, I am now convinced that authoring is also a team sport. I would not have made it through this experience without the support, guidance, and at times patience of the team. I would like to thank executive editor Laura Lewin and editorial assistant Olivia Basegio for their countless hours and limitless e-mails to help keep the project on schedule.

I would also like to thank my development editor, Michael Thurston, and technical editors, Maija Mednieks, Zigurd Mednieks, and David Whittaker, for helping me transform my unfinished, random, and meandering thoughts into something directed and cohesive. The support of the team is what truly made this a rewarding experience, and it would not have been possible without all of you.

Last, I would like to thank my beautiful wife and wonderful daughters. Your patience and support have meant more than I can express.

About the Author

Adam Stroud is an Android developer who has been developing apps for Android since 2010. He has been an early employee at multiple start-ups, including Runkeeper, Mustbin, and Chef Nightly, and has led the Android development from the ground up. He has a strong passion for Android and open source and seems to be attracted to all things Android.

In addition to writing code, he has written other books on Android development and enjoys giving talks on a wide range of topics, including Android gaining root access on Android devices. He loves being a part of the Android community and getting together with other Android enthusiasts to "geek out."

Adam is currently the technical cofounder and lead Android developer at a new start-up where he oversees the development of the Android app.

Relational Databases

The relational database model is one of the more popular models for databases today. Android comes with a built-in database called SQLite that is designed around the relational database model. This chapter covers some of the basic concepts of a relational database. It starts with a brief history of databases, then moves to a discussion of the relational model. Finally, it covers the evolution of database languages. This chapter is meant for the reader who is largely unfamiliar with the concept of a relational database. Readers who feel comfortable with the concepts of a relational database can safely move on to chapters that discuss the unique features of the SQLite database system that comes bundled with Android.

History of Databases

Like other aspects of the world of computing, modern databases evolved over time. While we tend to talk about NoSQL and relational databases nowadays, it is sometimes important to know "how we got here" to understand why things work the way they do. This section of the chapter presents a little history of how the database evolved into what it is today.

> **Note**
>
> This section of the chapter presents information that may be of interest to some but seem superfluous to others. Feel free to move on to the next section to get into the details of how databases work on Android.

The problem of storing, managing, and recalling data is not a new one. Even decades before computers, people were storing, managing, and recalling data. It is easy to think of a paper-based system where important data was manually written, then organized and stored in a filing cabinet until it would need to be recalled. I need only to look in the corner of my basement to be reminded of the days when this was a common paradigm for data storage.

The paper-based approach has obvious limitations, the main one being its ability to scale as the amount of data grows. As the amount of data increases, so does the amount of time it takes to both manage the data store and recall data from the data store.

A paper-based approach also implies a highly manual process for data storage and retrieval, making it slow and error prone as well taking up a lot of space.

Early attempts to offload some of this process onto machines followed a very similar approach. The difference was that instead of using hard copies of the data written on paper, data was stored and organized electronically. In a typical electronic-file-based system, a single file would contain multiple entries of data that was somehow related to other data in the file.

While this approach did offer benefits over older approaches, it still had many problems. Typically, these file stores were not centralized. This led to large amounts of redundant data, which made processing slow and took large amounts of storage space. Additionally, problems with incompatible file formats were also frequent because there was rarely a common system in charge of controlling the data. In addition, there were often difficulties in changing the structure of the data as the usage of the data evolved over time.

Databases were an attempt to address the problems of decentralized file stores. Database technology is relatively new when compared to other technological fields, or even other areas of computer science. This is primarily because the computer itself had to evolve to a point where databases provided enough utility to justify their expense. It wasn't until the early to mid-1960s that computers became cheap enough to be owned by private entities as well as possess enough power and storage capacity to allow the concept of a database to be useful.

The first databases used models that are different from the relational model discussed in this chapter. In the early days, the two main models in widespread use were the network model and the hierarchical model.

Hierarchical Model

In the hierarchical model data is organized into a tree structure. The model maintains a one-to-many relationship between child and parent records with each child node having no more than one parent. However, each parent node may have multiple children. An initial implementation of the hierarchical model was developed jointly by IBM and Rockwell in the 1960s for the Apollo space program. This implementation was named the IBM Information Management System (IMS). In addition to providing a database, IMS could be used to generate reports. The combination of these two features made IMS one of the major software applications of its time and helped establish IBM as a major player in the computer world. IMS is still a widely used hierarchical database system on mainframes.

Network Model

The network model was another popular early database model. Unlike the hierarchical model, the network model formed a graph structure that removed the limitation of the one-to-many parent/child node relationship. This structure allowed the model to represent more complex data structures and relations. In addition, the network model was standardized by the Conference on Data Systems Language (CODASYL) in the late 1960s.

The Introduction of the Relational Model

The relational database model was introduced by Edgar Codd in 1970 in his paper "A Relational Model of Data for Large Shared Data Banks." The paper outlined some of the problems of the models of the time as well as introduced a new model for efficiently storing data. Codd went into details about how a relational model solved some of the shortcomings of the current models and discussed some areas where a relational model needed to be enhanced.

This was viewed as the introduction to relational databases and caused the idea to be improved and evolve into the relational database systems that we use today. While very few, if any, modern database systems strictly follow the guidelines that Codd outlined in his paper, they do implement most of his ideas and realize many of the benefits.

The Relational Model

The relational model makes use of the mathematical concept of a relation to add structure to data that is stored in a database. The model has a foundation based in set theory and first-order predicate logic. The cornerstone of the relational model is the relation.

Relation

In the relational model, conceptual data (the modeling of real-world data and its relationships) is mapped into relations. A relation can be thought of as a table with rows and columns. The columns of a relation represent its **attributes**, and the rows represent an entry in the table or a **tuple**. In addition to having attributes and tuples, the relational model mandates that the relation have a formal name.

Let's consider an example of a relation that can be used to track Android OS versions. In the relation, we want to model a subset of data from the Android dashboard (https://developer.android.com/about/dashboards/index.html). We will name this relation os.

The relation depicted in Table 1.1 has three attributes—version, codename, and api—representing the properties of the relation. In addition, the relation has four tuples tracking Android OS versions 5.1, 5.0, 4.4, and 4.3. Each tuple can be thought of as an entry in the relation that has properties defined by the relation attributes.

Table 1.1 The os Relation

version	codename	api
5.1	Lollipop	22
5.0	Lollipop	21
4.4	KitKat	19
4.3	Jelly Bean	18

Attribute

The attributes of a relation provide the data points for each tuple. In order to add structure to a relation, each attribute is assigned a **domain** that defines what data values can be represented by the attribute. The domain can place restrictions on the type of data that can be represented by an attribute as well as the range of values that an attribute can have. In the previous example, the api attribute is limited to the domain of integers and is said to be of type integer. Additionally, the domain of the api attribute can be further reduced to the set of positive integers (an upper bound can also be defined if the need arises).

The concept of a domain for a relation is important to the relational model as it allows the relation to establish constraints on attribute data. This becomes useful in maintaining data integrity and ensuring that the attributes of a relation are not misused. In the relation depicted in Table 1.1, a string api value could make certain operations difficult or allow operations to produce unpredictable results. Imagine adding a tuple to the os relation that contains a nonnumeric value for the api attribute, then asking the database to return all os versions with an api value that is greater than 19. The results would be unintuitive and possibly misleading.

The number of attributes in a relation is referred to as its **degree**. The relation in Table 1.1 has a degree of three because it has three attributes. A relation with a degree of one is called a **unary** relation. Similarly, a relation with a degree of two is **binary**, and a relation with a degree of three is called **ternary**. A relation with a degree higher than three is referred to as an **n-ary** relation.

Tuples

Tuples are represented by rows in the tabular representation of a relation. They represent the data of the relation containing values for the relation's attributes.

The number of tuples in a relation is called its **cardinality**. The relation in Table 1.1 has a cardinality of four since it contains four tuples.

An important point regarding a relation's cardinality and its degree is the level of volatility. A relation's degree helps define its structure and will change infrequently. A change in the degree is a change in the relation itself.

In contrast, a relation's cardinality will change with high frequency. Every time a tuple is added or removed from a relation, the relation's cardinality changes. In a large-scale database, the cardinality could change several times per second, but the degree may not change for days at a time, or indeed ever.

Intension/Extension

A relation's attributes and the attributes' domains and any other constraints on attribute values define a relation's **intension**. A relation's tuples define its **extension**. Since intension and extension are related to cardinality and degree respectively, it is easy to see that a relation's intension will also remain fairly static whereas it extension is dynamic, changing as tuples are added, deleted, and modified. A relation's degree is a property of its intension, and its cardinality is a property of its extension.

Schema

The structure of a relation is defined by its relational **schema**. A schema is a list of attributes along with the specification of the domain for those attributes. While the tabular form of a relation (Table 1.1) allows us to deduce the schema of a relation, a schema can also be specified in text. Here is the text representation of the schema from Table 1.1:

```
os(version, codename, api)
```

Notice the name of the relation along with the list of the attributes. In addition, the primary key is sometimes indicated with bold column names. Primary keys are discussed later in the chapter.

Properties of a Relation

Each relation in the relational model must follow a set of rules. These rules allow the relation to effectively represent real-world data models as well as address some of the limitations of older database systems. Relations that adhere to the following set of rules conform to a property known as the **first normal form**:

- **Unique name**: Each relation must have a name that uniquely identifies it. This allows the relation to be identified in the system.
- **Uniquely named attributes**: In addition to a uniquely named relation, each attribute in a relation must have a unique name. Much like the relation name, the attribute's unique name allows it to be identified.
- **Single-valued attributes**: Each attribute in a relation can have at most one value associated with it per tuple. In the example in Table 1.1, each api level attribute has only a single integer value. Including a tuple that has multiple values (19 and 20) is considered bad form.
- **Domain-limited attribute values**: As discussed previously, the value of each attribute for a tuple must conform to the attribute's domain. The domain for an attribute defines the attribute's "legal" values.
- **Unique tuples**: There should be no duplicate tuples in the relation. While there may be parts of a tuple that have common values for a subset of the relation's attributes, no two tuples should be identical.
- **Insignificant attribute ordering**: The order of the attributes in a relation has no effect on the representation of the relation of the tuples defined in the relation. This is because each attribute has a unique name that is used to refer to that attribute.

  For example, in Table 1.1, if the column ordering of the codename and api attributes were switched, the relation would remain the same. This is because the attributes are referred to by their unique names rather than their column ordering.
- **Insignificant tuple ordering**: The order of the tuples in a relation has no effect on the relation. While tuples can be added and removed, their ordering has no significance for the relation.

Relationships

Most conceptual data models require a relational model that contains multiple relations. Fortunately, the relational model allows relationships between multiple relations to be defined to support this. In order to define relationships between two relations, keys must be defined for them. A **key** is a set of attributes that uniquely identify a tuple in a relation. A key is frequently used to relate one relation to another and allows for complex data models to be represented as a relational model.

- **Superkey**: A superkey is a set of attributes that uniquely identify a tuple in a relation. There are no limits placed on the number of attributes used to form a superkey. This means that the set of all attributes should define a superkey that is used for all tuples.

- **Candidate key**: A candidate key is the smallest set of attributes that uniquely identify a tuple in a relation. A candidate key is like a superkey with a constraint placed on the maximum number of attributes. No subset of attributes from a candidate key should uniquely identify a tuple. There may be multiple candidate keys in a relation.

- **Primary key**: The primary key is a candidate key that is chosen to be the primary key. It holds all the properties of a candidate key but has the added distinction of being the primary key. While there may be multiple candidate keys in a relation that all uniquely identify a single row, there can be only *one* primary key.

- **Foreign key**: A foreign key is a set of attributes in a relation that map to a candidate key in another relation.

The foreign key is what allows two relations to be related to one another. Such relationships can be any of three different types:

- **One-to-one relationship**: The one-to-one relationship maps a single row in table A to a single row in table B. Additionally, the row in table B *only* maps back to the single row in table A (see Figure 1.1).

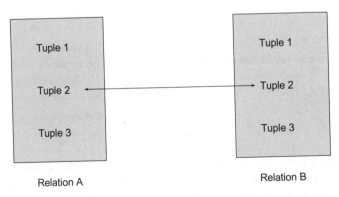

Figure 1.1   One-to-one relationship

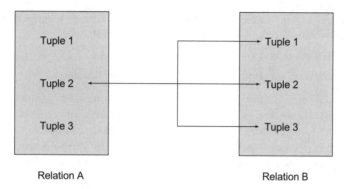

Figure 1.2 One-to-many relationship

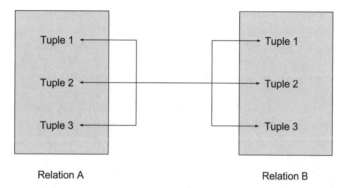

Figure 1.3 Many-to-many relationship

- **One-to-many relationship**: A one-to-many relationship maps a single row in table A to multiple other rows in table B. However, each row in table B maps to only a *single* row in table A (see Figure 1.2).

- **Many-to-many relationship**: A many-to-many relationship maps multiple rows in table A to multiple rows in table B and maps multiple rows in table B to multiple rows in table A (see Figure 1.3).

Referential Integrity

When using relationships in the relational model, it is important to ensure that a foreign key in a referenced table can be resolved to a tuple in the referring table. This concept is known as **referential integrity**. Most relational database management systems help to enforce referential integrity so that tables don't have foreign keys that cannot be resolved.

The concept of relationships is of great importance to the relational model as it allows the attributes of a relation to be atomic. For example, let's consider a conceptual data model that tracks mobile device information in addition to the os relation from Table 1.1. The relational schema for the database now looks like the following:

os(**version**, codename, api)

device(**version**, manufacturer, os_version, os_codename, os_api)

The device relation has attributes that define the characteristics of the hardware and the software. In addition, the os relation contains the characteristics of the OS software. If tuples are added, the tabular form of the relations would look like Table 1.2.

While the relation looks innocent enough, it has duplicate attributes that do not fit into a normalized form of the relational model. Specifically, values for the os_version, os_codename, and os_api attributes are repeated in multiple tuples in the relation. In addition, the same values are part of the os relation from Table 1.1. Now, imagine that an attribute of the os relation needs to be updated. In addition to directly modifying the os relation, each tuple of the device relation that references the os information needs to be updated. Duplicate copies of the data require multiple update operations when the data changes.

To solve this issue and make relations conform to a normal form, we can replace the os_version, os_codename, and os_api attributes in the device relation with the primary key from the os relation. This allows tuples in the device relation to *reference* tuples in the os relation. As mentioned previously, the primary key is a candidate key that is selected as the primary key.

The os relation has two candidate keys: the version and the api attributes. Notice that the codename attribute is *not* a candidate key as it does not uniquely identify a tuple in the relation (multiple tuples share the codename "Lollipop"). For this example, we use version as the primary key for the os relation. Using version as the primary key for os, we can rewrite the device relation to use the os foreign key to add the normalized relationship to the device relation. The updated device relation now looks like Table 1.3.

Table 1.2 device Relation

version	manufacturer	os_version	os_codename	os_api
Galaxy Nexus	Samsung	4.3	Jelly Bean	18
Nexus 5	LG	5.1	Lollipop	21
Nexus 6	Motorola	5.1	Lollipop	21

Table 1.3 Normalized device Relation

version	manufacturer	os_version
Galaxy Nexus	Samsung	4.3
Nexus 5	LG	5.1
Nexus 6	Motorola	5.1

With the updated structure, an update to the os relation is immediately reflected across the database since the duplicate attributes have been replaced by a reference to the os relation. Additionally, the device relation does not lose any os information since it can use the os_version attribute to look up attributes from the os relation.

Relational Languages

Thus far in the discussion of the relational model, we have focused on model structure. Tables, attributes, tuples, and domains provide a way to format the data so it fits the model, but we also need a way to both query and manipulate that model.

The two languages most used to manipulate a relational model are **relational algebra** and **relational calculus**. While relational algebra and relational calculus seem different, it is important to remember that they are equivalent. Any expression that can be written in one can also be written in the other.

Relational calculus, and to some extent relational algebra, is the basis for higher-level manipulation languages like SQL and SEQUEL. While a user does not directly use relational algebra or relational calculus to work with a database (higher-level languages are used instead), it is important to have at least a basic understanding of them to better comprehend what the higher-level languages are doing.

Relational Algebra

Relational algebra is a language that describes *how* the database should run a query in order to return the desired results. Because relational algebra describes how to run a query, it is referred to as a procedural language.

A relational algebra expression consists of two relations that act as operands and an operation. The operation produces an additional relation as output without any side effects on the input operands. Relations are closed under relational algebra, meaning that both the inputs and the outputs of an expression are relations. The closure property allows expressions to be nested using the output of one expression to be the input of another.

All relational algebra operations can be broken down into a base set of five operations. While other operations do exist, any operation outside the base set can be expressed in terms of the base set of operations. The base set of operations in relational algebra consists of **selection**, **projection**, **Cartesian product**, **union**, and **set difference**.

Relational algebra operations can operate on either a single relation (unary) or a pair of relations (binary). While most operations are binary, the selection and projection operations operate on a single relation and are unary.

In addition to the base operations, this section discusses the **intersection** and **join** operations.

To provide an example of relational algebra operations, consider the simple relations defined in Tables 1.4 and 1.5.

Table 1.4 Relation A

Color
Red
White
Blue

Table 1.5 Relation B

Color
Orange
White
Black

Table 1.6 A ∪ B

Color
Red
White
Blue
Orange
Black

Table 1.7 A ∩ B

Color
White

Union (A ∪ B)

The union operator produces a relation that includes all the tuples in the operand relations (see Table 1.6). It can be thought of as an "or" operation in that the output relation has all the members that are in either relation A OR relation B.

Intersection (A ∩ B)

The intersection operator produces a relation that includes all tuples in both relation A and relation B (see Table 1.7).

Difference (A − B)

The difference operator produces a relation that contains the tuples that are members of the left operand without the tuples that are members of the right operand (see Table 1.8).

Cartesian Product (A × B)

The Cartesian product produces a relation that includes all possible ordered pairings of all tuples from operand A with all tuples from operand B (see Table 1.9). The degree of the output relation is the sum of the degree of each operand relation. The cardinality of the output relation is the product of the cardinalities of the input relations. In our example, both relations A and B have a degree of 1. Therefore, the output relation has a degree of $1 + 1 = 2$. Similarly, both relations A and B have a cardinality of three, so the output relation has a degree of $3 * 3 = 9$.

Selection ($\sigma_{predicate}(A)$)

Selection produces a relation with only the tuples from the operand that satisfy a given predicate. Remember that, unlike the previous operations, selection is a unary operation and operates on only a single relation.

As an example of the selection operation, we again consider the os relation from earlier in the chapter. In the example, the os relation is being searched for all tuples that contain an api value that is greater than 19 (see Table 1.10).

Table 1.8 A − B

Color
Red
Blue

Table 1.9 A × B

A. Color	B. Color
Red	Orange
Red	White
Red	Black
White	Orange
White	White
White	Black
Blue	Orange
Blue	White
Blue	Black

Table 1.10 $\sigma_{api>19}$ (os)

version	codename	api
5.1	Lollipop	22
5.0	Lollipop	21

Table 1.11 ($\Pi_{codename}$(os))

codename
Lollipop
KitKat
Jelly Bean

Table 1.12   *A* ⋈ *B*

device.version	device.manufacturer	os.version	os.codename	os.api
Galaxy Nexus	Samsung	4.3	Jelly Bean	18
Nexus 5	LG	5.1	Lollipop	21
Nexus 6	Motorola	5.1	Lollipop	21

Projection ($\Pi_{a1, a2,...,an}$(A))

Projection produces a relation containing only the attributes that are specified on the operand. The output relation has the values from the attributes listed in the operand, and the operation removes the duplicates.

Like selection, projection is also a unary operation working on a single input relation. As an example, we again use the relation depicted in Table 1.1. This time, only the values for the attribute codename are included in the resulting relation (see Table 1.11).

Joins

The join relations can be considered a class of relations that are similar to the Cartesian product of two operand relations. Usually, a query does not need to return the complete pairing of tuples from the two operands that are produced by the Cartesian product. Instead, it is usually more useful to limit the output relation to only those pairings that meet certain criteria. This is where the different join operations are useful.

Natural join is a useful join variant as it conceptually allows two relations to be combined into a single relation connecting the relations over a set of common attributes. For example, if we consider the os relation in Table 1.1 and the normalized device relation in Table 1.3, we can produce a relation that combines the two relations using the device.os_version and os.version attributes from each of the input relations. The results are depicted in Table 1.12.

Notice how the result of the natural join is the same unnormalized relation as in Table 1.2. By using a join operation, we are now able to perform additional operations on the output relation to produce the same results that would have been obtained if the data was combined in one table.

Natural join is really a specific type of **theta join** that uses the equality operation over a set of attributes. Theta join allows the use of any operation to combine the two operand relations. Equality (producing a natural join) is just one of the most common cases.

Relational Calculus

Relational calculus is another relational language that can be used to query and modify a relational model. Codd made the proposal for tuple relational calculus after his paper that introduced the relational model.

As discussed previously, relational algebra describes how data should be retrieved. Using relational calculus, we can describe *what* needs to be retrieved and leave the details of how the data is retrieved to the database. Because relational calculus is concerned with describing what to retrieve, it can be classified as a declarative language.

There are two forms of relational calculus: **tuple relational calculus** and **domain relational calculus**. Both forms are described in the following sections.

Tuple Relational Calculus

In tuple relational calculus, the tuples of a relation are evaluated against a predicate. The output of an expression is the relation that contains the tuples that make the predicate true. Again, with relational calculus, we only need to specify what we want and let the system determine the best way to fulfill the request.

If we again consider the os relation listed in Table 1.1, we can formulate a tuple relational calculus query in words. It would read something like this:

Return all tuples from the relation os where the codename is "Lollipop."

Notice that this is the same query that we, in the previous section, defined using relational algebra. While the text representation is generally how humans think about tuple relational calculus, we often use a shorthand notation to define the relation. The shorthand notation for this query would be

$$\{x|os(x) \wedge x.codename = `Lollipop'\}$$

This query would return all attributes for tuples that satisfy the predicate. We can also limit the attributes that are returned by the query. A query that would return only the codename when it is equal to "Lollipop" would look like this:

$$\{x.codename|os(x) \wedge x.codename = `Lollipop'\}$$

Domain Relational Calculus

Domain relational calculus evaluates the *domain* of the attributes in a relation as opposed to the tuples as in tuple relational calculus.

Database Languages

While the structure of a relational database is important, it is also necessary to be able to manipulate the data that is housed in the database. In his 1970 paper, Codd started describing a sub-language called ALPHA based on predicate calculus declaring relations, their attributes, and their domains.

ALPHA

While the ALPHA language was never developed, it did lay the foundation for modern-day languages used by most relational database systems today. It is important to point out that it was not Codd's intent to provide a full implementation of such a language in a paper that introduced the relational model. Instead, he presented some of the concepts and features that such a language would include. In addition, he described the language's relationship with a higher-level language as a "proof of concept" about what the language could do with a relational model.

The features of ALPHA that Codd described included the retrieval, modification, insertion, and deletion of data.

In addition to describing what the language could do, Codd went into the details of what the language should not do. Since the main objective of the language is to interact with a relational data model, the semantics of the language specify what data to retrieve as opposed to how to retrieve it. This is an important detail and is a language feature that has been carried through to modern-day SQL.

ALPHA was described as a "sub-language" that would exist along with another higher-level "host" language. This implies that ALPHA was never meant to be a complete language on its own. For example, features like arithmetic functions would be intentionally left out of ALPHA as they would be implemented in the host language and called from ALPHA.

QUEL

QUEL was a database language developed at UC Berkeley based on Codd's ALPHA language. It was shipped as part of the Ingres DBMS and has roots in POSTQUEL which was shipped with early versions of the Postgres database. QUEL was included as part of early relational databases but has more recently been supplanted by SQL in most modern relational database systems.

SEQUEL

Structured English QUEry Language (SEQUEL) was the name given to SQL when it was originally developed by IBM. However, due to trademark infringements, the name was shortened to Structured Query Language (SQL). SEQUEL was the first commercial language to be implemented based on Codd's ALPHA language.

As discussed earlier in the chapter, SQLite is the database system included as part of Android. In addition to implementing a way to store relational data, it includes an interpreter for the SQL high-level database language.

Summary

Relational databases offer a powerful mechanism to both store and operate on data. The introduction of the relational model by Edgar Codd in 1970 allowed database technology to overcome many of the limitations that existed in earlier file-based models.

The relational model, along with relational algebra and relational calculus, allows a database to be queried and perform operations on the data it stores. By including the concepts that define the relational languages in higher-level languages such as QUEL, SEQUEL, and SQL, developers are able to harness the power of a relational database to help support their software.

The next chapter dives into the details of the most popular database language: SQL.

2
An Introduction to SQL

Structured Query Language (SQL) is one programming language used to interact with a relational database, and it is the language used in SQLite. The language supports the ability to define database structure, manipulate data, and read the data contained in the database.

Although SQL has been standardized by both the American National Standards Institute (ANSI) and the International Organization for Standardization (ISO), vendors frequently add proprietary extensions to the language to better support their platforms. This chapter primarily focuses on SQL as it is implemented in SQLite, the database system that is included in Android. Most of the concepts in this chapter do apply to SQL in general, but the syntax may not be the same for other database systems.

This chapter covers three areas of SQL:

- Data Definition Language (DDL)
- Data Manipulation Language (DML)
- Queries

Each area has a different role in a database management system (DBMS) and a different subset of commands and language features.

Data Definition Language

Data Definition Language (DDL) is used to define the structure of a database. This includes the creation, modification, and removal of database objects such as tables, views, triggers, and indexes. The entire collection of DDL statements defines the **schema** for the database. The schema is what defines the structural representation of the database. The following SQL commands are usually used to build DDL statements:

- CREATE: Creates a new database object
- ALTER: Modifies an existing database object
- DROP: Removes a database object

The following sections describe how the CREATE, ALTER, and DROP commands can be used with different database objects.

Tables

Tables, as discussed in Chapter 1, "Relational Databases," provide the relations in a relational database. They are what house the data in the database by providing rows representing a data item, and columns representing attributes of each item. Table 2.1 shows an example of a table that contains device information.

SQLite supports the CREATE, ALTER, and DROP commands with regard to tables. These commands allow tables to be created, mutated, and deleted respectively.

CREATE TABLE

The CREATE TABLE statement begins by declaring the name of the table that will be created in the database, as shown in Figure 2.1. Next, the statement defines the columns of the table by providing a column name, data type, and any constraints for the column. Constraints place limits on the values that can be stored in a given attribute of a table.

Table 2.1 Device Table

model	nickname	display_size_inches
Nexus One	Passion	3.7
Nexus S	Crespo	4.0
Galaxy Nexus	Toro	4.65
Nexus 4	Mako	4.7

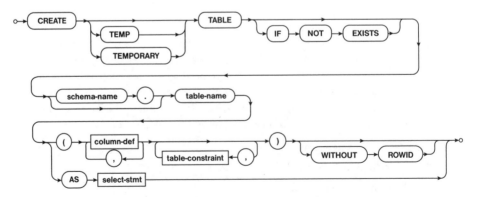

Figure 2.1 Overview of the CREATE TABLE statement

Source: sqlite.org

Listing 2.1 shows a CREATE TABLE statement that creates a table named device with three columns: model, nickname, and display_size_inches.

Listing 2.1 Creating the device Table

```
CREATE TABLE device (model TEXT NOT NULL,
                     nickname TEXT,
                     display_size_inches REAL);
```

> **Note**
>
> The discussion of SQL data types is deferred to Chapter 3, "An Introduction to SQLite." For now, it is enough to know that TEXT represents a text string and REAL a floating-point number.

If the SQL statement from Listing 2.1 is run and returns without an error, the device table is created with three columns: model, nickname, and display_size_inches of types TEXT, TEXT, and REAL respectively. In addition, the table has a constraint on the model column to ensure that every row has a non-null model name. The constraint is created by appending NOT NULL to the end of the column name in the CREATE statement. The NOT NULL constraint causes SQLite to throw an error if there is an attempt to insert a row into the table that contains a null value for the model column.

At this point, the table can be used to store and retrieve data. However, as time passes, it is often necessary to make changes to existing tables to support the changing needs of software. This is done with an ALTER TABLE statement.

ALTER TABLE

The ALTER TABLE statement can be used to modify an existing table by either adding new columns or renaming the table. However, the ALTER TABLE statement does have limitations in SQLite. Notice from Figure 2.2 that there is no way to rename or remove a column from a table. This means that once a column is added, it will always be a part of the table. The only way to remove a column is to remove the entire table and re-create

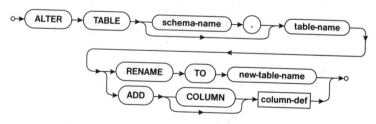

Figure 2.2   Overview of the ALTER TABLE statement

Source: sqlite.org

the table without the column to be removed. Doing this, however, also removes all the data that was in the table. If the data is needed when the table is re-created, an app must manually copy the data from the old table into the new table.

As an example, the SQL code to add a new column to the `device` table is shown in Listing 2.2. The new column is named `memory_mb` and it is of type `REAL`. It is used to track the amount of memory in a device.

Listing 2.2 Adding a New Row to the `device` Table

```
ALTER TABLE device ADD COLUMN memory_mb REAL;
```

DROP TABLE

The `DROP TABLE` statement is the simplest table operation; it removes the table from the database along with all the data it contains. Figure 2.3 shows an overview of the `DROP TABLE` statement. In order to remove a table, the `DROP TABLE` statement needs only the name of the table to be removed.

The `device` table can be removed with the statement shown in Listing 2.3.

Listing 2.3 Removing the `device` Table

```
DROP TABLE device;
```

Care should be taken when using the `DROP TABLE` statement. Once the `DROP TABLE` statement completes, the data is irrevocably removed from the database.

Indexes

An index is a database object that can be used to speed up queries. To understand what an index is, a discussion of how databases (SQLite in this case) find rows in a table is helpful.

Suppose an app needs to find a device with a specific model from the `device` table shown in Table 2.1. The application code would run a query against the table, passing the desired model name. Without an index, SQLite would then have to examine every row in the table to find all rows that match the model name. This is referred to as a **full table scan** as the entire table is being read. As the table grows, a full table scan takes more time as the database needs to inspect an increasing number of rows. It would take significantly more time to perform a full table scan on a table with four million rows than on a table with only four rows.

Figure 2.3 Overview of the `DROP TABLE` statement

Source: sqlite.org

Table 2.2 `device` Table with `rowid`

rowid	model	nickname	display_size_inches
1	Nexus One	Passion	3.7
2	Nexus S	Crespo	4.0
3	Galaxy Nexus	Toro	4.65
5	Nexus 4	Mako	4.7

An index can speed up a query by keeping track of column values in an additional table that can be quickly scanned to avoid a full table scan. Table 2.2 shows another version of the `device` table presented in Table 2.1.

Notice the new column in Table 2.2 called `rowid`. SQLite automatically creates this column when creating a table unless you specifically direct it not to. While an app will logically consider the `device` table to look like Table 2.1 (without the `rowid`), in memory the `device` table actually looks more like Table 2.2 with the `rowid` included.

> **Note**
>
> The `rowid` column can also be accessed using standard SQL queries.

The `rowid` is a special column in SQLite and can be used to implement indexes. The `rowid` for each row in a table is guaranteed to be an increasing integer that uniquely identifies the row. However, notice in Table 2.2 that the `rowid` values may not be consecutive. This is because `rowid`s are generated as rows are inserted to a table, and `rowid` values are not reused when rows are removed from a table. In Table 2.2, a row with a `rowid` of 4 was inserted into the table at one point but has since been deleted. Even though `rowid`s may not be consecutive, they remain ordered as rows are added to the table.

Using the `rowid`, SQLite can quickly perform a lookup on a row since internally it uses a B-tree to store row data with the `rowid` as the key.

> **Note**
>
> Using the `rowid` to query a table also prevents the full table scan. However, `rowid`s are usually not convenient to use as they rarely have any other purpose in an app's business logic.

When an index is created for a table column, SQLite creates a mapping of the row values for that column and the corresponding `rowid`. Table 2.3 shows such a mapping for the `model` column of the `device` table.

Notice that the model names are sorted. This allows SQLite to perform a binary search to find the matching model. Once it is found, SQLite can access the `rowid` for the model and use that to perform the lookup of the row data in the `device` table without the need for a full table scan.

Table 2.3 Index on `model`

model	rowid
Galaxy Nexus	3
Nexus 4	5
Nexus One	1
Nexus S	2

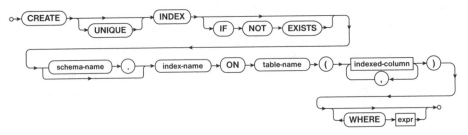

Figure 2.4   Overview of the CREATE INDEX statement

Source: sqlite.org

Figure 2.5   Overview of the DROP INDEX statement

Source: sqlite.org

CREATE INDEX

The CREATE INDEX statement needs a name as well as a column definition for the index. In the simplest case, the index has a column definition that includes a single column that is frequently used to search a table during queries. Figure 2.4 shows the structure of the CREATE INDEX statement.

Listing 2.4 shows how to create an index on the model column of the device table.

Listing 2.4 Creating an Index on model

```
CREATE INDEX idx_device_model ON device(model);
```

Unlike tables, indexes cannot be modified once they are created. Therefore, the ALTER keyword cannot be applied to indexes. To modify an index, the index must be deleted with a DROP INDEX statement and then re-created with a CREATE INDEX statement.

DROP INDEX

The DROP INDEX statement, as shown in Figure 2.5, has the same form as other DROP statements such as DROP TABLE. It needs only the name of the index to be removed.

Listing 2.5 shows how to drop the index that was created in Listing 2.4.

Listing 2.5 Deleting the Index on `model`

```
DROP INDEX idx_device_model;
```

Views

A view can be thought of as a *virtual* table in a database. Like a table, it can be queried against to get a result set. However, it does not physically exist in the database in the same way that a table does. Instead, it is the stored result of a query that is run to generate the view. Table 2.4 shows an example of a view.

Notice that the view from Table 2.4 contains only a subset of the columns of the `device` table. Even if more columns are added to the table, the view will remain the same.

> **Note**
>
> SQLite supports only read-only views. This means that views can be queried but do not support the `DELETE`, `INSERT`, or `UPDATE` operations.

CREATE VIEW

The `CREATE VIEW` statement assigns a name to a view in a similar manner to other `CREATE` statements (`CREATE TABLE`, `CREATE VIEW`, etc.), as shown in Figure 2.6. In addition to a name, the `CREATE VIEW` statement includes a way to define the content of the view. The view's content can be defined by a `SELECT` statement, which returns the columns

Table 2.4 Device Name View

`model`	`nickname`
Nexus One	Passion
Nexus S	Crespo
Galaxy Nexus	Toro
Nexus 4	Mako

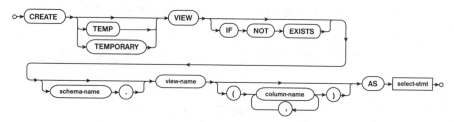

Figure 2.6 Overview of the `CREATE VIEW` statement

Source: sqlite.org

to be included in the view as well as places limits on which rows should be included in the view.

Listing 2.6 shows the SQL code needed to create the view from Table 2.4. The code creates a view named `device_name` which includes the `model` and `nickname` columns from the `device` table. Because the `SELECT` statement has no `WHERE` clause, all rows from the `device` table are included in the view.

Listing 2.6 Creating the `device_name` View

```
CREATE VIEW device_name AS SELECT model, nickname FROM device;
```

> **Note**
>
> `SELECT` statements are covered in more detail later in the chapter.

Views in SQLite are read-only and don't support the `DELETE`, `INSERT`, or `UPDATE` operations. In addition, they cannot be modified with an `ALTER` statement. As with indexes, in order to modify a view, it must be deleted and re-created.

DROP VIEW

`DROP VIEW` works like the other `DROP` commands that have been discussed thus far. It takes the name of the view to be deleted and removes it. The details of the `DROP VIEW` statement can be seen in Figure 2.7.

Listing 2.7 removes the `device_name` view that was created in Listing 2.6.

Listing 2.7 Removing the `device_name` View

```
DROP VIEW device_name;
```

Triggers

The final database object that can be manipulated by DDL is a trigger. Triggers provide a way to perform an operation in response to a database event. For example, a trigger can be created to run an SQL statement whenever a row is added or deleted in the database.

CREATE TRIGGER

Like other `CREATE` statements discussed previously, the `CREATE TRIGGER` statement assigns a name to a trigger by providing the name to the `CREATE TRIGGER` statement.

Figure 2.7 Overview of the `DROP VIEW` statement
Source: sqlite.org

After the name, an indication of *when* the trigger needs to run is defined. This definition of when a trigger should run has two parts: the operation that causes the trigger to run, and when the trigger should run in relation to that operation. For example, a trigger can be declared to run before, after, or instead of any DELETE, INSERT, or UPDATE operation. The DELETE, INSERT, and UPDATE operations are part of SQL's DML, discussed later in the chapter. Figure 2.8 shows an overview of the CREATE TRIGGER statement.

Listing 2.8 shows the creation of a trigger on the device table that sets the insertion time of any newly inserted rows.

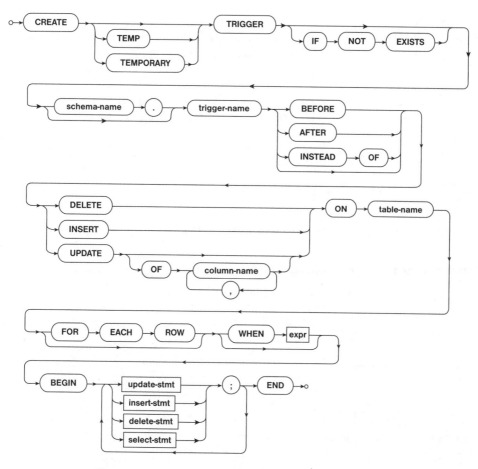

Figure 2.8 Overview of the CREATE TRIGGER statement

Source: sqlite.org

Listing 2.8 Creating a Trigger on the device Table

```
ALTER TABLE device ADD COLUMN insert_date INTEGER;

CREATE TRIGGER insert_date AFTER INSERT ON device

  BEGIN

    UPDATE device

    SET insert_date = datetime('now');

    WHERE _ROWID_ = NEW._ROWID_;

  END;
```

Before the insertion date can be tracked, the insert_date column must be added to the device table. This is done with an ALTER TABLE statement prior to the trigger being created (the insert_date column needs to exist before it can be referenced in the trigger definition).

After the ALTER TABLE statement has been run, the device table will contain the values shown in Table 2.5.

Notice that the value of insert_date is null for all rows. This is because the column was added after the table was created and the ALTER TABLE statement did not specify a default value to add to existing rows.

Now that the trigger is defined, the following INSERT statement can be run to insert a new row in the table:

```
INSERT INTO device (model, nickname, display_size_inches)

  VALUES ("new_model", "new_nickname", 4);
```

Table 2.6 shows the rows that are now in the device table.

Table 2.5 Adding insert_date

model	nickname	display_size_inches	insert_date
Nexus One	Passion	3.7	\<null\>
Nexus S	Crespo	4.0	\<null\>
Galaxy Nexus	Toro	4.65	\<null\>
Nexus 4	Mako	4.7	\<null\>

Table 2.6 Inserting a Row

model	nickname	display_size_inches	insert_date
Nexus One	Passion	3.7	\<null\>
Nexus S	Crespo	4.0	\<null\>
Galaxy Nexus	Toro	4.65	\<null\>
Nexus 4	Mako	4.7	\<null\>
new_model	new_nickname	4	2015-07-13 04:52:20

Notice that the new row has a timestamp to indicate when it was added. This column was populated by the insert_date trigger automatically when the INSERT statement was run. Let's dive a little deeper into the details of the trigger to explore how it works.

The first line of the trigger simply assigns it a name and dictates that it should be run after an INSERT statement on the device table:

```
CREATE TRIGGER insert_date AFTER INSERT ON device
```

The actual details of the trigger are between the BEGIN and END statements:

```
BEGIN
    UPDATE device
    SET insert_date = datetime('now')
    WHERE _ROWID_ = NEW._ROWID_;
END;
```

The previous statements cause an UPDATE statement to run, setting the insert_date to the current time. The UPDATE statement defines which table to operate on (device) and what values to set (column insert_date to the current date and time). The interesting part of the insert_date trigger is the WHERE clause in the UPDATE statement:

```
WHERE _ROWID_ = NEW._ROWID_;
```

Recall from the discussion of indexes that rows in an SQLite database have a rowid that is added by the database automatically and that this rowid column can be accessed. The WHERE clause in the UPDATE statement accesses this rowid column by using NEW._ROWID_. _ROWID_ is the special name of the column that can be used to access the rowid for a given row.

This WHERE clause causes the UPDATE statement to run only when the WHERE clause evaluates to true. In the insert_date trigger, this happens only when the row being manipulated by the trigger is the current row. Failure to include the WHERE clause causes the UPDATE statement to run on every row of the table.

To ensure that the current row matches the row being inserted, the NEW keyword is used. In a trigger, NEW represents the updated column values of the row being updated. In a similar fashion, OLD can be used to access the old values of a row that is being processed.

Triggers cannot be altered. In order for them to be modified, they need to be deleted and re-created.

DROP TRIGGER

The DROP TRIGGER statement works like the other DROP statements introduced in this chapter. As shown in Figure 2.9, it takes the name of the trigger that should be removed and deletes it.

Listing 2.9 removes the insert_date trigger.

Listing 2.9 Removing the DROP TRIGGER Statement

```
DROP TRIGGER insert_date;
```

Figure 2.9   Overview of the DROP TRIGGER statement
Source: sqlite.org

The previous sections provided an overview of the DDL that is supported by SQLite. Using the DDL, it is possible to define database objects that can be used to store data in a local database. The next section discusses ways to manipulate data that can be stored in a database.

> **Warning**
>
> While triggers can be an attractive feature of SQL, it is important to understand that they are not without their faults. Because the database runs a trigger automatically in response to an action performed on the database, a trigger may produce unexpected side effects. It may not always be obvious to application code that a trigger has been added to a table, and that could cause a database operation initiated by the trigger to have unintended results. In a lot of cases, it may be better for the app to move certain logic to the application code rather than add the same functionality in a trigger.

Data Manipulation Language

Data Manipulation Language (DML) is used to read and modify the data in a database. This includes inserting and updating rows in tables. Once the structure of the database has been defined with DDL, DML can be used to alter the data in the table. The main difference between DDL and DML is that DDL is used to define the structure of the data in a database, whereas DML is used to process the data itself.

DML consists of three operations that can be applied to rows in a table:

- INSERT: Adds a row to a table
- DELETE: Removes a row from a table
- UPDATE: Modifies the attribute values for a row in a table

INSERT

The INSERT statement is used to add rows to a table. Specifying what data should be inserted into the table and which columns that data should be inserted into can be done in three ways: using the VALUES keyword, using a SELECT statement, and using the DEFAULT keyword. Figure 2.10 shows an overview of the INSERT statement.

VALUES

When using the VALUES keyword, the INSERT statement must specify the values to be instated for each row. This is done by using two lists in the INSERT statement to specify

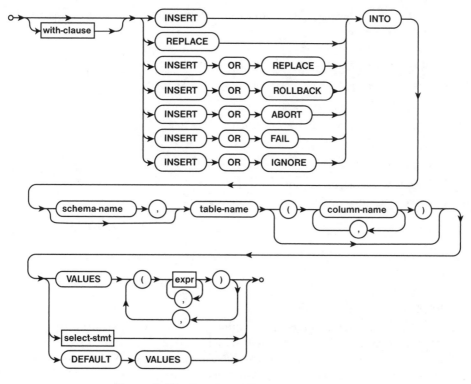

Figure 2.10   Overview of the INSERT statement

Source: sqlite.org

the destination column and the value for the column. The order must match so that the column name and the value have the same offset in the list.

When using the VALUES keyword with the INSERT statement, only a single row can be inserted into a table per INSERT statement. This means that multiple INSERT statements are needed in order to insert multiple rows into a table.

SELECT

Using the SELECT statement to specify row content in an INSERT statement causes the row that is inserted to contain the result set returned by the SELECT statement. When using this form of the INSERT statement, it is possible to insert multiple rows with one INSERT statement.

DEFAULT

The DEFAULT keyword is used to insert a row into the table that contains only default values for each column. When defining a table, it is possible to assign a default value for each column.

Listing 2.10 shows a basic example of using multiple INSERT statements to populate the data into the device table that was presented in Table 2.1.

Listing 2.10　Populating the Table with Multiple INSERT Statements

```
INSERT INTO device (model, nickname, display_size_inches)
    VALUES ("Nexus One", "Passion", 3.7);

INSERT INTO device (model, nickname, display_size_inches)
    VALUES ("Nexus S", "Crespo", 4.0);

INSERT INTO device (model, nickname, display_size_inches)
    VALUES ("Galaxy Nexus", "Toro", 4.65);

INSERT INTO device (model, nickname, display_size_inches)
    VALUES ("Nexus 4", "Mako", 4.7);
```

After rows have been inserted into a table, they can be altered using an UPDATE statement.

UPDATE

An UPDATE statement is used to modify data that already exists in a table. Like the INSERT statement, the table name, affected columns, and the new values for the affected columns must be specified. In addition, a WHERE clause may be specified to limit the manipulation to only specific rows. If a WHERE clause is not present in the UPDATE statement, all rows of the table will be manipulated. Figure 2.11 shows an overview of the UPDATE statement.

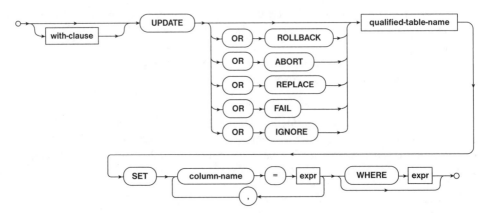

Figure 2.11　Overview of the UPDATE statement

Source: sqlite.org

Listing 2.11 shows an example of an UPDATE statement that processes all rows of a table. The UPDATE statement sets the model column to "Nexus" for all rows of the table.

Listing 2.11 Processing All Rows with **UPDATE**

```
UPDATE device SET model = "Nexus";
```

Listing 2.12 makes use of the WHERE clause to update specific rows of the table. The UPDATE statement sets the model name to "Nexus 4" for all rows that have a device_size_inches greater than 4.

Listing 2.12 Using **UPDATE** with a **WHERE** Clause

```
UPDATE device SET model = "Nexus 4" WHERE device_size_inches > 4;
```

DELETE

The DELETE statement, shown in Figure 2.12, is used to remove rows from a table. Like the UPDATE statement, it can be used with a WHERE clause to remove only specific rows. If the WHERE clause is not used, the DELETE statement removes all rows from a table. The table will still exist in the database; it will just be empty.

Listing 2.13 shows a DELETE statement that removes all rows from the device table where the display_size_inches is greater than 4.

Listing 2.13 Removing Rows with **DELETE**

```
DELETE FROM device WHERE display_size_inches > 4;
```

Now that DDL and DML have been discussed, it is time to start looking at the parts of SQL that allow queries to be run against a database. This is done with the SELECT statement.

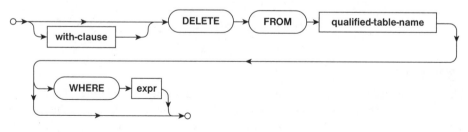

Figure 2.12   Overview of the DELETE statement

Source: sqlite.org

Queries

In addition to defining database structure and manipulating data in a database, SQL provides a way to read the data. In most cases, this is done by querying the database using a SELECT statement. Running database queries is heavily based on the relational algebra and relational calculus concepts that were discussed in Chapter 1.

Figure 2.13 shows the structure for the SELECT statement in SQL.

The SELECT statement can be fairly complicated as can be seen in Figure 2.13. In most cases, it starts with the SELECT keyword and is followed by the projection of the query. Recall from Chapter 1 that the projection is the subset of columns in the table. For the SELECT statement, the projection is the list of columns that should be returned from the table. The projection either can list the desired columns or may use a * to represent all the columns of the table.

After the desired columns have been specified, a SELECT statement must include a FROM clause to indicate where the input data is located. Listing 2.14 contains two queries that return data from the device table. The first query uses the * character to return all columns from the table, and the second query lists a subset of columns to be returned from the device table.

Listing 2.14 SELECT Statement

```
SELECT * FROM device;

SELECT model, nickname FROM device;
```

The result set returned from each of the queries in Listing 2.14 includes all of the rows of the table. To limit the query to specific rows, the WHERE clause can be added to a SELECT statement.

The WHERE clause describes which rows the query should return. The WHERE clause in a SELECT statement works the same way as a WHERE clause in an UPDATE or DELETE statement. Listing 2.15 shows a SELECT statement that returns all columns for rows that contain a display_size_inches value that is greater than 4.

Listing 2.15 Using SELECT with a WHERE Clause

```
SELECT * FROM device WHERE display_size_inches > 4;
```

ORDER BY

The query in Listing 2.15 returns the list of rows using the default ordering. That can be changed by using the ORDER BY clause in a SELECT statement. The ORDER BY clause directs the database how to order the result set that is returned by the query. In the simplest case, the ORDER BY clause can use the value of a column to dictate how the result set should be ordered.

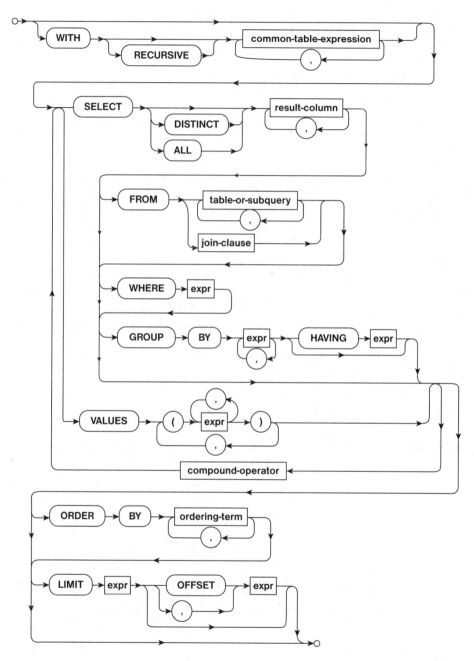

Figure 2.13 SELECT statement structure

Source: sqlite.org

Listing 2.16 shows a query that returns every row from the device table ordered by model. The results of the query are shown in Table 2.7.

Listing 2.16 Ordering Rows with ORDER BY

```
SELECT * FROM device ORDER BY model;
```

Notice that the result set is now in alphabetical order by model name.

In addition to the result set being ordered, the way it is ordered can be controlled in an ORDER BY clause by appending either the ASC keyword or the DESC keyword after the ORDER BY clause. ASC and DESC control how the ORDER BY clause sorts the result set (ascending or descending order). The query in Listing 2.16 made use of the ASC ordering, which is the default if neither ASC nor DESC is provided in the query. Appending a DESC to the end of the ORDER BY clause causes the result to be reversed as shown in Table 2.8.

Joins

Joins provide a way to include data from multiple tables in a single query. In many cases, tables in a database contain related data. Rather than repeat the data in a single table, it is preferable to create multiple tables to store the data and allow the tables to reference each other. With this structure, using a JOIN when querying allows data from both tables to be combined in a single result set.

As an example, let's extend the database that has been discussed in this chapter. Currently it has a single device table that tracks the properties of various mobile devices. Suppose the database also needs to track the manufacturer of each device, and each

Table 2.7 Alphabetical Order by model

model	nickname	display_size_inches
Galaxy Nexus	Toro	4.65
Nexus 4	Mako	4.7
Nexus One	Passion	3.7
Nexus S	Crespo	4

Table 2.8 Reverse Alphabetical Order by model

model	nickname	display_size_inches
Nexus S	Crespo	4
Nexus One	Passion	3.7
Nexus 4	Mako	4.7
Galaxy Nexus	Toro	4.65

Table 2.9 Duplicate Manufacturer Information

model	nickname	display_size_ inches	manuf_short_ name	manuf_long_ name
Nexus One	Passion	3.7	HTC	HTC Corporation
Nexus S	Crespo	4.0	Samsung	Samsung Electronics
Galaxy Nexus	Toro	4.65	Samsung	Samsung Electronics
Nexus 4	Mako	4.7	LG	LG Electronics

manufacturer has a short name and a long name. The device table could be altered to add two new columns to track this data. However, since a single manufacturer makes multiple devices, the details of each manufacturer would need to be duplicated in device rows. Table 2.9 shows the problem.

Since two devices, the Nexus S and the Galaxy Nexus, are made by the same company, they have identical values for the manuf_short_name and manuf_long_name columns. This becomes problematic should the name of the company need to be changed in the database. An app would then need to search for all occurrences of the manufacturer name and update the table. Also, if additional information needs to be tracked about the manufacturer, the device table must be updated to add the new column, and each row in the table needs to be updated to populate a value for the new attribute. This database structure simply does not scale well and is inefficient.

A better approach would be to add the manufacturer information to a second table and add a reference to a row in the manufacturer table to each row of the device table. Listing 2.17 shows the SQL to create the manufacturer table that contains columns for the short_name, long_name, and an automatically generated id.

Listing 2.17 Creating a **manufacturer** Table

```
CREATE TABLE manufacturer (id INTEGER PRIMARY KEY AUTOINCREMENT,

                           short_name TEXT,

                           long_name TEXT);
```

The CREATE TABLE statement in Listing 2.17 looks similar to the CREATE statements in previous examples with one exception, the id column. In Listing 2.17, the id attribute is declared as an INTEGER and the primary key of the table. This simply means that the id column must uniquely identify a single row in the table. The CREATE TABLE statement in Listing 2.17 also uses the AUTOINCREMENT keyword. This can be used with columns that are integer types to automatically increment the value as rows are inserted.

After running the INSERT statements in Listing 2.18, the manufacturer table contains the data in Table 2.10.

Listing 2.18 Inserting Manufacturers

```
INSERT INTO manufacturer (short_name, long_name)
    VALUES ("HTC", "HTC Corporation");
INSERT INTO manufacturer (short_name, long_name)
     VALUES ("Samsung", "Samsung Electronics");
INSERT INTO manufacturer (short_name, long_name)
     VALUES ("LG", "LG Electronics");
```

In order to "link" the tables together, the device table needs to have a column added to reference the id from the manufacturer table.

Listing 2.19 shows the ALTER TABLE statement that adds the column as well as the UPDATE TABLE statements that update the rows in the device table.

Listing 2.19 Adding a Manufacturer Reference to the device Table

```
ALTER TABLE device
  ADD COLUMN manufacturer_id INTEGER REFERENCES manufacturer(id);
UPDATE device SET manufacturer_id = 1 where model = "Nexus One";
UPDATE device SET manufacturer_id = 2
WHERE model IN ("Nexus S", "Galaxy Nexus");
UPDATE device SET manufacturer_id = 3 where model = "Nexus 4";
```

After running the SQL statements in Listing 2.19, the device table contains the data from Table 2.11.

Table 2.10 Manufacturer Table

id	short_name	long_name
1	HTC	HTC Corporation
2	Samsung	Samsung Electronics
3	LG	LG Electronics

Table 2.11 Duplicate Manufacturer Information

model	nickname	display_size_inches	manufacturer_id
Nexus One	Passion	3.7	1
Nexus S	Crespo	4.0	2
Galaxy Nexus	Toro	4.65	2
Nexus 4	Mako	4.7	3

Now, each device has a `manufacturer_id` that references a row in the `manufacturer` table.

Now that the two tables are defined and populated, a `JOIN` between them can be performed in a `SELECT` statement. Listing 2.20 shows a `SELECT` statement that combines all the data from the two tables.

Listing 2.20 Joining the Tables with JOIN

```
SELECT model, nickname, display_size_inches, short_name, long_name

FROM device

JOIN manufacturer

ON (device.manufacturer_id = manufacturer.id);
```

The `SELECT` statement in Listing 2.20 returns the rows from both the `device` and `manufacturer` tables in the projection. The `FROM` clause in the `SELECT` statement is where the `JOIN` operation happens.

The following code fragment indicates that the `device` and `manufacturer` tables should be joined where the `manufacturer_id` from the `device` table matches the value of the `id` column from the `manufacturer` table:

```
FROM device JOIN manufacturer ON (device.manufacturer_id = manufacturer.id)
```

The outcome of the `SELECT` statement in Listing 2.20 is a single result that combines the data from two different tables as if they were a single table.

Summary

SQL contains different types of statements to perform operations on a database. Data Definition Language (DDL) includes the SQL commands and statements needed to define a schema for a database using various database objects such as tables, views, triggers, and indexes. The operations included in DDL are `CREATE`, `ALTER`, and `DROP`.

Data Manipulation Language (DML) contains SQL language features needed to work with the data in tables. These include the `INSERT`, `UPDATE`, and `DELETE` statements.

Once a database has been defined and populated with data, the `SELECT` statement can be used to query the database. A query defines which table columns should be returned as the result along with which rows from the database should be selected for inclusion in the result set.

Chapter 3, "An Introduction to SQLite," goes into more details about SQLite, which is the SQL database implementation included in Android.

An Introduction to SQLite

Previous chapters discussed the basics of general SQL and relational databases. The Android SDK contains a relational database system called SQLite that can be used to store and retrieve an app's internal data. SQLite is a lightweight database system, making it ideal for use in resource-constrained environments like mobile devices. This chapter discusses some of the features that make SQLite unique when compared to other database systems, and it discusses some of its limitations.

SQLite Characteristics

Unlike larger database systems (MySQL, PostgreSQL, etc.), SQLite does not require a server/client architecture. Instead, it is completely server-less and self-contained. It runs in a single process, making it ideal for a mobile environment. All the SQLite functionality resides in process via a library that is part of the Android framework.

Each process that uses SQLite uses a single file to store its database content. However, SQLite does make use of some temporary files to support transactions, a topic that is discussed later in the chapter. The use of a single file to store all database content (tables, views, data, etc.) makes SQLite data storage simple and convenient.

Because the database file format is system agnostic, it can be read and written to across different environments. This can be a real convenience for developers because it allows them to copy an app's SQLite database from a mobile device to a development machine and inspect its contents. Additionally, an app can include an SQLite database file to help bootstrap the database during the install/initialization process.

SQLite Features

While SQLite is lightweight, it does provide a set of features that are present in larger database systems. It does not include *all* the features of more robust systems, but it does provide a large enough feature set to handle most use cases that arise in mobile development. Using SQLite, it is possible to add structure to data by making use of DDL to create tables and views. In addition, constraints can be added to the table by using primary/foreign keys. SQLite also includes support for cascading deletes and updates with foreign key support. Also, features such as atomic transaction and multithread support, which are found in larger database systems, are supported in SQLite.

Where SQLite differs from other database systems is in what it does not support as well as the way it implements data types. It has limited support for the JOIN operations as well as ALTER TABLE operations. Data types in SQLite are also more fluid than those found in other systems.

Foreign Key Support

SQLite supports foreign key constraints across tables to help ensure data integrity. Using foreign key constraints can help ensure that changes to the database span multiple tables when UPDATE or DELETE operations are performed. For example, should a row from the parent table be deleted, SQLite can ensure that any rows that reference that row in other tables are also deleted. While this can be done using triggers or application code, using a foreign key with the CASCADE operator can often be a cleaner approach.

Foreign key support was added to SQLite version 3.6.19. This is problematic for versions of Android older than 2.2 as they contained SQLite version 3.5.9 as part of the Android SDK. This means that foreign key support does not work in versions of Android older than 2.2. For these versions of Android, database integrity can be maintained by using either triggers or having the application code perform all the necessary database actions when rows are either updated or deleted.

The Android Debug Bridge (adb) utility can be used to display the version of SQLite that is present on an Android device using the following command:

```
adb -s <device_id> shell sqlite3 –version
```

While adb is not something that is generally used in app code, it can be used to determine which version of SQLite is present on a device or emulator that represents the minimum SDK level that is supported by an app. adb is covered in more detail in Chapter 4, "SQLite in Android."

Full Text Search

SQLite supports full-text search (FTS), allowing an app to query the database for all rows that contain a specified string or token. In order to enable full-text support, a virtual table must be created using one of the FTS modules. These modules are used to create tables that have a built-in full-text index. It is this full-text index that allows the tables to be efficiently searched for textual strings. The SQL code to create a table with FTS support enabled is shown in Listing 3.1.

Listing 3.1 Creating an FTS Table

```
CREATE VIRTUAL TABLE person USING fts4(first_name, middle_name, last_name);
```

The SQL code in Listing 3.1 creates a table named person that has three columns—first_name, middle_name, and last_name—that support full-text search.

Once the virtual table is created, it can be used like any other database table with SQL operations like INSERT, DELETE, DROP, and UPDATE.

To enable FTS support, either the FTS3 or the FTS4 module must be used (FTS1 and FTS2 are considered deprecated and should be avoided). These modules are similar, but they do have some differences. FTS4 is considered an enhancement to FTS3 and contains optimizations that allow FTS queries to have better performance. The performance enhancements are achieved by use of shadow tables. The shadow tables also require the FTS4 module to use more space than the FTS3 module.

In general, FTS4 is the recommended module to use to support FTS on a table. However, FTS4 was added to SQLite version 3.7.4 and is available only on Android devices running Android 3.0 and later.

Atomic Transactions

SQLite supports atomic transactions. To ensure the atomicity of transactions, SQLite can run in one of two modes: journal mode or write-ahead-log (WAL) mode. Each mode allows SQLite to write to a file that is external to the main database file. This use of an external file is one of the primary ways SQLite supports atomic transactions.

Journal Mode

When performing a transaction in journal mode, SQLite first writes all the current database content into a journal file, then updates the original database file with the changes from the transaction. If a transaction needs to be rolled back, the journal file's contents can be replayed back into the original database file. When the content from the journal file is replayed into the database file, the database is returned to the previous state. When the changes need to be committed to the database, the journal file is simply removed from the file system.

The external journal file is located in the same directory as the database file and has the same base name as the database file, with `-journal` appended to it.

Write-Ahead-Log (WAL) Mode

When WAL mode is enabled, SQLite still makes use of an additional file to support atomic transactions, but the role of the files changes. When using WAL, the changes in the transaction are written to an external file while the main database file remains unchanged. A commit can occur by simply writing a commit record to the external WAL file. This means that in WAL mode, a commit can occur without ever actually touching the main database file. Allowing commits to occur without a need to change the database file allows read and write operations to be performed simultaneously because they are performed on two different files. The read operation is performed on the main database file and the write operation is performed on the WAL file.

At some point the data from the WAL file needs to be added to the main database file. This is called a **checkpoint**. SQLite, by default, performs a checkpoint when the WAL file reaches a certain size. The checkpoint operation happens automatically without intervention from an app.

Enabling WAL in SQLite does have performance implications that developers need to be mindful of. While there are both advantages and disadvantages to enabling WAL, most of the disadvantages are limited by the fact that the app using the SQLite database is running on Android, which imposes certain limitations. For example, all access to a WAL-enabled database must happen from processes on the same machine. While this might be a concern for larger software systems, it is not a concern for Android apps since all database access likely already happens from the same process. In addition, apps don't directly communicate with an SQLite database. Instead, they use an Android SDK API which also helps limit the negative effects of enabling WAL. Enabling WAL can make database access faster for most use cases because WAL allows read and write operations to happen simultaneously. The downside of WAL is that it can be slower in scenarios where read operations have a high frequency and write operations have a low frequency. Enabling WAL also causes SQLite to perform an extra operation, the checkpoint.

Multithread Support

SQLite supports multiple threading modes: **single-thread**, **multithread**, and **serialized**. In the single-thread mode, SQLite is not thread-safe because all of its internal mutexes are disabled. When running in single-thread mode, access to the database needs to be controlled by the application client to ensure that data does not get corrupted. Multithread mode adds a level of multithread support to SQLite. However, thread safety is guaranteed only if the same connection is not used in multiple threads at the same time. The serialized mode is the default thread for SQLite. In this mode, SQLite access is thread-safe for all access.

An important point to keep in mind when using SQLite in Android is that the Android SDK provides additional thread-safety support. Specifically, the `SQLiteDatabase` class provides thread-safe access as long as the same instance is used for all database access.

What SQLite Does Not Support

While SQL is a language used by relational database systems, not all features of the language may be supported by all database systems. SQLite is no different, and some of the limitations are in place to ensure that SQLite remains a lightweight database solution. The following sections reveal some of the areas where SQLite has limited support.

Limited JOIN Support

SQLite does provide support for an SQL `JOIN` operation, but it is limited to the `RIGHT JOIN` and the `FULL OUTER JOIN`. Specifically, the `LEFT JOIN` is not supported. This limitation is easy to work with, but it is something to keep in mind when designing a database schema and writing queries.

Read-Only Views

Views can be a convenient way to consistently present insight into the data stored in a database. While views can be used in SQLite, they *cannot* be used to manipulate data. SQLite does not support using `INSERT`, `UPDATE`, or `DELETE` from within a view. However, triggers can be used to perform the data manipulation when an INSERT, UPDATE, or DELETE operation is attempted.

Limited ALTER TABLE Support

Table modification operations are limited to renaming tables (RENAME TABLE) and adding columns (ADD COLUMN). SQLite does not support removing columns (DROP COLUMN), changing the data type of a column (ALTER COLUMN), or adding constraints to a column.

Should a column data type need to be modified, or a constraint need to be added to a column, a new column can be added to the table. After the new column is added, the data can be migrated from the old column and the old column must then be ignored.

SQLite Data Types

Unlike most other database systems, SQLite does not have rigid data typing. In most other database systems, the type of data stored in a table is defined by the data type of the column. In SQLite, the type of a piece of data is more a property of the actual data value rather than the declared type of the column itself. SQLite allows a database schema to provide a hint as to what type of data a column contains, but the database makes the typing determination from the actual data.

Storage Classes

In addition to having more static data typing, SQLite has a slightly different model of data storage from most other database systems. Rather than have multiple different types that can represent similar types of data, SQLite uses data storage classes. While other database systems might have SMALLINT, INTEGER, or BIGINT to represent different types of integer values, SQLite has only the INTEGER storage class. In the case of the INTEGER type, SQLite uses different types to store the actual data in the database file depending on its magnitude. However, that specific typing information can be ignored at the application level since SQLite always returns an INTEGER storage class value when the database file is read.

Storage classes allow SQLite to be more flexible with data typing because they are more general. That being said, a developer can think of a storage class as a data type in other database systems and can usually use them the same way. Following are the types of storage classes supported by SQLite:

- INTEGER: Used to store integer values. SQLite stores the value in 1, 2, 3, 4, 6, or 8 bytes in the database file.
- REAL: Used to store floating-point values in the database file. All REAL values are stored as 8-byte IEEE floating-point numbers.
- TEXT: Used to store strings in the database file. The stored strings are encoded using the database encoding.
- BLOB: Typically used to store binary data in the database. Technically, the BLOB storage class stores data in the database file exactly as it is received in SQL.
- NULL: Used to store null values in the database file.

Type Affinity

While SQLite stores column data based on the actual data rather than the column type, it does allow the CREATE statement to make a suggestion as to which kind of data the column will hold. This is called **type affinity**. This is only a suggestion, however. Because of SQLite's dynamic data typing, any kind of data can be stored in any column independent of what type the column is declared as, or what type of data is already contained in the column. Following is a list of column affinities that are supported in SQLite:

- TEXT
- NUMERIC
- INTEGER
- REAL
- BLOB

In an effort to make SQLite's data typing system compatible with SQL syntax, SQLite calls a CREATE TABLE operation to specify more specific data types that are used in other database systems. For example, the SQL in Listing 3.2 is valid in SQLite even though it uses a type affinity that is not in the previous list.

Listing 3.2 Using Standard SQL Types

```
CREATE TABLE person (first_name VARCHAR(255),
                     age INT,
                     height_in_feet DOUBLE);
```

While some of the types used in Listing 3.2 are not explicitly defined in the SQLite typing system, SQLite uses type affinity to assign the appropriate storage class. In the case of Listing 3.2, INT has a type affinity of INTEGER, VARCHAR(255) has a type affinity of TEXT, and DOUBLE has a type affinity of REAL. This allows the same SQL code that would work on other database systems to also work with SQLite and still fit into its dynamic typing system.

Summary

SQLite is a very popular database system primarily because it has a really small footprint and still provides many of the features of much larger database systems. The "Lite" part of SQLite should refer to the size of the library rather than to a lack of functionality. These properties make SQLite a good choice for mobile development and are one of the reasons it was included in the Android SDK.

By supporting features like foreign keys, full-text search, multithread access, and atomic transactions, SQLite provides the functionality to support a wide number of Android apps. Becoming familiar with some of the unique features of SQLite such as its dynamic data types, limited JOIN support, and read-only views can take some time. The limitations of SQLite can also make database development slightly more challenging than working with more robust database systems.

The next chapter dives into more of the specifics of using SQLite on the Android platform.

4

SQLite in Android

Previous chapters discussed general database use and how SQLite works. This information is invaluable when working with databases in most environments. This chapter focuses on working with an SQLite database in Android. It covers some of the tools that can be used to interact with a database, and it introduces the Android APIs that can be used to add database support to an Android app.

Data Persistence in Phones

On Android, there are multiple ways that data can be persisted. For data that is highly structured and needs to be accessed efficiently, persisting data in SQLite may be a good solution. SQLite is not only lightweight, but it also provides fast access to data in the form of SQL queries.

Other methods of persisting data in Android, like preferences and/or direct file access, may be more convenient, but they don't provide the power that a relational database and SQL can provide. For larger sets of data, the added complexity of adding SQLite database support may be well worth the time and effort.

Android Database API

The Android SDK contains multiple classes that provide a level of abstraction between an app and the details of working with SQLite. These classes are located in the `android.database.sqlite` package. Two of the most basic classes that are used to work with SQLite databases are `SQLiteOpenHelper` and `SQLiteDatabase`. These classes provide a Java API for low-level database access on Android.

SQLiteOpenHelper

The `SQLiteOpenHelper` class is used to manage the SQLite database file for a process. Recall from Chapter 3, "An Introduction to SQLite," that SQLite stores an entire database in a single file. `SQLiteOpenHelper` is responsible for creating the SQLite database as well as configuring the connections to the database and performing upgrade operations. `SQLiteOpenHelper` is the main access point for an SQLite database in Android. While `SQLiteOpenHelper` does not directly support manipulating the database via SQL, it does provide methods to get an `SQLiteDatabase` instance that supports interacting with the database through SQL.

Because `SQLiteOpenHelper` is an abstract class, an app must provide a subclass that implements the `SQLiteOpenHelper.onCreate()` and `SQLiteOpenHelper.onUpgrade()` methods as well as one of the constructor methods.

SQLiteOpenHelper Constructors

The `SQLiteOpenHelper` class contains two constructor methods:

- `public SQLiteOpenHelper(Context context,`
                          `String name,`
                          `SQLiteDatabase.CursorFactory factory,`
                          `int version)`
- `public SQLiteOpenHelper(Context context`
                          `String name,`
                          `SQLiteDatabase.CursorFactory factory,`
                          `int version,`
                          `DatabaseErrorHandler errorHandler)`

Each constructor accepts a `Context`, a `String`, a `SQLiteDatabase.CursorFactory`, and an `int`. The `CursorFactory` is used to generate cursor objects in response to database query operations. Making this value `null` applies the default implementation.

The `String` parameter is used to define the name of the database file. The value of this parameter is the name of the SQLite database file that is stored in the Android file system. This name is usually not important to an app's Java code as an app typically does not interact with the SQLite database file directly. The database file name is important if the database needs to be inspected with external developer tools.

The `int` parameter defines the current schema version of the database. As the functionality of an app changes, the database may also need to evolve to support added functionality. It is typical for tables and/or views to be added to a database as the app evolves over time and gains functionality. Since requiring a user to uninstall/reinstall an app in order to upgrade leads to a bad experience, the `SQLiteOpenHelper` uses the schema version to trigger an upgrade process to allow the developer to provide a lightweight upgrade process for the user. When the schema needs to change, an incremented value can be passed to the constructor, and the `SQLiteOpenHelper` calls `onUpgrade()` to allow the database to be upgraded by the app.

The only difference between the constructors is that one includes a `DatabaseErrorHandler` in the parameter list, which can be used to perform a custom action when Android detects that the database is corrupt.

Listing 4.1 shows a snippet of a class that extends `SQLiteOpenHelper` and its constructor.

Listing 4.1 Implementing the **SQLiteOpenHelper** Constructor

```
/* package */ class DevicesOpenHelper extends SQLiteOpenHelper {
    private static final String TAG = DevicesOpenHelper.class.getSimpleName();
    private static final int SCHEMA_VERSION = 1;
    private static final String DB_NAME = "devices.db";

    private final Context context;

    private static DevicesOpenHelper instance;

    public synchronized static DevicesOpenHelper getInstance(Context context) {
        if (instance == null) {
            instance = new DevicesOpenHelper(context.getApplicationContext());
        }

        return instance;
    }
    /**
     * Creates a new instance of the simple open helper.
     *
     * @param context Context to read assets. This will be helped by the
➡instance.
     */
    private DevicesOpenHelper(Context context) {
        super(context, DB_NAME, null, SCHEMA_VERSION);

        this.context = context;
    }
```

Forcing an app to use the same instance of SQLiteOpenHelper can provide added thread safety if the database is accessed from multiple threads. Using the singleton pattern is one way to ensure that only one instance of the open helper is used throughout the app. In Listing 4.1, the DevicesOpenHelper is implemented as a singleton to ensure that all database access throughout the app uses the same instance to assure thread safety.

The `DevicesOpenHelper` also uses constants to define the database name and schema version, which are passed to the constructor of the parent class. The database file name is unlikely to change throughout the life of the app. However, the schema version will almost certainly change. If the schema needs to be updated, the global constant `SCHEMA_VERSION` should be manually incremented in the `DevicesOpenHelper` class to reflect a new version. This ensures that the `onUpgrade()` method is called to perform the upgrade operation.

SQLiteOpenHelper.onCreate()

The `SQLiteOpenHelper.onCreate()` method is used to create the database that the app will use. Like the `Activity.onCreate()` and `Fragment.onCreate()` methods, it is called only once when the database is being created for the first time. The `SQLiteOpenHelper.onCreate()` method is the place where DDL can be used to create tables and views in the database. In addition, DML can be used to initialize any data the app might need. While the `SQLiteOpenHelper` class cannot perform an SQL operation on its own, the `SQLiteOpenHelper.onCreate()` method is passed an `SQLiteDatabase` object that can perform SQL operations on the database.

Listing 4.2 shows the implementation of `DevicesOpenHelper.onCreate()`.

Listing 4.2 Implementing `DevicesOpenHelper.onCreate()`

```
@Override
public void onCreate(SQLiteDatabase db) {

    for (int i = 1; i <= SCHEMA_VERSION; i++) {

        applySqlFile(db, i);

    }

}
```

The `DevicesOpenHelper.onCreate()` method makes multiple calls to the `applySql()` method, passing the `SQLiteDatabase` instance as well as the schema version. The `applySql()` method reads an SQL file from the assets resource and sends all the SQL statements from the file to the database.

Because the `DevicesOpenHelper.onCreate()` method is called only when the database is first created, the method loops through all the schema version files to create the latest version of the schema in the database. For the device database sample app, all the schema version files build upon each other, so it is necessary to run them all to have a complete database schema.

The `DevicesOpenHelper.onCreate()` uses asset files to read SQL statements to send to the database. However, the SQL statements needed to create the database can also be generated in Java code and sent, as `Strings`, to the `SQLiteDatabase` object.

SQLiteOpenHelper.onUpgrade()

The `SQLiteOpenHelper.onUpgrade()` method is called when Android detects that a database upgrade is needed. Android keeps track of the current schema version that is passed to the constructor of `SQLiteOpenHelper` by using SQLite's `PRAGMA user_version`.

SQLite PRAGMAs can be used to keep track of data that does not belong in a table because the PRAGMA data describes properties of the database itself. The user_version PRAGMA can be used by any application to store application-specific version data.

When the SQLiteOpenHelper detects that the current schema version is older than the version passed to the constructor, it calls the SQLiteOpenHelper.onUpgrade() method. Listing 4.3 shows the implementation of DevicesOpenHelper.onUpgrade().

Listing 4.3 Implementing `DevicesOpenHelper.onUpgrade()`

```java
@Override
public void onUpgrade(SQLiteDatabase db, int oldVersion, int newVersion) {
    for (int i = (oldVersion + 1); i <= newVersion; i++) {
        applySqlFile(db, i);
    }
}
```

The onUpgrade() method is similar to the onCreate() method. Both use the applySql() method to read a series of SQL files and apply the SQL statements to the database. The only difference between onCreate() and onUpgrade() is that onUpgrade() is passed both the old schema version and the new schema version. This allows the onUpgrade() method to process only SQL files that have not already been processed.

Listing 4.4 shows the implementation of applySql() that is used in both onCreate() and onUpgrade().

Listing 4.4 Implementing `applySql()`

```java
private void applySqlFile(SQLiteDatabase db, int version) {
    BufferedReader reader = null;

    try {
        String filename = String.format("%s.%d.sql", DB_NAME, version);
        final InputStream inputStream = context.getAssets().open(filename);
        reader = new BufferedReader(new InputStreamReader(inputStream));

        final StringBuilder statement = new StringBuilder();

        for (String line; (line = reader.readLine()) != null;) {
            if (BuildConfig.DEBUG) {
                Log.d(TAG, "Reading line -> " + line);
            }
```

```
                // Ignore empty lines
                if (!TextUtils.isEmpty(line) && !line.startsWith("--")) {
                    statement.append(line.trim());
                }

                if (line.endsWith(";")) {
                    if (BuildConfig.DEBUG) {
                        Log.d(TAG, "Running statement " + statement);
                    }

                    db.execSQL(statement.toString());
                    statement.setLength(0);
                }
            }

        } catch (IOException e) {
            Log.e(TAG, "Could not apply SQL file", e);
        } finally {
            if (reader != null) {
                try {
                    reader.close();
                } catch (IOException e) {
                    Log.w(TAG, "Could not close reader", e);
                }
            }
        }
    }
}
```

The applySql() method takes an SQLiteDatabase instance as a parameter as well as an int to indicate the schema version file that should be read. Using the DATABASE_NAME constant and the schema version number, applySql() accesses the SQL file as an asset resource. It then reads each non-empty and non-comment line in the file until it finds a line that ends with a semicolon. These lines are concatenated to form an SQL statement that is then passed the SQLiteDatabase.execSQL(), which sends the statement to the actual SQLite database. The SQLiteDatabase.execSQL() method takes a String representing raw SQL and runs the statements on the database.

Database schema versions are handled by keeping multiple SQL files as asset resources and giving them a naming convention that includes the schema version in the file name. Figure 4.1 shows the SQL resources in Android Studio.

The SQL files in Figure 4.1 represent the different database schema versions. Each of the SQL files follows a naming convention of `devices.db.<schema_version>.sql`. The `applySql()` method looks for the file with the given schema version, reads its content, and sends the SQL statements to the database.

When extending `SQLiteOpenHelper`, the `onCreate()` and `onUpgrade()` methods are the only methods that must be implemented because they are abstract. However, there are other methods that can be useful to override, such as `onConfigure()` and `onDowngrade()`.

SQLiteOpenHelper.onConfigure()

The `SQLiteOpenHelper.onConfigure()` method is used to configure a connection to the database. Because this method performs the connection configuration, it is called before any other methods that may be used to manipulate the database (`onCreate()`, `onUpgrade()`, `onDowngrade()`). Being called so early also means that the `onConfigure()` method should not be used to make changes to the database as the database may be in an unpredictable state until one of the `onCreate()`, `onUpgrade()`, or `onDowngrade()` methods is called.

Figure 4.1 SQL schema files

Listing 4.5 shows the implementation of DevicesOpenHelper.onConfigure().

Listing 4.5 Implementing `DevicesOpenHelper.onConfigure()`

```
@Override
@TargetApi(Build.VERSION_CODES.JELLY_BEAN)
public void onConfigure(SQLiteDatabase db) {
    super.onConfigure(db);

    setWriteAheadLoggingEnabled(true);
    db.setForeignKeyConstraintsEnabled(true);
}
```

The DevicesOpenHelper.onConfigure() method in Listing 4.5 enables write-ahead logging and foreign key support. This is also the method that can be used to set any PRAGMA values that may be needed for a database.

> **Note**
>
> The SQLiteOpenHelper.onConfigure() method was introduced in API 16. Any devices running on an older version of Android need to handle the database connection configuration in a different way.

`SQLiteOpenHelper.onDowngrade()`

The SQLiteOpenHelper.onDowngrade() method is similar to the SQLiteOpenHelper.onUpgrade() method, except it handles the case where the current schema version is higher than the new version. It has the same parameter list as the SQLiteOpenHelper.onUpgrade() method, including two int parameters representing the current and new schema version values.

Putting It All Together

Listing 4.6 shows the entire implementation of DevicesOpenHelper.

Listing 4.6 Entire Implementation of `DevicesOpenHelper`

```
/* package */ class DevicesOpenHelper extends SQLiteOpenHelper {
    private static final String TAG =DevicesOpenHelper.class.getSimpleName();
    private static final int SCHEMA_VERSION = 3;
    private static final String DB_NAME = "devices.db";


    private final Context context;
```

```java
private static DevicesOpenHelper instance;

public synchronized static DevicesOpenHelper getInstance(Context ctx) {
    if (instance == null) {
        instance = new DevicesOpenHelper(ctx.getApplicationContext());
    }

    return instance;
}
/**
 * Creates a new instance of the simple open helper.
 *
 * @param context Context to read assets. This will be helped by the
 *                instance.
 */
private DevicesOpenHelper(Context context) {
    super(context, DB_NAME, null, SCHEMA_VERSION);

    this.context = context;

    // This will happen in onConfigure for API >= 16
    if (Build.VERSION.SDK_INT < Build.VERSION_CODES.JELLY_BEAN) {
        SQLiteDatabase db = getWritableDatabase();
        db.enableWriteAheadLogging();
        db.execSQL("PRAGMA foreign_keys = ON;");
    }
}


@Override
public void onCreate(SQLiteDatabase db) {
    for (int i = 1; i <= SCHEMA_VERSION; i++) {
        applySqlFile(db, i);
    }
}
```

```java
@Override
public void onUpgrade(SQLiteDatabase db,
                      int oldVersion,
                      int newVersion) {
    for (int i = (oldVersion + 1); i <= newVersion; i++) {
        applySqlFile(db, i);
    }
}

@Override
@TargetApi(Build.VERSION_CODES.JELLY_BEAN)
public void onConfigure(SQLiteDatabase db) {
    super.onConfigure(db);

    setWriteAheadLoggingEnabled(true);
    db.setForeignKeyConstraintsEnabled(true);
}

private void applySqlFile(SQLiteDatabase db, int version) {
    BufferedReader reader = null;

    try {
        final InputStream inputStream =
                context.getAssets().open(filename);
        reader =
                new BufferedReader(new InputStreamReader(inputStream));

        final StringBuilder statement = new StringBuilder();

        for (String line; (line = reader.readLine()) != null;) {
            if (BuildConfig.DEBUG) {
                Log.d(TAG, "Reading line -> " + line);
            }

            // Ignore empty lines
            if (!TextUtils.isEmpty(line) && !line.startsWith("--")) {
```

```
                    statement.append(line.trim());
                }


            if (line.endsWith(";")) {
                if (BuildConfig.DEBUG) {
                    Log.d(TAG, "Running statement " + statement);
                }


                db.execSQL(statement.toString());
                statement.setLength(0);
            }
        }


    } catch (IOException e) {
        Log.e(TAG, "Could not apply SQL file", e);
    } finally {
        if (reader != null) {
            try {
                reader.close();
            } catch (IOException e) {
                Log.w(TAG, "Could not close reader", e);
            }
        }
    }
    }
}
```

SQLiteDatabase

As discussed previously in this chapter, the SQLiteOpenHelper class is used to help manage creating and upgrading a database in Android. However, in order to actually use the database, an app needs to use additional classes that allow for interaction with the database. When using an open helper, the SQLiteDatabase class represents the connection to the database itself. SQLiteDatabase contains methods to interact with a database, including executing SQL statements. It is the class that will be used to perform typical SQL operations such as query(), create(), and delete() as well as allow for database configuration and transaction management.

Before an app can interact with an SQLiteDatabase connection, it must first get an instance of SQLiteDatabase. In most cases, apps use methods from SQLiteOpenHelper to get a reference to an SQLiteDatabase connection.

SQLiteOpenHelper contains two methods that return SQLiteDatabase connections: SQLiteOpenHelper.getReadableDatabase() and SQLiteOpenHelper.getWritableDatabase(). Both methods return an SQLiteDatabase or create one if necessary. However, as the method names indicate, getReadableDatabase() returns an SQLiteDatabase that can be used for read operations, and getWritableDatabase() returns an SQLiteDatabase that can be used for both reading and writing.

The actual database connection object that is returned by getReadableDatabase() and getWritableDatabase() is cached inside SQLiteOpenHelper to improve performance. Additionally, once a writable database connection is created, getReadableDatabase() actually returns the same connection as getWritableDatabase() since both methods return the cached version of the object.

Strategies for Upgrading Databases

The topic of database upgrades was briefly discussed earlier in this chapter. However, because it can be a complicated issue, it warrants more discussion.

The DevicesOpenHelper method presented in this chapter uses an upgrade approach that preserves the data in the database and uses external SQL files to manipulate the database for different schema versions. While this approach works, it may not be well suited for all use cases and can cause problems that developers should be aware of. In addition, there are other paradigms that can be used to handle SQL database upgrades such as dropping all database tables and re-creating them.

Rebuilding the Database

The simplest way to upgrade an existing application database is to drop all the tables and views in the database and simply re-create them. With this approach, there is no need to track schema versions. There is still a need to increment the schema version that is passed to the constructor of SQLiteOpenHelper, but that simply requires triggering SQLiteOpenHelper.onUpgrade() to run. The onUpgrade() method essentially clears out all database objects, then uses DDL to re-create the database.

While this is the simplest approach, it also destroys the data that is already in the database. Depending on the needs of the app, and the architecture of the entire system, this may not be much of an issue. For example, if an app is repeatedly pulling data from a remote Web service, it might not need to persist its local database across database upgrades. Removing all database objects, re-creating them, and then populating them with the data from a Web service may be perfectly acceptable at times. If so, perhaps the simplicity of this approach makes it worth implementing.

Manipulating the Database

While dropping and re-creating the entire database may be the simplest approach, it may not work in all cases. For example, an app may collect data that is provided by the user and not stored on any remote site. For these cases, simply manipulating the database with DDL might be a better approach.

Manipulating an already-existing database is the upgrade strategy that is used in the `DevicesOpenHelper` presented earlier in this chapter. Depending on the changes needed to the database, using DDL to change existing database objects may be enough. If the changes needed to update the schema are purely additive (adding a table and/or columns, for example), this approach often works. It is when existing database objects need to be changed that this approach may get complicated.

Recall from Chapter 3 that the `ALTER TABLE` statement poses some limitations on the operations it can perform in SQLite. Specifically, `ALTER TABLE` does not support `DROP COLUMN` or `ALTER COLUMN`. If there is no way to alter or drop a column, columns that are no longer used by the app remain in the table. This is not necessarily problematic, but it can potentially cause the table to use more disk space. In addition, because the column still exists in the table, the column can accidentally be accessed by application code without having the database throw an error.

A typical approach to achieving the equivalent `ALTER COLUMN` functionality is to create a new column and copy the data from the old column to the new column for each row in the table. With this approach, the table is once again left with a column that is not being used, leading to increased disk usage and opening the door for programming errors.

The addition of extra columns along with the inability to drop old columns can also have a much more menacing side effect than simply taking up more space and allowing for accidental usage of the old column. It would be convenient to simply ignore the old column and let it reside in the database, but remove all references to the column in app code. Unfortunately, if the column contains a constraint that prevents null values from being entered when a row is added, this may not be possible. To prevent an error from SQLite, the application code needs to populate a column with a non-null constraint with *some* non-meaningful value.

To alleviate some of these problems, some apps may be able to simply remove one or more tables, re-create them, and restore the data.

Copying and Dropping Tables

One way to circumvent the problem of having columns that are no longer used in a database, either because of the lack of `DROP COLUMN` or to work around the lack of `ALTER COLUMN` support, is to create a new table that has the desired columns under a different name. When creating this new table, the data from the old table can be copied to the new table. After the data is copied, the old table can be dropped and the new table can be renamed to match the name of the old table. This approach allows a table to be manipulated without losing any data. It also bypasses the limitations imposed by lack of `DROP COLUMN` and `ALTER COLUMN` support.

As an example, suppose a database has a table created with the SQL statements from Listing 4.7.

Listing 4.7 Example Table

```
CREATE TABLE data_table (column1 TEXT NOT NULL,
                         column2 TEXT NOT NULL,
                         column3 TEXT NOT NULL);


INSERT INTO data_table
VALUES ('row1_column1', 'row1_column2', 'row1_column3');


INSERT INTO data_table
VALUES ('row2_column1', 'row2_column2', 'row2_column3');


INSERT INTO data_table
VALUES ('row3_column1', 'row3_column2', 'row3_column3');
```

Even though the `data_table.column3` column is no longer needed, it may cause problems with app code because it has the `NOT NULL` constraint on it. Any attempt to add a row to the table requires some value to be inserted into `data_table.column3`. Ideally, what needs to happen is that `column3` needs to be removed from the table so the application code does not need to worry about inserting a value into it.

Listing 4.8 shows the SQL code that implements the copy and `DROP` approach that was discussed previously.

Listing 4.8 Copying and Dropping a Table

```
CREATE TABLE temp_table AS SELECT column1, column2 FROM data_table;


DROP TABLE data_table;
ALTER TABLE temp_table RENAME TO data_table;
```

Copying the data to a new table and giving it the same name as the old table helps to ensure that the queries used by the application code still work; they just return a smaller result set.

Database Access and the Main Thread

Performing long-running tasks on the main thread is always a concern with Android development. Spending too much time on the main thread can cause the UI to become slow or even hang. Android best practices tend to recommend refraining from any disk access on the main thread out of fear of causing a poor user experience. Even though

SQLite data access is typically fast, the database does reside in a file on the disk and should not be accessed from the main thread.

While typical Android threading techniques can be used to offload database operations from the main thread, the Android SDK also provides the loader framework to help. Specifically, the `CursorLoader` can be used to painlessly access a database off the main thread and perform UI tasks on the main thread. An in-depth discussion of the use of a `CursorLoader` comes in Chapter 5, "Working with Databases in Android."

Exploring Databases in Android

When developing an Android app that uses a database, it is often necessary to access the database in order to inspect its data. Because Android uses SQLite as the database system, any tool that supports SQLite can be used to interact with and manipulate an app's database. Additionally, the Android SDK provides the tools to inspect a database that is on a mobile device, as well as copy the database to a development machine so that other tools can be used to interact with it. There are also third-party tools, like Facebook's Stetho, that can be used to access a database in an app.

Accessing a Database with `adb`

The Android Debug Bridge (`adb`) is a very valuable tool for any Android developer. One of the things `adb` can do is open a shell to a device or emulator. The shell provides command-line access to the device, allowing a developer to perform some basic operations. Also included in the Android SDK is the `sqlite3` tool that can be used to interact with a database on a device through the shell. Once a shell is opened to a device, the `sqlite3` command-line tool can be used to open the database and send it commands.

Introduction to `adb`

The following code snippet shows how to use `adb` to open a shell to a device:

```
<path_to_android_sdk_dir>/platform-tools/adb shell
```

If there are multiple devices (emulators or actual devices) connected to the machine, `adb` needs to be provided with the ID of the target device. `adb` can be used to get a list of devices, and their IDs, that are currently connected to the machine using the `adb devices` subcommand. Listing 4.9 shows an example of using `adb` to find all the devices currently connected to the machine.

Listing 4.9 Getting a List of Attached Devices

```
bash-4.3$ adb devices

List of devices attached

HT4ASJT00075     device

ZX1G22PJGX       device


bash-4.3$
```

While the device IDs are displayed to the screen, it is not always clear which device is represented by a given ID. Passing –1 to the adb devices command causes adb to print additional information to help identify different devices. Listing 4.10 shows usage of the adb devices command with the –1 flag.

Listing 4.10 Getting a List of Attached Devices with Device Names

```
bash-4.3$ adb devices -l

List of devices attached

HT4ASJT00075              device product:volantis model:Nexus_9 device:flounder

ZX1G22PJGX               device product:shamu model:Nexus_6 device:shamu


bash-4.3$
```

With the addition of the –1 flag, it is now clear which device is represented by which ID so that the shell can be opened on the correct device.

Once the ID for the desired device has been determined, the adb shell command can be used along with the –s flag to indicate which device is the target for the adb command. The following snippet shows use of the adb shell command with the –s flag:

```
adb -s HT4ASJT00075 shell
```

> **Note**
>
> The –s flag passed to the adb command applies to adb itself and not the subcommand of shell. This means that the –s flag can be used with any adb subcommand.

Once a shell to the desired device is connected, the file system hierarchy can be navigated using standard Linux commands, such as cd to change directories and ls to retrieve a directory listing.

Permissions and the Android File System

When using the adb shell command, it is important to remember that the Android environment is heavily based on Linux. Each app is treated like a user on a Linux system with a home directory and permissions set on the home directory to disallow other apps from reading its private data. This is an intentional security feature that is built into Android in the same way that this is a security feature built into Linux to protect user data. On Android, apps have home directories in the /data/data folder. The actual name of the app's home directory is the same as the package name that uniquely identifies the app in the system. Listing 4.11 shows a part of a directory listing of /data/data, including the permissions of each subdirectory.

Listing 4.11 /data/data Directory Listing

```
root@generic_x86_64:/ # ls -l /data/data

drwxr-x--x u0_a0   u0_a0    2015-12-16 14:04 com.android.backupconfirm
```

```
drwxr-x--x u0_a15    u0_a15    2015-12-16 14:04 com.android.backuptester
drwxr-x--x u0_a17    u0_a17    2015-12-16 14:04 com.android.browser
drwxr-x--x u0_a18    u0_a18    2015-12-16 14:04 com.android.calculator2
drwxr-x--x u0_a19    u0_a19    2015-12-16 14:04 com.android.calendar
drwxr-x--x u0_a33    u0_a33    2015-12-16 14:04 com.android.camera
drwxr-x--x u0_a20    u0_a20    2015-12-16 14:04 com.android.captiveportallogin
drwxr-x--x u0_a21    u0_a21    2015-12-16 14:04 com.android.certinstaller
drwxr-x--x u0_a2     u0_a2     2016-03-24 20:40 com.android.contacts
drwxr-x--x u0_a22    u0_a22    2015-12-16 14:04 com.android.customlocale2
drwxr-x--x u0_a3     u0_a3     2015-12-16 14:05 com.android.defcontainer
drwxr-x--x u0_a23    u0_a23    2015-12-16 14:04 com.android.deskclock
drwxr-x--x u0_a24    u0_a24    2015-12-16 14:04 com.android.development
drwxr-x--x u0_a4     u0_a4     2015-12-16 14:04 com.android.dialer
drwxr-x--x u0_a1     u0_a1     2015-12-16 14:04 com.android.providers.calendar
drwxr-x--x u0_a2     u0_a2     2015-12-16 14:04 com.android.providers.contacts
drwxr-x--x u0_a5     u0_a5     2015-12-16 14:04 com.android.providers.media
```

In Listing 4.11, each directory in the listing represents the home directory of an app that is installed on the device. The home directory is where local data, such as databases, preferences, and cache information, is saved. Because the data is specific to the app, Android assigns permissions that prevent other apps from accessing local app data. The permissions for the directories in /data/data (rwxr-x-–x) allow any app to enter the directory but not add or remove anything in the directory. Only the app that "owns" the directory can add or remove content from the directory.

Drilling down into an app directory a little deeper provides more detail on how Android protects files. Listing 4.12 shows the permissions of files in the databases directory of /data/data/com.android.providers.contacts.

Listing 4.12 File Permissions

```
root@generic_x86_64:/ # ls -l \
> data/data/com.android.providers.contacts/databases
-rw-rw---- u0_a2    u0_a2      348160 2016-03-24 20:42 contacts2.db
-rw-rw---- u0_a2    u0_a2           0 2016-03-24 20:42 contacts2.db-journal
-rw-rw---- u0_a2    u0_a2      348160 2015-12-16 14:04 profile.db
-rw-rw---- u0_a2    u0_a2       16928 2015-12-16 14:04 profile.db-journal
root@generic_x86_64:/ #
```

Notice that in Listing 4.12 the file permissions (rw-rw----) are even more restrictive than the directory permissions. The file permissions for every file in the databases directory ensure that no other app can read or write to the file.

File permissions are important when exploring a device with adb because when the adb shell is launched, it may be launched as an "unprivileged" user. In Linux terms, an unprivileged user means that the user account used to run the shell is not able to override any of the permissions of the files or directories on the device. If a file has permissions that prevent it from being read for all users except the app that owns the file, the adb shell is not able to read the file. This means that the adb shell is not able to perform tasks like read and write to databases in an app's home directory.

While the adb shell does tend to run as an unprivileged user on most devices, it is run as the "root" user on the emulator, or if the device is "rooted" (modified to allow apps and programs to run as root). On Linux systems, the root user can override file and directory permissions. It can be thought of as an administrative account with almost limitless access to the system and its contents.

When the adb shell is run as root, it has access to an app's private files and directories. This is important because it means that on an emulator or rooted device, the adb shell is able to access an app-private database. However, the adb shell is not able to access app-private databases on a device that is not rooted. Because most devices are not rooted, accessing a database on most devices can be problematic.

> **Note**
>
> All the adb shell commands listed in this chapter were run on either the Android emulator or a rooted device. The commands used to read and copy files from an app's home directory are not able to run on a non-rooted device/emulator due to a lack of permissions.

Finding a Database Location with adb

To connect to an app's SQLite database, the location of the SQLite database file must be known. Recall from Chapter 3 that SQLite stores an entire database in a single file (with the possibility of some temporary files used for transaction support). The database file is stored in the app's home directory.

An example of accessing an app's database would be accessing the database of one of Android's internal databases: the contacts database. Before the contacts database can be accessed, the location of the database file must be known. The database file location can be determined using adb.

As for most system-level databases, Android provides a content provider to access the contacts database. While the concept of content providers will be explored more deeply in later chapters, for now it is enough to know that a content provider provides a data abstraction layer and contains an **authority** that uniquely identifies the type of data in the ContentProvider. This authority is typically defined in a contract class that provides the public API for using a ContentProvider.

In the case of the contacts content provider, the contract class is ContactsContract. Examining the documentation for the ContactsContract class

(https://developer.android.com/reference/android/provider/ContactsContract.
html#AUTHORITY) reveals that ContactsContract defines an AUTHORITY constant
which has a value of com.android.contacts. We can use the value of ContactsCon-
tract.AUTHORITY along with adb shell dumpsys to find the location of the database
that supports the contacts ContentProvider.

The adb shell dumpsys subcommand can be used to display information about the
Android system. Listing 4.13 shows how to use adb shell dumpsys to get information
about the registered content providers in the system as well as a snippet of the output
from the command.

Listing 4.13 adb shell dumpsys Subcommand

```
bash-4.3$ adb shell dumpsys activity providers

ACTIVITY MANAGER CONTENT PROVIDERS (dumpsys activity providers)

...

* ContentProviderRecord{2f0e81e u0 com.android.providers.contacts/.Contacts
➥Provider2}
    package=com.android.providers.contacts process=android.process.acore
    proc=ProcessRecord{ad8d91a 11766:android.process.acore/u0a2}
    launchingApp=ProcessRecord{ad8d91a 11766:android.process.acore/u0a2}
    uid=10002 provider=android.content.ContentProviderProxy@c8028ff
    authority=contacts;com.android.contacts

...


bash-4.3$
```

The output from the adb shell dumpsys subcommand provides all the content
provider information for the entire device, listing all the providers provided by the
various apps that are installed. To find the correct content provider entry, the authority
field from the adb shell dumpsys output needs to be examined. Specifically, the
ContentProviderRecord with an authority that includes com.android.contacts
provides the details needed to find the contacts SQLite database file. The correct
ContentProviderRecord is highlighted in Listing 4.13.

In most cases, the adb shell dumpsys command prints a lot of information that needs
to be searched to find the correct authority string. After the ContentProviderRecord
is identified, the package of the app that provides the content provider can be resolved.
In the case of the contacts content provider, the package name for the app that provides
the content provider is com.android.providers.contacts. Once the package name is
known, finding the actual SQLite database file is easy since it is in the home directory
of the app. In this case, the home directory is /data/data/com.android.providers.
contacts.

Listing 4.14 shows using the cd command to change to the contacts provider app home directory, then using the ls command to perform a directory listing.

Listing 4.14 Home Directory Listing

```
root@generic_x86_64:/ # cd /data/data/com.android.providers.contacts

root@generic_x86_64:/data/data/com.android.providers.contacts # ls

cache

code_cache

databases

files

shared_prefs

root@generic_x86_64:/data/data/com.android.providers.contacts #
```

The contents of the contacts content provider app can be seen in Listing 4.14. The directory /data/data/com.android.providers.contacts contains the following entries:

- cache
- code_cache
- databases
- files
- shared_prefs

The cache and code_cache directories are used to store temporary information. The files directory is where app-specific files get stored. shared_prefs contains the XML files used to persist preferences in Android, and the databases directory is used to store the SQLite database files for the app. Recall from the discussion of SQLiteOpenHelper that the name of the database is specified when opening the database. The file in the database directory matches the file names used in the SQLiteOpenHelper class. Listing 4.15 shows a directory listing of the databases directory for the contacts provider app.

Listing 4.15 databases Directory Listing

```
root@generic_x86_64:/data/data/com.android.providers.contacts# ls databases

contacts2.db

contacts2.db-journal

profile.db

profile.db-journal

root@generic_x86_64:/data/data/com.android.providers.contacts#
```

In Listing 4.15, there are two database files in the databases directory that make up the contacts database, contacts2.db and profile.db. Each database file also has a journal file to support transactions. With the knowledge of the location of the database file, the sqlite3 command can now be used to connect to the database in the shell.

Connecting to a Database with sqlite3

The sqlite3 command is part of the SQLite package and is included in the Android SDK. To use the sqlite3 command to connect to a database, simply pass the database file name as an argument to sqlite3. Listing 4.16 shows how to use the sqlite3 command to connect to the contacts database from Listing 4.15.

Listing 4.16 Connecting to the Contacts Database

```
root@generic_x86_64:/data/data/com.android.providers.contacts # sqlite3 \
> databases/contacts2.db
SQLite version 3.8.10.2 2015-05-20 18:17:19
Enter ".help" for usage hints.
sqlite>
```

Once the connection to the database has been made, sqlite3 displays a prompt. Notice in Listing 4.16 that the sqlite3 program provides a hint at how to get help: typing .help and pressing Enter. Listing 4.17 shows what is printed when the .help command is issued to sqlite3.

Listing 4.17 Issuing .help to sqlite3

```
sqlite> .help
.backup ?DB? FILE      Backup DB (default "main") to FILE
.bail on|off           Stop after hitting an error.  Default OFF
.binary on|off         Turn binary output on or off.  Default OFF
.clone NEWDB           Clone data into NEWDB from the existing database
.databases             List names and files of attached databases
.dbinfo ?DB?           Show status information about the database
.dump ?TABLE? ...      Dump the database in an SQL text format
                         If TABLE specified, only dump tables matching
                         LIKE pattern TABLE.
.echo on|off           Turn command echo on or off
.eqp on|off            Enable or disable automatic EXPLAIN QUERY PLAN
.exit                  Exit this program
.explain ?on|off?      Turn output mode suitable for EXPLAIN on or off.
                         With no args, it turns EXPLAIN on.
```

```
.fullschema              Show schema and the content of sqlite_stat tables
.headers on|off          Turn display of headers on or off
.help                    Show this message
.import FILE TABLE        Import data from FILE into TABLE
.indexes ?TABLE?         Show names of all indexes
                             If TABLE specified, only show indexes for tables
                             matching LIKE pattern TABLE.
.limit ?LIMIT? ?VAL?     Display or change the value of an SQLITE_LIMIT
.log FILE|off            Turn logging on or off.  FILE can be stderr/stdout
.mode MODE ?TABLE?       Set output mode where MODE is one of:
                             ascii    Columns/rows delimited by 0x1F and 0x1E
                             csv      Comma-separated values
                             column   Left-aligned columns.  (See .width)
                             html     HTML <table> code
                             insert   SQL insert statements for TABLE
                             line     One value per line
                             list     Values delimited by .separator strings
                             tabs     Tab-separated values
                             tcl      TCL list elements
.nullvalue STRING        Use STRING in place of NULL values
.once FILENAME           Output for the next SQL command only to FILENAME
.open ?FILENAME?         Close existing database and reopen FILENAME
.output ?FILENAME?       Send output to FILENAME or stdout
.print STRING...         Print literal STRING
.prompt MAIN CONTINUE    Replace the standard prompts
.quit                    Exit this program
.read FILENAME           Execute SQL in FILENAME
.restore ?DB? FILE       Restore content of DB (default "main") from FILE
.save FILE               Write in-memory database into FILE
.scanstats on|off        Turn sqlite3_stmt_scanstatus() metrics on or off
.schema ?TABLE?          Show the CREATE statements
                             If TABLE specified, only show tables matching
                             LIKE pattern TABLE.
```

```
.separator COL ?ROW?    Change the column separator and optionally the row
                           separator for both the output mode and .import
.shell CMD ARGS...      Run CMD ARGS... in a system shell
.show                   Show the current values for various settings
.stats on|off           Turn stats on or off
.system CMD ARGS...     Run CMD ARGS... in a system shell
.tables ?TABLE?         List names of tables
                           If TABLE specified, only list tables matching
                           LIKE pattern TABLE.
.timeout MS             Try opening locked tables for MS milliseconds
.timer on|off           Turn SQL timer on or off
.trace FILE|off         Output each SQL statement as it is run
.vfsname ?AUX?          Print the name of the VFS stack
.width NUM1 NUM2 ...    Set column widths for "column" mode
                           Negative values right-justify
sqlite>
```

Typing `.help` lists all the commands that `sqlite3` supports. Notice that each of the commands starts with a period. This is a common pattern with `sqlite3`. Besides `.help`, one of the most important commands for `sqlite3` is `.quit`, which exits the `sqlite3` shell and returns the user to the Android shell.

After a database connection is established, the `sqlite3` command can be used to execute SQL statements against the database. Since the schema of the database (which defines the tables) is not known, it is useful to get a list of tables that can be used in a query before running a query. The output of the `.help` command in Listing 4.17 reveals that `sqlite3` contains the `.tables` command, which shows the list of tables in the database. Listing 4.18 shows the output of running the `.tables` command.

Listing 4.18 Running `.tables`

```
qlite> .tables
_sync_state            phone_lookup           view_data
_sync_state_metadata   photo_files            view_data_usage_stat
accounts               pre_authorized_uris    view_entities
agg_exceptions         properties             view_groups
android_metadata       raw_contacts           view_raw_contacts
```

calls	search_index	view_raw_entities
contacts	search_index_content	view_stream_items
data	search_index_docsize	view_v1_contact_methods
data_usage_stat	search_index_segdir	view_v1_extensions
default_directory	search_index_segments	view_v1_group_membership
deleted_contacts	search_index_stat	view_v1_groups
directories	settings	view_v1_organizations
groups	status_updates	view_v1_people
mimetypes	stream_item_photos	view_v1_phones
name_lookup	stream_items	view_v1_photos
nickname_lookup	v1_settings	visible_contacts
packages	view_contacts	voicemail_status
sqlite>		

Now that the list of tables is known, `sqlite3` can be used to run a query. Listing 4.19 shows running a query to return all the rows of the `raw_contacts` table.

Listing 4.19 Querying the `raw_contacts` Table

```
sqlite> select _id, display_name, display_name_alt from raw_contacts;
1|Bob Smith|Smith, Bob
2|Rob Smith|Smith, Rob
3|Carol Smith|Smith, Carol
4|Sam Smith|Smith, Sam
sqlite>
```

While the output from Listing 4.19 is useful, sometimes it is convenient to show the column names along with the query results. This can be done by using the `.headers` command in the SQLite command prompt. The `.headers` command controls whether the column names are shown as column headers in the query results. The default is to hide the headers. Listing 4.20 shows the use of the `.headers` command to turn the headers on. It also shows running a query again to show all the data from the table.

Listing 4.20 Enabling Column Headers

```
sqlite> .headers on
sqlite> select _id, display_name, display_name_alt from raw_contacts;
_id|display_name|display_name_alt
1|Bob Smith|Smith, Bob
```

```
2|Rob Smith|Smith, Rob

3|Carol Smith|Smith, Carol

4|Sam Smith|Smith, Sam

sqlite>
```

Notice the bold text in Listing 4.20, which highlights the column names in the query results. The addition of the headers can make it easier to determine which column in the result set represents which column in the table definition.

One additional tweak to the output of sqlite3 that can make reading query results easier is to enable columns. This can be done with the .mode command. sqlite3 supports many different output types when returning query results. It can output in an ASCII format or HTML, generate SQL INSERT statements based on the current contents of the data, or just provide a more intuitive column structure. To make the result set more readable, the .mode command can be passed the column parameter. Listing 4.21 shows how to enable the column mode, and it shows the result set from running a query against the raw_contacts table.

Listing 4.21 Enabling Columns

```
sqlite> .mode column

sqlite> select _id, display_name, display_name_alt from raw_contacts;

_id         display_name  display_name_alt

----------  ------------  ----------------

1           Bob Smith     Smith, Bob

2           Rob Smith     Smith, Rob

3           Carol Smith   Smith, Carol

4           Sam Smith     Smith, Sam

sqlite>
```

A Shorthand Approach to adb and sqlite3

The previous listings showed how to use adb to traverse the Android system tree and use sqlite3 to access a database. If the location of the database is known, probably because the package name of the app is known, a shorthand version of adb shell and sqlite3 can be used to connect to the database and run SQL commands. The shorthand approach can be more convenient than explicitly starting a shell, then connecting to the database, because it allows for use of typical shell features (history, pipes, redirection, etc.) that are traditionally part of a shell on a development machine.

To use the shorthand approach, adb shell is passed a command to run inline, and it returns the results. To access a database, the adb shell command is passed sqlite3 along with the path to the database. Listing 4.22 shows the combined execution of adb shell and sqlite3.

Listing 4.22 Combining adb shell and sqlite3

```
bash-4.3$ adb shell sqlite3 \
> /data/data/com.android.providers.contacts/databases/contacts2.db \
> '"select _id, display_name, display_name_alt from raw_contacts;"'
1|Bob Smith|Smith, Bob
2|Rob Smith|Smith, Rob
3|Carol Smith|Smith, Carol
4|Sam Smith|Smith, Sam
bash-4.3$
```

Notice in Listing 4.22 that the output from the query has lost its formatting from previous examples. The formatting can be enabled by passing the –column and –header flags to the sqlite3 command. These are needed because with the shorthand approach, the SQLite shell is not entered. Instead, the SQL command is run, the results are printed, and then sqlite3 exits. Listing 4.23 shows the shorthand approach with the formatting added.

Listing 4.23 Combining adb shell and sqlite3 with Formatting Added

```
bash-4.3$ adb shell sqlite3 -column -header \
> /data/data/com.android.providers.contacts/databases/contacts2.db \
> '"select _id, display_name, display_name_alt from raw_contacts;"'
_id         display_name  display_name_alt
----------  ------------  ----------------
1           Bob Smith     Smith, Bob
2           Rob Smith     Smith, Rob
3           Carol Smith   Smith, Carol
4           Sam Smith     Smith, Sam
bash-4.3$
```

With the column formatting and the headers added, the output is equivalent to running the query with the sqlite3 interactive shell.

For common queries, it can be convenient to add the combined shorthand adb shell sqlite3 command in a script that can be rerun easily. This allows complex queries to be persisted and easily run from a development machine while the SQLite database file still resides on the device.

Using Third-Party Tools to Access Android Databases

The `adb` and `sqlite3` commands provide lightweight and convenient access to Android databases. However, they lack the features of some more robust database access tools such as a graphical interface and code completion, both of which can make development easier. When a more feature-filled database tool is desired, the SQLite database must be transferred to a development machine where it can be accessed by the database application. The `adb` command supports pulling files from and pushing files to and from an Android device from a connected development machine.

To copy a file from a mobile device to a development machine, the `adb pull` command can be used. Listing 4.24 shows copying the databases containing the contact information to the local directory.

Listing 4.24 Pulling Contact Information with `adb pull`

```
bash-4.3$ adb pull \
> /data/data/com.android.providers.contacts/databases
pull: building file list...
pull: /data/data/com.android.providers.contacts/databases
/contacts2.db-journal -> ./contacts2.db-journal
pull: /data/data/com.android.providers.contacts/databases
/contacts2.db -> ./contacts2.db
5 files pulled. 0 files skipped.
1745 KB/s (713248 bytes in 0.399s)
bash-4.3$
```

When the database folder has been copied to the development machine, any database tool that supports SQLite can be used to access the database by reading the main SQLite database file.

While using `adb` to pull the database from a device does allow powerful tools to be used to access the database, it means that the database needs to be copied whenever the mobile device makes changes to the database. This added step can be a little cumbersome. Luckily, there is at least one tool, Stetho, that provides more functionality than `sqlite3` while reading the database directly from the device.

Accessing a Database with Stetho

Stetho (https://facebook.github.io/stetho/) is a tool written and maintained by Facebook for Android debugging. Stetho uses the Chrome browser's developer tools to provide access to information that can be useful when debugging an Android app. While there is a lot of data that Stetho can provide access to, the focus for this chapter is on database access.

In order to use Stetho, it must be added to the target Android project and initialized in the app. In addition, Stetho functionality is typically enabled only for debug builds as there are probably very few compelling reasons to have it enabled for release builds. This means that Stetho can be used to debug/inspect apps that are being developed but will likely not help in accessing any data, including SQLite databases, for apps that are downloaded via Google Play.

Because of this limitation, this chapter looks at using Stetho with an app that is used to track devices.

Before Stetho can be initialized, it must be added to the project `build.gradle` file which causes the library to be downloaded. Listing 4.25 shows the `build.gradle` snippet that includes Stetho as a dependency.

Listing 4.25 Adding Stetho to `build.gradle`

```
dependencies {
    // other dependencies
    compile 'com.facebook.stetho:stetho:1.3.1'}
}
```

With the dependency added to the `build.gradle` file, Stetho now needs to be initialized. The recommended place to initialize Stetho is on the `Application` class's `onCreate()` method. Because Stetho functionality should be enabled only for debug builds, it is usually a good idea to inspect the `BuildConfig.DEBUG` flag to conditionally enable it. Listing 4.26 shows the `Application` class that is used in the device database app.

Listing 4.26 Device Database `Application` Class

```
public class DeviceDatabaseApplication extends Application {
    @Override
    public void onCreate() {
        super.onCreate();

        if (BuildConfig.DEBUG) {
            Stetho.initializeWithDefaults(this);
        }
    }
}
```

With Stetho initialized, the Chrome browser can be used to inspect a running application. To inspect the app details provided by Stetho, start the Chrome Web browser and enter "chrome://inspect" into the address bar. Figure 4.2 displays what should appear in Chrome.

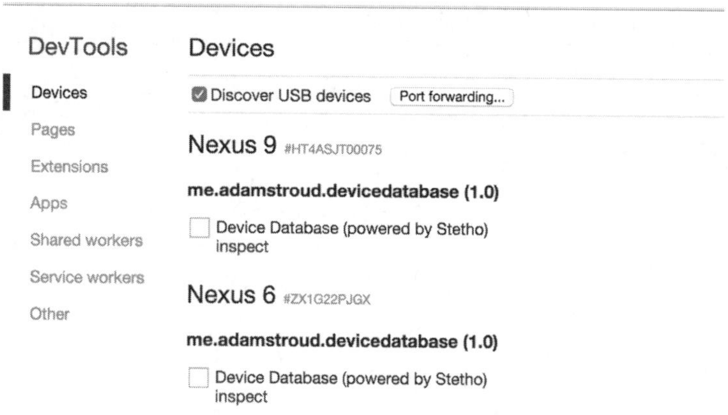

Figure 4.2   Stetho device list screen

Figure 4.2 shows all of the devices that are currently attached to the development machine as well as the package name of the app that is configured to use Stetho. In this case, Figure 4.2 indicates that Chrome can attach to either a Nexus 6 or a Nexus 9 device, both of which are running the device database app. To start viewing the data provided by Stetho, click the "inspect" link under the desired device to open the Developer Tools window for the device. Figure 4.3 shows the Developer Tools window for the Nexus 6.

To access the database information on the device, click the "Resources" tab at the top of the screen, then expand the Web SQL tree in the left panel. Under the Web SQL tree, there is an entry for the database file(s) for the app. For the device database, the file is named devices.db as can be seen from the entry under Web SQL. Expanding the device tree shows the tables in the database that can be inspected by simply clicking on them. In Figure 4.3, all the rows in the manufacturer table are being displayed. This view can be useful for inspecting the contents of a table in a graphical tool without going through the trouble of pulling the database from the device.

In addition to viewing table contents, Stetho allows a developer to send SQL statements to the database. To open up the SQL editor, click the database file name instead of a table. Figure 4.4 shows the SQL Editor in Stetho.

The Stetho SQL Editor provides a prompt that allows SQL statements to be typed in and run inline. Once a statement is run, the result of the statement is shown below it. This allows for complex queries such as JOINs to be built while connected to the database.

Accessing a database in Android can be invaluable when developing an app. Whether wrestling with the SQL syntax that will be used by Java code, or debugging a problem in the app, using tools like adb and Stetho can be vital.

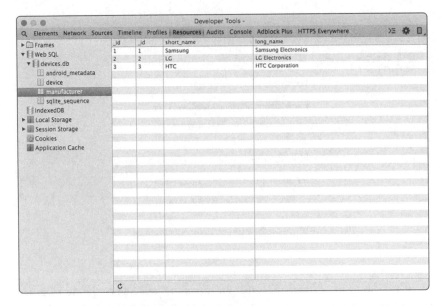

Figure 4.3 Developer Tools window

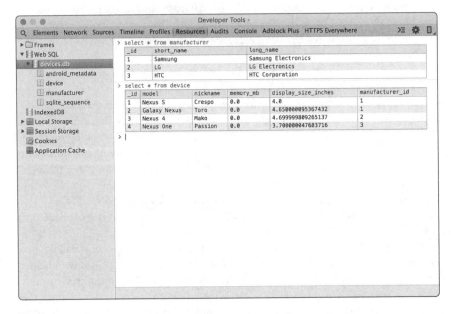

Figure 4.4 Stetho SQL Editor

Summary

The use of SQLite is becoming more frequent with complex apps. To support the need to have a database to store internal data for an app, Android provides tools to ease the complexity of working with SQLite. Tools like adb along with adb shell and adb shell dumpsys can make interacting with a database on a device possible. In addition, adb can be used to transfer a database from a device to a development machine so that more powerful tools may be used to interact with the database.

To further abstract the details of communicating with an SQLite database, Android also provides APIs that support different lifecycle events of a database. The SQLiteOpenHelper class provides convenience methods for creating, upgrading, and downgrading a database as well as configuring the connection to the database. The SQLiteDatabase class provides methods for executing raw SQL statements in SQLite.

This chapter provided some of the higher-level details for working with SQLite in Android. The rest of the book gets more into the specifics of how to implement different parts of the Android SQLite API.

Working with Databases in Android

The previous chapter introduced the SQLiteOpenHelper and SQLiteDatabase classes and discussed how to create databases. Of course, this is only the first step as a database is not very useful until it contains data and allows software to run queries against that data. This chapter explains how that is done in Android by discussing which Android SDK classes can be used to manipulate a database as well as query a database.

Manipulating Data in Android

The Android SDK contains many classes to support database operations. Along with the classes to support create, read, update, and delete (CRUD) operations, the SDK contains classes to help generate the queries that read the database. Following are the classes introduced in this chapter and a summary of how they are used to work with databases in Android:

- SQLiteDatabase: Represents a database in Android. It contains methods to perform standard database CRUD operations as well as control the SQLite database file used by an app.

- Cursor: Holds the result set from a query on a database. An app can read the data from a cursor and display it to a user or perform business logic based on the data contained in the cursor.

- ContentValues: A key/value store that inserts data into a row of a table. In most cases, the keys map to the column names of the table, and the values are the data to enter into the table.

- CursorLoader: Part of the loader framework that handles cursor objects.

- LoaderManager: Manages all loaders for an activity or fragment. The LoaderManager contains the API for initializing and resetting a loader that may be used by Android components.

Working with SQL is a vital part of working with databases in Android. In Chapter 2, "An Introduction to SQL," we saw how SQL is used to both create and upgrade a database. SQL can also be used to read, update, and delete information from a database in Android. The Android SDK provides useful classes to assist in creating SQL statements, while also supporting the use of Java string processing to generate SQL statements.

Working with SQL in Android involves calling methods on an `SQLiteDatabase` object. This class contains methods for building SQL statements as well as convenience methods to make issuing SQL statements to the database easy.

In a typical database use case, inserting data into the database is the step that follows creating the database. This makes sense since a database is useful only after it contains data. The steps to create a database were covered in the previous chapter, so this discussion starts with inserting data into a database.

Inserting Rows into a Table

The `SQLiteDatabase` class contains multiple convenience methods that can be used to perform insert operations. In most cases, one of the following three methods is used to perform an insert operation:

- `long insert(String table, String nullColumnHack, ContentValues values)`

- `long insertOrThrow(String table, String nullColumnHack, ContentValues values)`

- `long insertWithOnConflict(String table, String nullColumnHack, ContentValues values, int conflictAlgorithm)`

Notice that the parameter lists for all the variations of the insert methods contain (as the first three parameters) a `String tableName`, a `String nullColumnHack`, and `ContentValues values`. `SQLiteDatabase.insertWithOnConflict()` contains a fourth parameter which will be discussed soon. The common three parameters for the insert methods are

- `String table`: Gives the name of the table on which to perform the insert operation. This name needs to be the same as the name given to the table when it was created.

- `String nullColumnHack`: Specifies a column that will be set to `null` if the `ContentValues` argument contains no data.

- `ContentValues values`: Contains the data that will be inserted into the table.

`ContentValues` is a maplike class that matches a value to a `String` key. It contains multiple overloaded put methods that enforce type safety. Here is a list of the put methods supported by `ContentValues`:

- `void put(String key, Byte value)`

- `void put(String key, Integer value)`

- `void put(String key, Float value)`

- `void put(String key, Short value)`

- void put(String key, byte[] value)
- void put(String key, String value)
- void put(String key, Double value)
- void put(String key, Long value)
- void put(String key, Boolean value)

Each put method takes a String key and a typed value as parameters. When using ContentValues to insert data into a database, the key parameter must match the name of the column for the table that is targeted by the insert.

In addition to the overloaded put methods just listed, there is also a put(ContentValues other) method that can be used to add all the values from another ContentValues object, and a putNull(String key) method that adds a null value to a column of a table.

In a typical use case, a new instance of ContentValues is created and populated with all the values that should be inserted into the table. The ContentValues object is then passed to one of the insert methods from SQLiteDatabase. Listing 5.1 shows typical ContentValues usage.

Listing 5.1 Inserting Data with `SQLiteDatabase.insert()`

```
int id = 1;
String firstName = "Bob";
String lastName = "Smith";


ContentValues contentValues = new ContentValues();
contentValues.put("id", id);
contentValues.put("first_name", firstName);
contentValues.put("last_name", lastName);


SQLiteDatabase db = getDatabase();
db.insert("people", null, contentValues);
```

The code in Listing 5.1 passes a null for the value of the nullColumnHack to the SQLiteDatabase.insert() method. This is primarily because the code in Listing 5.1 "knows" what values were used to populate the values parameter and can ensure that there is at least one column represented in the ContentValues object. However, this is not always the case, and this is why the nullColumnHack parameter exists.

To explain nullColumnHack, consider the case where a ContentValues object that is inserted into a table contains no key/value pairs. This would amount to attempting to perform an insert operation without specifying any columns to insert data into. Such an insert statement is illegal in SQL because an insert statement *must* specify at least one column to insert data into. The nullColumnHack parameter can be used to guard against the "empty ContentValues" use case by specifying the name of a column that should be set to null in the case that the ContentValues object contains no data. Like the keys in the ContentValues instance, the string value for nullColumnHack must match the name of a column in the table that is targeted by the insert statement.

Listing 5.2 contains a usage of the nullColumnHack parameter. After the code in Listing 5.2 is run, column last_name will contain a value of null.

Listing 5.2 Specifying Null Columns with nullColumnHack

```
ContentValues contentValues = new ContentValues();

SQLiteDatabase db = getDatabase();

db.insert("people", "last_name", contentValues);
```

All three insert methods of SQLiteDatabase return a long. The value returned by the methods is the row ID of the inserted row, or a value of -1 if there was an error performing the insert.

Both Listings 5.1 and 5.2 used the simplest insert method to put a row into a table of the database, SQLiteDatabase.insert(). This method attempts to perform the insert and returns -1 if there is an error. The other two insert methods can be used to handle error cases differently.

SQLiteDatabase.insertOrThrow() is similar to SQLiteDatabase.insert(). However, it throws an SQLException if there was an error inserting the row. SQLiteDatabase.insertOrThrow() takes the same parameter list and has the same return type as SQLiteDatabase.insert(). It takes a String as the table parameter, a String as the nullColumnHack parameter, and a ContentValues object as the values parameter.

SQLiteDatabase.insertWithConflict(String table, String nullColumnHack, ContentValues values, int conflictAlgorithm) operates a little differently from the other two insert methods. It supports **conflict resolution** during the insert operation. Insertion conflicts occur when an attempt is made to insert a row into a table that would produce duplicates in a column that has the UNIQUE constraint applied to it, or duplicate data for the primary key. For example, consider the database table represented by Table 5.1.

Table 5.1 Example Database Table

first_name	last_name	id*
Bob	Smith	1
Ralph	Taylor	2
Sabrina	Anderson	3
Elizabeth	Hoffman	4
Abigail	Elder	5

In Table 5.1, the `id` column is the primary key and must hold a unique value for all rows across the entire table. Therefore, an attempt to insert a row containing an id of 1 would be an illegal operation in SQL because it would cause a `UNIQUE` constraint violation.

In this scenario, the two previous insert methods would indicate the error by either returning a value of -1 (`SQLiteDatabase.insert()`) or throwing an exception (`SQLiteDatabase.insertOrThrow()`). However, `SQLiteDatabase.insertWithOnConflict()` takes a fourth `int` parameter that can be used to tell the method how to handle the insertion conflict. The conflict resolution algorithms are defined as constants in `SQLiteDatabase` and can be one of the following:

- `SQLiteDatabase.CONFLICT_ROLLBACK`: Aborts the current insert statement. If the insert was part of a transaction, any previous statements are also undone and the value of `SQLiteDatabase.CONFLICT_FAIL` is returned by the `insertWithOnConflict()` method.

- `SQLiteDatabase.CONFLICT_ABORT`: Aborts the current statement. If the statement was part of a transaction, all previous statements are left untouched.

- `SQLiteDatabase.CONFLICT_FAIL`: Similar to `SQLiteDatabase.CONFLICT_ABORT`. In addition to aborting the current statement, this flag causes the method to return `SQLITE_CONSTRAINT` as a return code.

- `SQLiteDatabase.CONFLICT_IGNORE`: Skips the current statement and all other statements in the transaction are processed. When using this flag, no error value is returned.

- `SQLiteDatabase.CONFLICT_REPLACE`: Removes conflicting rows currently in the table, and the new row is inserted. An error will not be returned when using this flag.

- `SQLiteDatabase.NONE`: No conflict resolution is applied.

Updating Rows in a Table

Once data has been inserted into a database, it often needs to be updated. Like the three insert methods discussed previously, `SQLiteDatabase` has a couple of update methods that can be used to perform update operations on tables in a database:

- `int update(String table, ContentValues values, String whereClause, String[] whereArgs)`

- `int updateWithOnConflict(String table, ContentValues values, String whereClause, String[] whereArgs, int conflictAlgorithm)`

Much like the insert methods, both update methods take the same first four parameters, and `updateWithOnConflict()` takes a fifth parameter to define how a conflict should be resolved.

The common parameters for the update methods are

- `String table:` Defines the name of the table on which to perform the update. As with the insert statements, this string needs to match the name of a table in the database schema.
- `ContentValues values:` Contains the key/value pairs that map the columns and values to be updated by the update statement.
- `String whereClause:` Defines the WHERE clause of an UPDATE SQL statement. This string can contain the "?" character that will be replaced by the values in the whereArgs parameter.
- `String[] whereArgs:` Provides the variable substitutions for the whereClause argument.

Listing 5.3 shows an example of the `SQLiteDatabase.update()` call.

Listing 5.3 Example Update Call

```
String firstName = "Robert";


ContentValues contentValues = new ContentValues();
contentValues.put("first_name", firstName);


SQLiteDatabase db = getDatabase();
db.update("people", contentValues, "id = ?", new String[] {"1"});
```

Listing 5.3 updates the first name of the person that has an `id` of 1. The code first creates and populates a `ContentValues` object to hold the values that will be updated. It then makes the call to `SQLiteDatabase.update()` to issue the statement to the database. The rows are selected for the `update()` method using the `whereClause` and `whereArgs` parameters, which are in bold in Listing 5.3. The "?" in the `whereClause` parameter of the `update()` method serves as a placeholder for the statement. The `whereArgs` parameter, containing an array of strings, holds the value(s) that will replace the placeholder(s) when the statement is sent to the database. Since Listing 5.3 contains only a single placeholder, the string array only needs to be of size 1. When multiple placeholders are used, they will be replaced in order using the values from the string array. Passing `null` values for the `whereClause` and `whereArgs` parameters will cause the update statement to be run against *every* row in the table.

Table 5.2 shows the result of running the code in Listing 5.3 on Table 5.1. The changes to the row with `id` 1 are in bold.

The basic `whereClause` in Listing 5.3 matches the value of a single column. When using either update method, any legal SQL `whereClause` can be used to build the statement.

Table 5.2 `person` Table after Call to `update()`

first_name	last_name	id*
Robert	Smith	1
Ralph	Taylor	2
Sabrina	Anderson	3
Elizabeth	Hoffman	4
Abigail	Elder	5

Both update methods in `SQLiteDatabase` return an integer that represents the number of rows that were affected by the update statement.

Replacing Rows in a Table

In addition to insert and update operations, `SQLiteDatabase` supports the SQL replace operation with the `SQLiteDatabase.replace()` methods. In SQLite, a replace operation is an alias for `INSERT OR REPLACE`. It inserts the row if it does not already exist in a table, or updates the row if it already exists.

> **Note**
>
> This is different from an update operation because an update operation does not insert a row if it does not already exist.

There are two versions of the `replace()` method in `SQLiteDatabase`: `SQLiteDatabase.replace()` and `SQLiteDatabase.replaceOrThrow()`. Both methods have the same parameter list:

- `String table`: The name of the table on which to perform the operation
- `String nullColumnHack`: The name of a column to set a null value in case of an empty `ContentValues` object
- `ContcentValues initialValues`: The values to insert into the table

Both `replace()` methods return a `long` indicating the row ID of the new row, or a value of `-1` if an error occurs. In addition, `replaceOrThrow()` can also throw an exception in the case of an error.

Listing 5.4 shows an example of the `SQLiteDatabase.replace()` call.

Listing 5.4 Example Replace Call

```
String firstName = "Bob";


ContentValues contentValues = new ContentValues();
contentValues.put("first_name", firstName);
contentValues.put("id", 1);
```

```
SQLiteDatabase db = getDatabase();
db.replace("people", null, contentValues);
```

Table 5.3 shows the state of the `people` table after running the `SQLiteDatabase.replace()` call in Listing 5.4. Notice that the `last_name` attribute for the first row is now blank. This is because there was a conflict when processing the `SQLiteDatabase.replace()` method. The `ContentValues` object passed to `SQLiteDatabase.replace()` specified a value of 1 for the `id` attribute. The conflict arises because the `id` attribute is the primary key for the table, and there is already a row that contains an `id` of 1. To resolve the conflict, the `SQLiteDatabase.replace()` method removes the conflicting row and inserts a new row containing the values specified in the `ContentValues` object. Because the `ContentValues` object passed to `SQLiteDatabase.replace()` contains values for only the `first_name` and `id` attributes, only those attributes are populated in the new row.

Deleting Rows from a Table

Unlike the update and insert operations, `SQLiteDatabase` has only a single method for deleting rows: `SQLiteDatabase.delete(String table, String whereClause, String[] whereArgs)`. The `delete()` method's signature is similar to the signature of the `update()` method. It takes three parameters representing the name of the table from which to delete rows, the `whereClause`, and a string array of `whereArgs`. The processing of the `whereClause` and the `whereArgs` for the `delete()` method matches the `whereClause` processing for the `update()` method. The `whereClause` parameter contains question marks as placeholders, and the `whereArgs` parameter contains the values for the placeholders. Listing 5.5 shows a `delete()` method example.

Listing 5.5 Example Delete Method

```
SQLiteDatabase db = getDatabase();
db.delete("people", "id = ?", new String[] {"1"});
```

Table 5.3 `person` Table after `replace()` Call

first_name	last_name	id*
Bob		1
Ralph	Taylor	2
Sabrina	Anderson	3
Elizabeth	Hoffman	4
Abigail	Elder	5

Table 5.4 Row Deleted from the Table

first_name	last_name	id*
Ralph	Taylor	2
Sabrina	Anderson	3
Elizabeth	Hoffman	4
Abigail	Elder	5

The results of running the code in Listing 5.5 are shown in Table 5.4, where there is no longer a row with an id of 1.

Transactions

All of the previously discussed insert, update, and delete operations manipulate tables and rows in a database. While each operation is atomic (will either succeed or fail on its own), it is sometimes necessary to group a set of operations together and have the set of operations be atomic. There are times when a set of related operations should be allowed to manipulate the database only if all operations succeed to maintain database integrity. For these cases, a database transaction is usually used to ensure that the set of operations is atomic. In Android, the SQLiteDatabase class contains the following methods to support transaction processing:

- void beginTransaction(): Begins a transaction
- void setTransactionSuccessful(): Indicates that the transaction should be committed
- void endTransaction(): Ends the transaction causing a commit if setTransactionSuccessful() has been called

Using a Transaction

A transaction is started with the SQLiteDatabase.beginTransaction() method. Once a transaction is started, calls to any of the data manipulation method calls (insert(), update(), delete()) may be made. Once all of the manipulation calls have been made, the transaction is ended with SQLiteDatabase.endTransaction(). To mark the transaction as successful, allowing all the operations to be committed, SQLiteDatabase.setTransactionSuccessful() must be called before the call to SQLiteDatabase.endTransaction() is made. If endTransaction() is called without a call to setTransactionSuccessful(), the transaction will be rolled back, undoing all of the operations in the transaction.

Because the call to setTransactionSuccessful() affects what happens during the endTransaction() call, it is considered a best practice to limit the number of non–database operations between a call to setTransactionSuccessful() and endTransaction(). Additionally, do not perform any additional database manipulation

operations between the call to setTransactionSuccessful() and endTransaction().
Once the call to setTransactionSuccessful() is made, the transaction is marked as
clean and is committed in the call to endTransaction() even if errors have occurred after
the call to setTransactionSuccessful().

Listing 5.6 shows how a transaction should be started, marked successful, and ended in
Android.

Listing 5.6 Transaction Example

```
SQLiteDatabase db = getDatabase();

db.beginTransaction();


try {

    // insert/update/delete

    // insert/update/delete

    // insert/update/delete

    db.setTransactionSuccessful();

} finally {

    db.endTransaction();

}
```

Database operations that happen in a transaction as well as the call to
setTransaction() should take place in a try block with the call to endTransaction()
happening in a finally block. This ensures that the transaction will be ended even if an
unhandled exception is thrown while modifying the database.

Transactions and Performance

While transactions can help maintain data integrity by ensuring that multiple data
manipulation operations occur atomically, they can also be used purely to increase database
performance in Android. Like any operation performed in Java, there is overhead that is
associated with running SQL statements inside a transaction. While a single transaction
may not inject large amounts of overhead into a data manipulation routine, it is important
to remember that *every* call to insert(), update(), and delete() is performed in its
own transaction. Thus inserting 100 records into a table would mean that 100 individual
transactions will get started, cleaned, and closed. This can cause a severe slowdown when
attempting to perform a large number of data manipulation method calls.

To make multiple data manipulation calls run as fast as possible, it is generally a good
idea to combine them into a single transaction manually. If the Android SDK determines
that a call to insert()/update()/delete() is already inside of an open transaction, it
will not attempt to start another transaction for the single operation. With a few lines

of code, an app can dramatically speed up data manipulation operations. It is common to see a speed increase of five to ten times when wrapping even 100 data manipulation operations into a single transaction. These performance gains can increase as the number and complexity of operations increase.

Running Queries

Previous sections of this chapter discussed inserting, updating, and deleting data from a database. The last piece of database CRUD functionality is retrieving data from the database. As with the insert and update database operations, SQLiteDatabase contains multiple methods to support retrieving data. In addition to a series of query convenience methods, SQLiteDatabase includes a set of methods that support more free-form "raw" queries that can be generated via standard Java string manipulation methods. There is also an SQLiteQueryBuilder class that can further aid in developing complex queries such as joins.

Query Convenience Methods

The simplest way to issue a query to a database in Android is to use one of the query convenience methods located in SQLiteDatabase. These methods are the overloaded variations of SQLiteDatabase.query(). Each variant of the query() method takes a parameter list that includes the following:

- String table: Indicates the table name of the query.
- String[] columns: Lists the columns that should be included in the result set of the query.
- String selection: Specifies the WHERE clause of the selection statement. This string can contain "?" characters that can be replaced by the selectionArgs parameter.
- String[] selectionArgs: Contains the replacement values for the "?" of the selection parameter.
- String groupBy: Controls how the result set is grouped. This parameter represents the GROUP BY clause in SQL.
- String having: Contains the HAVING clause from an SQL SELECT statement. This clause specifies search parameters for grouping or aggregate SQL operators.
- String orderBy: Controls how the results from the query are ordered. This defines the ORDER BY clause of the SELECT statement.

The table name, column list selection string, and selection arguments parameters operate in the same manner as other operations discussed earlier in the chapter. What is different about the query() methods is the inclusion of the GROUP BY, HAVING, and ORDER BY clauses. These clauses allow an app to specify additional query attributes in the same way that an SQL SELECT statement would.

Each query method returns a cursor object that contains the result set for the query. Listing 5.7 shows a query returning data from the `people` table used in previous listings.

Listing 5.7 Simple Query

```
SQLiteDatabase db = getDatabase();


Cursor result = db.query("people",
        new String[] {"first_name", "last_name"},
        "id = ?",
        new String[] {"1"},
        null,
        null,
        null);
```

Listing 5.7 returns the `first_name` and `last_name` columns for the row that has an id of 1. The query statement passes `null` values for the GROUP BY, HAVING, and ORDER BY clauses since the result set should be of size 1 and these clauses have no effect on a result set with size 1.

The `query()` method also supports passing a `null` value for the `columns` parameter which will cause the query to return all the table's columns in the result set. It is usually better to specify the desired table columns rather than letting the Android SDK return all columns from a table and making the caller ignore the columns it does not need.

To return all the rows from a table, pass `null` values for the `selection` and `selectionArgs` parameters. A query returning all rows in a table is shown in Listing 5.8; the result set is sorted by ID in descending order.

Listing 5.8 Returning All Rows in a Table

```
SQLiteDatabase db = getDatabase();


Cursor result = db.query("people",
        new String[] {"first_name", "last_name"},
        null,
        null,
        null,
        null,
        "id DESC");
```

Raw Query Methods

If the query() convenience methods do not provide enough flexibility for a query that an app needs to run, the SQLiteDatabase.rawQuery() methods can be used instead. Like the convenience query methods, the rawQuery() methods are an overloaded set of methods. However, unlike the query() methods, the rawQuery() methods take two parameters as input: a String parameter representing the query to run, and a String[] to support query placeholder substitution. Listing 5.9 shows the same query as Listing 5.6 using the rawQuery() method instead of the query() convenience method.

Listing 5.9 Using the `rawQuery()` Method

```
SQLiteDatabase db = getDatabase();

Cursor result = db.rawQuery("SELECT first_name, last_name " +
                            "FROM people " +
                            "WHERE id = ?",
           new String[] {"1"});
```

Like the query() method, rawQuery() returns a cursor containing the result set for the query. The caller can read and process the resulting cursor in the same way that it processes the result from the query() methods.

The rawQuery() method allows an app to have great flexibility and construct more complex queries using joins, sub-queries, unions, or any other SQL construct supported by SQLite. However, it also forces the app developer to build the query in Java code (or perhaps from reading a string resource), which can be cumbersome for really complex queries.

To aid in building more complex queries, the Android SDK contains the SQLiteQueryBuilder class. The SQLiteQueryBuilder class is discussed in more detail in the next chapter with the discussion of ContentProviders.

Cursors

Cursors are what contain the result set of a query made against a database in Android. The Cursor class has an API that allows an app to read (in a type-safe manner) the columns that were returned from the query as well as iterate over the rows of the result set.

Reading Cursor Data

Once a cursor has been returned from a database query, an app needs to iterate over the result set and read the column data from the cursor. Internally, the cursor stores the rows of data returned by the query along with a position that points to the current row of data in the result set. When a cursor is returned from a query() method, its position points to the spot *before* the first row of data. This means that *before* any rows of data can be read from the cursor, the position must be moved to point to a valid row of data.

The Cursor class provides the following methods to manipulate its internal position:

- boolean Cursor.move(int offset): Moves the position by the given offset
- boolean Cursor.moveToFirst(): Moves the position to the first row
- boolean Cursor.moveToLast(): Moves the position to the last row
- boolean Cursor.moveToNext(): Moves the cursor to the next row relative to the current position
- boolean Cursor.moveToPosition(int position): Moves the cursor to the specified position
- Cursor.moveToPrevious(): Moves the cursor to the previous row relative to the current position

Each move() method returns a boolean to indicate whether the operation was successful or not. This flag is useful for iterating over the rows in a cursor.

Listing 5.10 shows the code to read data from a cursor containing all the data from the people table.

Listing 5.10 Reading Cursor Data

```
SQLiteDatabase db = getDatabase();


String[] columns = {"first_name",
        "last_name",
        "id"};


Cursor cursor = db.query("people",
        columns,
        null,
        null,
        null,
        null,
        null);


while(cursor.moveToNext()) {
    int index;

    index = cursor.getColumnIndexOrThrow("first_name");
    String firstName = cursor.getString(index);
```

```
index = cursor.getColumnIndexOrThrow("last_name");
String lastName = cursor.getString(index);


index = cursor.getColumnIndexOrThrow("id");
long id = cursor.getLong(index);


//... do something with data
}
```

The code in Listing 5.10 uses a `while` loop to iterate over the rows in the cursor returned from the `query()` method. This pattern is useful if the code performing the iteration "controls" the cursor and has sole access to it. If other code can access the cursor (for example, if the cursor is passed into a method as a parameter), the cursor should also be set to a known position as the current position may not be the position ahead of the first row.

Once the cursor's position is pointing to a valid row, the columns of the row can be read from the cursor. To read the data, the code in Listing 5.10 uses two methods from the cursor class: `Cursor.getColumnIndexOrThrow()` and one of the type `get()` methods from the `Cursor` class.

The `Cursor.getColumnIndexOrThrow()` method takes a `String` parameter that indicates which column to read from. This `String` value needs to correspond to one of the strings in the `columns` parameter that was passed to the `query()` method. Recall that the `columns` parameter determines what table columns are part of the result set. `Cursor.getColumnIndexOrThrow()` throws an exception if the column name does not exist in the cursor. This usually indicates that the column was not part of the `columns` parameter of the `query()`. The `Cursor` class also contains a `Cursor.getColumnIndex()` method that does not throw an exception if the column name is not found. Instead, `Cursor.getColumnIndex()` returns a `-1` value to represent an error.

Once the column index is known, it can be passed to one of the cursor's `get()` methods to return the typed data of the row. The `get()` methods return the data from the column in the row which can then be used by the app. The `Cursor` class contains the following methods for retrieving data from a row:

- `byte[] Cursor.getBlob(int columnIndex)`: Returns the value as a `byte[]`
- `double Cursor.getDouble(int columnIndex)`: Returns the value as a `double`
- `float Cursor.getFloat(int columnIndex)`: Returns the value as a `float`
- `int Cursor.getInt(int columnIndex)`: Returns the value as an `int`
- `long Cursor.getLong(int columnIndex)`: Returns the value as a `long`
- `short Cursor.getShort(int columnIndex)`: Returns the value as a `short`
- `String Cursor.getString(int columnIndex)`: Returns the value as a `String`

Managing the Cursor

The internals of a cursor can contain a lot of resources such as all the data returned from the query along with a connection to the database. Because of this, it is important to handle a cursor appropriately and tell it to clean up when it is no longer in use to prevent memory leaks. To perform the cleanup, the Cursor class contains the Cursor.close() method, which needs to be called when an activity or fragment no longer needs the cursor.

In versions of Android before 3.0, cursor maintenance was left to developers. They either had to handle the closing of the cursor themselves or had to make sure they informed an activity that it was using a cursor so the activity would close the cursor at an appropriate time.

Android 3.0 introduced the loader framework that takes care of managing cursors for activities/fragments. To support older versions of Android, the loader framework has also been backported and added to the support library. When using the loader framework, apps no longer need to worry about calling Cursor.close() or informing an activity/fragment of a cursor that it needs to manage.

CursorLoader

The previous section discussed the low-level details of how to perform database operations in Android using SQLiteDatabase. However, it did not discuss the fact that databases on Android are stored on the file system, meaning that accessing a database from the main thread should be avoided in order to keep an app responsive for the user. Accessing a database from a non-UI thread typically involves some type of asynchronous mechanism, where a request for database access is made and the response to the request is delivered at some point in the future. Because views can be updated only from the UI thread, apps need to make calls to update views on the UI thread even though the results to a database query may be delivered on a different thread.

Android provides multiple tools for executing potentially long-running code off the UI thread while having results processed in the UI thread. One such tool is the loader framework. For accessing databases, there is a specialized component of the Loader called CursorLoader, which, in addition to managing a cursor's lifecycle with regard to an activity lifecycle, also takes care of running queries in a background thread and presenting the results on the main thread, making it easy to update the display.

Creating a CursorLoader

There are multiple pieces to the CursorLoader API. A CursorLoader is a specialized member of Android's loader framework specifically designed to handle cursors. In a typical implementation, a CursorLoader uses a ContentProvider to run a query against a database, then returns the cursor produced from the ContentProvider back to an activity or fragment.

Note

ContentProviders are discussed in detail in Chapter 6, "Content Providers." For now, it is enough to know that they abstract the functionality provided by SQLiteDatabase away from an activity (or fragment) so the activity does not need to worry about making method calls on an SQLiteDatabase object.

An activity only needs to use the LoaderManager to start a CursorLoader and respond to callbacks for CursorLoader events.

In order to use a CursorLoader, an activity gets an instance of the LoaderManager. The LoaderManager manages all loaders for an activity or fragment, including a CursorLoader.

Once an activity or fragment has a reference to its LoaderManager, it tells the LoaderManager to initialize a loader by providing the LoaderManager with an object that implements the LoaderManager.LoaderCallbacks interface in the LoaderManager. initLoader() method. The LoaderManager.LoaderCallbacks interface contains the following methods:

- Loader<T> onCreateLoader(int id, Bundle args)
- void onLoadFinished(Loader<T>, T data)
- void onLoaderReset(Loader<T> loader)

LoaderCallbacks.onCreate() is responsible for creating a new loader and returning it to the LoaderManager. To use a CursorLoader, LoaderCallbacks.onCreate() creates, initializes, and returns a CursorLoader object that contains the information necessary to run a query against a database (through a ContentProvider).

Listing 5.11 shows the implementation of the onCreateLoader() method returning a CursorLoader.

Listing 5.11 Implementing onCreateLoader()

```
@Override
public Loader<Cursor> onCreateLoader(int id, Bundle args) {
    Loader<Cursor> loader = null;
    switch (id) {
        case LOADER_ID_PEOPLE:
            loader = new CursorLoader(this,
                    PEOPLE_URI,
                    new String[] {"first_name", "last_name", "id"},
                    null,
                    null,
                    "id ASC");
```

```
            break;
    }


    return loader;
}
```

In Listing 5.11, the onCreateLoader() method first checks the ID it was passed to know which loader it needs to create. It then instantiates a new CursorLoader object and returns it to the caller.

The constructor of CursorLoader can take parameters that allow the CursorLoader to run a query against a database. The CursorLoader constructor called in Listing 5.11 takes the following parameters:

- Content context: Provides the application context needed by the loader
- Uri uri: Defines the table against which to run the query
- String[] projection: Specifies the SELECT clause for the query
- String selection: Specifies the WHERE clause which may contain "?" as placeholders
- String[] selectionArgs: Defines the substitution variables for the selection placeholders
- String sortOrder: Defines the ORDER BY clause for the query

The last four parameters, projection, selection, selectionArgs, and sortOrder, are similar to parameters passed to the SQLiteDatabase.query() discussed earlier in this chapter. In fact, they also do the same thing: define what columns to include in the result set, define which rows to include in the result set, and define how the result set should be sorted.

Once the data is loaded, Loader.Callbacks.onLoadFinished() is called, allowing the callback object to use the data in the cursor. Listing 5.12 shows a call to onLoadFinished().

Listing 5.12 Implementing onLoadFinished()

```
@Override
public void onLoadFinished(Loader<Cursor> loader, Cursor data) {
while(data.moveToNext()) {
    int index;


    index = data.getColumnIndexOrThrow("first_name");
    String firstName = data.getString(index);
```

```
    index = data.getColumnIndexOrThrow("last_name");

    String lastName = data.getString(index);


    index = data.getColumnIndexOrThrow("id");

    long id = data.getLong(index);


    //... do something with data
}
```

Notice how similar the code in Listing 5.12 is to the code in Listing 5.10 where a direct call to SQLiteDatabase.query() was made. The code to process the results of the query is nearly identical. Also, when using the LoaderManager, the activity does not need to worry about calling Cursor.close() or making the database query on a non-UI thread. That is all handled by the loader framework.

There is one other important point to note about onLoadFinished(). It is not only called when the initial data is loaded; it is also called when changes to the data are detected by the Android database. There is one line of code that needs to be added to the ContentProvider to trigger this, and that is discussed next chapter. However, having a single point in the code that receives query data and can update the display can be really convenient. This architecture allows activities to easily react to changes in data without the developer worrying about explicitly notifying the activities of changes to the data. The LoaderManager handles the lifecycle and knows when to requery and pass the data to the LoaderManager.Callbacks when it needs to.

There is one more method in the LoaderManager.Callbacks interface that needs to be implemented to use a CursorLoader: LoaderManager.Callbacks. onLoaderReset(Loader<T> loader). This method is called by the LoaderManager when a loader that was previously created is reset and its data should no longer be used. For a CursorLoader, this typically means that any references to the cursor that was provided by onLoadFinished() need to be discarded as they are no longer active. If a reference to the cursor is not persisted, the onLoadReset() method can be empty.

Starting a CursorLoader

Now that the mechanics of using a CursorLoader have been discussed, it is time to focus on how to start a data load operation with the LoaderManager. For most use cases, an activity or a fragment implements the LoaderManager.Callbacks interface since it makes sense for the activity/fragment to process the cursor result in order to update its display. To start the load, LoaderManager.initLoader() is called. This ensures that the loader is created, calling onCreateLoader(), loading the data, and making a call to onLoadFinished().

Both activities and fragments can get their `LoaderManager` object by calling `getLoaderManager()`. They can then start the load process by calling `LoaderManager.initLoader()`. `LoaderManager.initLoader()` takes the following parameters:

- `int id`: The ID of the loader. This is the same ID that is passed to `onCreateLoader()` and can be used to identify a loader (see Listing 5.11).

- `Bundle args`: Extra data that might be needed to create the loader. This is also passed to `onCreateLoader()` (see Listing 5.11). This value can be null.

- `LoaderManager.LoaderCallbacks callbacks`: An object to handle the `LoaderManager` callbacks. This is typically the activity or fragment that is making the call to `initLoader()`.

The call to `initLoader()` should happen early in an Android component's lifecycle. For activities, `initLoader()` is usually called in `onCreate()`. Fragments should call `initLoader()` in `onActivityCreated()` (calling `initLoader()` in a fragment before its activity is created can cause problems).

Once `initLoader()` is called, the `LoaderManager` checks to see if there is already a loader associated with the ID passed to `initLoader()`. If there is no loader associated with the ID, `LoaderManager` makes a call to `onCreateLoader()` to get the loader and associate it with the ID. If there is currently a loader associated with the ID, `initLoader()` continues to use the preexisting loader object. If the caller is in the started state, and there is already a loader associated with the ID, and the associated loader has already loaded its data, then a call to `onLoadFinished()` is made directly from `initLoader()`. This usually happens only if there is a configuration change.

One detail to note about `initLoader()` is that it cannot be used to alter the query that was used to create the `CursorLoader` that gets associated with an ID. Once the loader is created (remember, the query is used to define the `CursorLoader`), it is reused only on subsequent calls to `initLoader()`. If an activity/fragment needs to alter the query that was used to create a `CursorLoader` with a given ID, it needs to make a call to `restartLoader()`.

Restarting a `CursorLoader`

Unlike the call to `LoaderManager.initLoader()`, a call to `LoaderManager.restartLoader()` disassociates a loader with a given ID and allows it to be re-created. This results in `onCreateLoader()` being called again, allowing a new `CursorLoader` object to be made which can contain a different query for a given ID. `LoaderManager.restartLoader()` takes the same parameter list as `initLoader()` (`int id`, `Bundle args`, `LoaderManager.Callbacks`, and `callbacks`) and discards the old loader. This makes `restartLoader()` useful for when the query of a `CursorLoader` needs to change. However, the `restartLoader()` method should not be used to simply handle activity/fragment lifecycle changes as they are already handled by the `LoaderManager`.

Summary

This chapter presented the basic API for working with databases in Android and built upon the concepts introduced in Chapter 4, "SQLite in Android," where database creation was discussed. By using SQLiteDatabase and its create(), insert(), update(), replace(), and delete() methods, an app is able to manipulate an internal database. In addition, an app can call the query and rawQuery() methods to retrieve the data from a database to perform actions on that data, or just display it to a user.

Query data is returned in the form of a cursor that can be iterated over to access the result set returned by a query.

While this chapter introduced some of the low-level "plumbing" needed to use an in-app database, there are higher-level components that allow apps to both abstract some of the data access details away from components that define and drive user interaction (activities and fragments) as well as allow data to be shared across apps and across processes. These concepts are introduced in the next chapter with the discussion of content providers.

6

Content Providers

This chapter builds upon the brief introduction to content providers presented in Chapter 5, "Working with Databases in Android." It discusses how to use a content provider to share data between internal parts of an app as well as with external apps. This chapter also discusses when it is appropriate to use a content provider, and it provides the code for a simple content provider implementation.

REST-Like APIs in Android

Content providers allow an app to expose structured data to other components of the same app and/or other apps. They also present an API similar to Representational State Transfer (REST) for accessing the data. Since the data in a content provider is usually retrieved using a URI, they also present a REST-like API for accessing data in Android.

RESTful APIs have become a popular way to implement Web services recently. A typical RESTful API makes use of a URL scheme convention and uses HTTP methods to retrieve and manipulate data. For example, a RESTful API may have a URL scheme convention of http://api.example.com/items that a client would use to address all of the concrete items the Web service supports. Sending an HTTP GET request to this URL would retrieve the entire list of items the Web service can provide. To get a single item, a client would append the ID of the item to the end of the URL. For example, to get the details of an item with ID 17, a client would send an HTTP GET request to the URL http://api.example.com/items/17. This would return the details of a single item in the serialization format the Web service supports.

Content providers work in a similar fashion. Specifying a URL tells a content provider which type of data to perform an operation (query, insert, update, delete) on. Usually, content providers follow the same pattern when defining their URIs as the RESTful pattern just described. The base URI for a set of data follows the general URI form of content://some_authority/items, and a specific member of the data can be accessed by appending the ID to the URI (content://some_authority/items/32).

> **Note**
>
> The actual format of the URI scheme that defines the API for a content provider can be specified by the content provider. Always follow the provider's documentation and URI specs.

Content URIs

Content provider URIs (also called content URIs) typically have the following formats:

- `content://authority/path`
- `content://authority/path/id`

The first part of the URI (`content://`) is referred to as the **scheme**. For content URIs, this is always `content://`.

The next part of the URI is referred to as the **authority**. The authority is specific to an individual content provider and allows Android to determine which content provider to route a request to. Because the authority for each content provider exists at the Android system level, it is important that all content providers use unique authorities to avoid naming collisions. A standard convention is to use an app's package name with `.provider` appended to the end to ensure uniqueness across the Android device.

The **path** portion of a content URI indicates the collection of data being targeted by a request. For example, content providers that are backed by a database may use the path to indicate a certain table in the database that a request is targeting.

The last part of a content URI is the ID. The ID can be used to uniquely identify an individual data member in a content URI path. For content providers that are backed by a database, the ID usually represents the primary key of the table that is defined by the path. The ID is optional, and when not used, a URI refers to the entire collection of data that is referred to by the path.

Exposing Data with a Content Provider

Content providers have the ability to expose multiple types of data to app components. In addition, the details of how the data is stored and retrieved can vary without these details being exposed to other app components. Content providers can expose data that is stored in a database or files stored on the file system, or even retrieve data from a remote Web server. The remainder of this chapter assumes a fairly common case for content providers, providing access to data that is stored in an SQLite database.

The next sections discuss the APIs that are used to communicate with a content provider and introduce some of the concepts that are necessary to work with content providers in Android.

The `ContentProvider` and the `ContentResolver` are the two major classes that apps interact with, both directly and indirectly, when working with the content provider API. The details of how each class is used and how they interact are discussed in the following sections.

Implementing a Content Provider

`android.content.ContentProvider` is the base class for all content providers in Android. Whether the concrete implementation that is provided by an app returns data from a database, provides access to a file on the file system, or exposes data from a Web service, it extends `android.content.ContentProvider`. All content providers must also implement, at minimum, the following abstract methods inherited from `android.content.ContentProvider`:

- `boolean onCreate()`
- `Uri insert(Uri uri, ContentValues values)`
- `int delete(Uri uri, String selection, String[] selectionArgs)`
- `String getType(Uri uri)`
- `Cursor query(Uri uri, String[] projection, String selection, String[] selectionArgs, String sortOrder)`
- `int update(Uri uri, ContentValues values, String selection, String[] selectionArgs)`

onCreate()

The `onCreate()` method is called at the beginning of a content provider's lifecycle and, like other Android components, can be a convenient place to perform initialization for the class. However, it is important to remember that the call to `onCreate()` happens on the main thread, so it is important to not perform any lengthy tasks in `onCreate()`. Also, unlike other Android components, the call to `ContentProvider.onCreate()` happens at app start-up as opposed to the first time the content provider is accessed. This means that any delays in finishing the method will cause the entire app to be delayed when starting up.

If a content provider is supported by an SQLite database, extra care should be used when initially accessing the database. It is important to remember that a database may be upgraded, if needed, when it is first accessed. This means that the `onCreate()` method of a content provider is *not* a good place to create a connection to a database as that could cause the database to be upgraded in the main thread while the app is started. Since the database is likely to reside on disk, it will almost certainly delay the initial app open routine.

`ContentProvider.onCreate()` returns a `boolean` indicating if the initialization was successful. A value of `true` indicates that the provider was successfully initialized, and a value of `false` indicates an error.

insert()

The `insert()` method is used to insert an entry into the database:

```
insert(Uri uri, ContentValues values)
```

The method takes two parameters: a URI declaring which table to perform the insertion on, and a `ContentValues` object that contains the values to be inserted into the table. After the row is inserted, this method should make a call to `ContentResolver.notifyChange()` to make other parts of the app, or other apps, aware that the table has been updated if they are using a content observer.

Recall from Chapter 5 that the content values used by the `SQLiteDatabase.insert()` method contain name/value pairs for the row to be inserted. The `ContentValues` object passed to `ContentProvider.insert()` works the same way. In fact, the `ContentValues` object passed to `ContentProvider.insert()` can be used as a parameter to `SQLiteDatabase.insert()` without modification to insert data into a table.

`ContentProvider.insert()` finishes by returning a `Uri` object that references the newly created row in the provider. This URI should be constructed in a way that allows an external caller to retrieve the newly inserted row from the content provider.

This method can be called on any thread, so it must ensure that all logic can execute safely when called by multiple threads.

delete()

The `ContentProvider.delete()` method removes the row from the table that is specified by the uri parameter:

```
delete(Uri uri, String selection, String[] selectionArgs)
```

The uri parameter may refer either to a table in the database (`content://authority/table`) or to a specific row of a table to be deleted (`content://authority/table/id`). When the URI refers to a table, the `delete()` method must use the `selection` and `selectionArgs` parameters to determine which row(s) should be deleted from the table.

Like the `ContentProvider.insert()` method, the `selection` and `selectionArgs` parameters can be passed to `SQLiteDatabase.delete()` without being manipulated by the `ContentProvider.delete()` method.

The `ContentProvider.delete()` method returns the number of rows that have been deleted by the call. This is usually the same value that is returned by `SQLiteDatabase.delete()`.

The `ContentProvider.delete()` method may also be called on any thread and needs to ensure that its operation happens in a thread-safe manner. It should call `ContentResolver.notifyChange()` to inform any observers that the table has changed.

getType()

The `ContentProvider.getType()` method returns the MIME type for the given URI:

```
getType(Uri uri)
```

When the URI refers to a table (`content://authority/table`), the method should return a `String` that starts with `vnd.android.cursor.dir/`. When the URI refers to a single row in a table (`content://authority/table/id`), the method should return a `String` that begins with `vnd.android.cursor.item`.

After the prefix that is dependent on the type of URI, the rest of the returned `String` should contain the content provider's authority and the table name from the URI. For example, if the input URI is `content://myAuthority/tableName/32`, the MIME type would be

```
vnd.android.cursor.item/myAuthority.tableName
```

This method can be called by any thread and must ensure thread safety.

> **Note**
>
> The discussion of MIME types applies only to content providers that are returning data from a database. If the content provider is exposing files to a client, the `getType()` method should return the MIME type of the file.

query()

The query() method performs a query against the content provider:

```
query(Uri uri,

       String[] projection,

       String selection,

       String[] selectionArgs,

       String sortOrder)
```

The URI in the parameter list specifies the table(s) against which to perform the query. All other parameters can be passed to an `SQLiteDatabase.query()` method, or used by an `SQLiteQueryBuilder` to build the query. The cursor resulting from either `SQLiteDatabase.query()` or `SQLiteQueryBuilder` should be returned by `ContentProvider.query()`.

The `ContentProvider.query()` method may be called from any thread.

update()

The update() method performs an update operation on the table specified by the URI:

```
update(Uri uri,

       ContentValues values,

       String selection,

       String[] selectionArgs)
```

The `ContentValues` parameter contains the updated column/value pairs for the table. The `selection` and `selectionArgs` parameters select which rows from the table the update should be applied to. The `values`, `selection`, and `selectionArgs` parameters can all be passed to an `SQLiteDatabase.update()` method without modification. The return value from `SQLiteDatabase.update()` should also be returned by `ContentProvider.update()`.

The `ContentProvider.update()` method should make a call to `ContentResolver.notifyChange()` to notify observers that the table data has changed. The method can be called from any thread.

bulkInsert() **and** applyBatch()

The methods discussed in the previous sections *must* be implemented because they are abstract methods of `android.content.ContentProvider` and failure to implement them results in a compile error. There are, however, two additional methods that *should* be overridden:

- `int bulkInsert(Uri uri, ContentValues[] values)`
- `ContentProviderResult applyBatch(ArrayList<ContentProviderOperations operations)`

Both methods are used to perform multiple operations on a database. The problem with their default implementations is that neither wraps the operations in a transaction, which means that neither method is atomic (individual operations can fail). Additionally, recall from Chapter 5 that when not wrapped in a transaction, every `SQLiteDatabase` modification operation starts a new transaction for the individual operation. This has severe impacts on runtime performance and makes both calls much slower than if they wrapped all operations in a single transaction.

In both cases, each method should, at minimum, be overridden to wrap a call to super in a transaction. Listing 6.1 shows the minimal override for both methods.

Listing 6.1 Adding Transaction Support to `bulkInsert()` and `applyBatch()`

```
@Override
public int bulkInsert(Uri uri, ContentValues[] values) {
    final SQLiteDatabase db = helper.getWritableDatabase();

    db.beginTransaction();

    try {
        final int count = super.bulkInsert(uri, values);
        db.setTransactionSuccessful();

        return count;
    } finally {
        db.endTransaction();
    }
}


@Override
public
ContentProviderResult[]
applyBatch(ArrayList<ContentProviderOperation> operations)
```

```
        throws OperationApplicationException {
    final SQLiteDatabase db = helper.getWritableDatabase();

    db.beginTransaction();

    try {
        final ContentProviderResult[] results =
                super.applyBatch(operations);
        db.setTransactionSuccessful();

        return results;
    } finally {
        db.endTransaction();
    }
}
```

In addition to inheriting from android.content.ContentProvider and implementing the required methods, a content provider needs to be listed in an app's manifest, specifically in the <application> element. Listing 6.2 shows the minimal entry for a content provider that is available only to the app containing it.

Listing 6.2 Content Provider Manifest Listing

```
<provider
    android:name=".provider.MyProvider"
    android:authorities="com.example.provider"
    android:exported="false" />
```

The <provider> element in Listing 6.2 declares a class named MyProvider as an available content provider for the app with the android:name attribute of the <provider> element. The android:authorities attribute lists the authorities that the content provider supports. Content authorities are used in URIs that are passed to a content resolver which will the send the request to the correct content provider. The android:authorities element is what binds an authority to a content provider.

The third attribute in the minimal <provider> element is the android:export attribute. This attribute defines whether the content provider can be used by other apps. In Listing 6.2, the content provider is available only to the local app. Allowing a content provider to be accessed by other apps will be discussed in detail later in the chapter.

With an implementation of an `android.content.ContentProvider` and an entry for that content provider in the manifest, an app is ready to start using the content provider. To use the content provider, an app must first access its content resolver.

Content Resolver

Requesting operations on a content provider (insert, update, delete, query) is usually not done on a content provider object directly. Instead, an app requests that a content resolver send operation requests to a content provider. A content resolver has methods that conceptually delegate responsibility to a content provider. To get a reference to a content resolver, an app makes a call to `Context.getResolver()`. Once the app has access to a content resolver, it can begin to make method calls on the content resolver to have a similar method called on a content provider. A content resolver has the following methods available to a client:

- `Uri insert(Uri uri, ContentValue values)`
- `int delete(Uri uri, String selection, String[] selectionArgs)`
- `String getType(Uri uri)`
- `Cursor query(Uri uri, String[] projection, String selection, String[] selectionArgs, String sortOrder)`
- `int update(Uri uri, ContentValues values, String selection, String[] selectionArgs)`
- `int bulkInsert(Uri uri, ContentValues[] values)`
- `ContentProviderResult[] applyBatch(String authority, ArrayList<ContentProviderOperation> operations)`

Notice that the methods in a content resolver map to the methods of the same signature on a content provider. This allows the content resolver to pass a method call, with its parameter list, to the content provider.

The reason it is useful to have a content resolver act as a delegate to a content provider, instead of making method calls on a content provider directly, is that a content resolver aids in marshaling method calls across Android process boundaries. This allows an app to make interprocess method calls without worrying about details such as data serialization or deserialization. This interprocess support is what allows a content provider to be implemented by one app and seamlessly used by another. In addition, this feature allows a single app to execute in two separate processes and easily read, write, and manipulate its data.

Exposing a Remote Content Provider to External Apps

The code introduced in the previous section builds the foundation for using a content provider in most cases. However, there is one other configuration detail that needs to be addressed in order to allow a content provider to expose its data to other apps. Recall from Listing 6.2 that the manifest entry would not allow the content provider to be exported to other Android apps (`android:exported` was set to `false` in the manifest). In order to allow the content provider to be used by other apps, the `exported` flag needs to be set to `true`. In addition, the manifest should assign permissions that external apps need to use in order to control the external access to the data.

By default, when a content provider is exported, all other apps can use the content provider for both read and write access unless the content provider declares a permission model in its `<provider>` element in the app's manifest. To declare the permission model, app developers must first decide what types of permissions they want for the content provider. The permissions for a content provider can vary in the granularity of the access they provide. A permission can be set ranging from access to the top-level content provider down to individual parts of the data a content provider exposes with finer-level permissions taking precedence.

By using permissions, a content provider gives the user the ability to decide which other apps have access to the data of the content provider. The user is presented with a UI that can explain which data-related permissions an external app is requesting and has the ability to decide whether to grant access to that data by an external app.

Provider-Level Permission

An app can declare a single read/write-level permission for the entire content provider. If an external app has this permission, it has read/write access to any of the data exposed by the content provider. This top-level permission is controlled by the `android:permission` attribute of the `<provider>` element in the app manifest.

Individual Read/Write Permissions

Adding different permissions to read and write operations of a content provider allows an app to provide more control over access to its data. Instead of declaring a single permission for read/write access to the entire content provider, an app can assign different permissions for read and write operations in its manifest.

To assign a read permission, an app uses the `android:readPermission` attribute of the `<provider>` element in the manifest. To assign a write permission, an app assigns a value to the `android:writePermission` attribute of the `<provider>` element. Using two permissions, an app can allow the ability to read its data while disallowing write access to its data.

Both `android:readPermission` and `android:writePermission` take precedence over `android:permission` of the `<provider>` element.

URI Path Permissions

Path permissions allow a content provider to assign individual permissions for different paths in its URIs, enabling the content provider to allow access to different sections of the data it exposes. Path permissions are set using the `<path-permission>` element as a child of the `<provider>` element. A `<path-permission>` element may have the following attributes:

- `android:path`: The full path for the URI to configure permissions for.
- `android:pathPrefix`: The beginning of the path that should be affected by the element. This is useful if multiple URI paths have the same beginning URI.
- `android:pathPattern`: A pattern to match the paths that should be affected by the element.
- `android:permission`: The permission to apply to the entire path. This affects both reading from and writing to the path and can be overridden by `android:readPermission` and `android:writePermission`.
- `android:readPermission`: The permission for reading the paths.
- `android:writePermission`: The permission for writing to the paths.

Content Provider Permissions

In addition to associating permissions with certain content provider actions, apps usually need to declare their own content-provider-related permissions. Creating app-specific permissions allows a content provider to have full control over its data access since it is unlikely that permissions already exist to fit the needs of a content provider.

To define a new permission for content provider use, an app needs to add a `<permission>` element to its manifest under the `<manifest>` element. The `<permission>` element can contain the following attributes:

- `android:description`: Text to describe the permission to the user. This can be longer than the label and should inform users about what action they may be enabling.
- `android:icon`: An icon that represents the permission.
- `android:label`: A name given to the permission that will be displayed to the user.
- `android:name`: The name given to the permission. This name is what will be used by the content provider entries in the manifest. The name needs to be unique across Android, so a good permission-naming pattern is to prefix the permission with the app package name (`com.example.myapp.mypermission`).
- `android:permissionGroup`: The group of which the permission is a member. It is not mandatory to add the permission to a group.
- `android:protectionLevel`: The risk level of granting the permission. This allows an app to dictate which other apps can be granted the permission:
  - `normal`: Permission presents a low level of risk to the system, user, or other apps. This is the default value.

- dangerous: Permission allows actions that present a higher level of risk to the user or the system such as exposing private information about the user to other apps.

- signature: Permission is granted only to apps that are signed by the same certificate as the app declaring the permission.

- signatureOrSystem: Permission is granted only if the app requesting the permission is signed with the same certificate as the app declaring the permission or the app requesting the permission is a "system" app (located on the /system partition of the device). This permission is usually reserved for device vendors.

Listing 6.3 shows the manifest declaration of two permissions and the use of the permissions in the declaration of a content provider.

Listing 6.3 Declaring Content Provider Permissions

```
<permission
    android:description="@string/permission_description_read_devices"
    android:name="me.adamstroud.devicedatabase.provider.READ_DEVICES" />


<permission
    android:description="@string/permission_description_write_devices"
    android:name="me.adamstroud.devicedatabase.provider.WRITE_DEVICES" />


<application
    android:allowBackup="true"
    android:icon="@mipmap/ic_launcher"
    android:label="@string/app_name"
    android:supportsRtl="true"
    android:theme="@style/AppTheme"
    android:name=".DeviceDatabaseApplication">


    <provider
        android:name=".provider.DevicesProvider"
        android:authorities="${applicationId}.provider"
        android:exported="false"
        android:readPermission=
```

```
                    "me.adamstroud.devicedatabase.provider.READ_DEVICES"
android:writePermission=
                    "me.adamstroud.devicedatabase.provider.WRITE_DEVICES"/>
```

Content Provider Contract

In order to expose a content provider's data, an app should also declare its contract. The content provider's contract is especially important if the data can be accessed by external apps as it defines the tables and rows that can be accessed using the content provider.

Using a content provider involves specifying URIs and columns that can be used when making queries. For a database-backed content provider, the database structure and especially table and column names are intimate details of the content provider that any external component should not need to worry about.

The contract class for a content provider is where an app can define the URIs as well as specific details of how the data is structured in the content provider. Think of the contract class as the external API for a content provider that should be published to external apps that need to use the content provider. By including constants in a contract class, an external app can easily use a content provider's API.

An easy way to define the contract class for a content provider is to store constants in a common place so they can be accessed by both local app components and external apps.

Listing 6.4 shows an example content provider implementation.

Listing 6.4 Implementing the Contract Class

```java
public final class DevicesContract {
    public static final String AUTHORITY =
            String.format("%s.provider", BuildConfig.APPLICATION_ID);

    public static final Uri AUTHORITY_URI = new Uri.Builder()
            .scheme(ContentResolver.SCHEME_CONTENT)
            .authority(AUTHORITY)
            .build();

    public interface Device extends BaseColumns {
        /* default */ static final String PATH = "device";
        public static final String MODEL = "model";
        public static final String NICKNAME = "nickname";
        public static final String MEMORY_MB = "memory_mb";
```

```
        public static final String DISPLAY_SIZE_INCHES =
                "display_size_inches";

        public static final String MANUFACTURER_ID = "manufacturer_id";

        public static final Uri CONTENT_URI =
                Uri.withAppendedPath(AUTHORITY_URI, PATH);
    }


    public interface Manufacturer extends BaseColumns {
        /* default */ static final String PATH = "manufacturer";
        public static final String SHORT_NAME = "short_name";
        public static final String LONG_NAME = "long_name";

        public static final Uri CONTENT_URI =
                Uri.withAppendedPath(AUTHORITY_URI, PATH);
    }


    public interface DeviceManufacturer extends Device, Manufacturer {
        /* default */ static final String PATH = "device-manufacturer";
        public static final String DEVICE_ID = "device_id";
        public static final String MANUFACTURER_ID = "manufacturer_id";

        public static final Uri CONTENT_URI =
                Uri.withAppendedPath(AUTHORITY_URI, PATH);
    }
}
```

Notice in Listing 6.4 that all information needed to use the content provider is listed in the contract class. This includes the content provider's authority URI as well as internal structures (interfaces in this implementation) to represent the logical structure of the data. Since this content provider exposes data stored in a database, each internal interface represents a table in the database and contains constants for the table's content URI and the columns in the table. This allows a client of the content provider to use the contents when making method calls on the content resolver.

Listing 6.5 shows an example of using the contract class to insert data into the database via a content provider. Usage of the contract class is shown in bold for clarity.

Listing 6.5 Inserting Data Using the Contract Class

```
final ContentValues contentValues = new ContentValues();


final String modelValue =
        modelView.getEditText().getText().toString();


final String nicknameValue =
        nicknameView.getEditText().getText().toString();


contentValues.put(DevicesContract.Device.MODEL, modelValue);

contentValues.put(DevicesContract.Device.NICKNAME, nicknameValue);


getContentResolver().insert(DevicesContract.Device.CONTENT_URI,
                            contentValues);
```

Because the contract class serves as the API definition for a content provider, serious thought should be given to contract changes. As with all APIs, introducing changes that cause older clients to break can cause headaches and pain for other developers.

Allowing Access from an External App

The content provider discussed thus far exposes data to external clients, has a configured set of permissions, and has a defined contract that other apps can use. There is one additional step that needs to be done in order to allow the content provider to export data externally.

Recall from Listing 6.2 that there is a <provider> entry in the manifest that can be used to determine if the content provider will be accessible from outside its current app. Listing 6.2 declares a content provider that *would not* be accessible from an external app. If the content provider needs to be available to other apps, the android:exported attribute needs to be set to true for the <provider> element as shown in Listing 6.6.

Listing 6.6 Exported Content Provider Manifest Listing

```
<provider
    android:name=".provider.MyProvider"
    android:authorities="com.example.provider"
    android:exported="true" />
```

At this point, all of the parts of a content provider that can be used to expose data to external apps have been discussed. If a content provider needs to expose data only in local parts of its app, there are some additional APIs that can be of use to app developers.

Implementing a Content Provider

The previous sections of this chapter discussed many of the details of content providers such as their APIs, manifest configurations, and how to access them. This section finally deals with the details of actually implementing a content provider, and it dissects the code for the example app content provider.

The DevicesProvider exposes the data in the device database app that was introduced in Chapter 4, "SQLite in Android." The app contains two tables, device and manufacturer, which need to be supported by the DevicesProvider. In addition, some of the activities in the device database need information from both the device and manufacturer tables. Instead of making clients query the tables individually, the DevicesProvider implements an INNER JOIN that clients can use.

Extending android.content.ContentProvider

As discussed previously, the first step in implementing a content provider is extending android.content.ContentProvider and implementing the abstract methods it declares. Listing 6.7 shows the class declaration as well as the constant declarations and all member variables for the content provider.

Listing 6.7 Content Provider Declaration

```
public class DevicesProvider extends ContentProvider {
    private static final String TAG =
            DevicesProvider.class.getSimpleName();


    private static final int CODE_ALL_DEVICES = 100;

    private static final int CODE_DEVICE_ID = 101;

    private static final int CODE_ALL_MANUFACTURERS = 102;

    private static final int CODE_MANUFACTURER_ID = 103;

    private static final int CODE_DEVICE_MANUFACTURER = 104;


    private static final SparseArray<String> URI_CODE_TABLE_MAP =
            new SparseArray<>();


    private static final UriMatcher URI_MATCHER =
            new UriMatcher(UriMatcher.NO_MATCH);
```

```
static {
    URI_CODE_TABLE_MAP.put(CODE_ALL_DEVICES,
            DevicesOpenHelper.Tables.DEVICE);

    URI_CODE_TABLE_MAP.put(CODE_DEVICE_ID,
            DevicesOpenHelper.Tables.DEVICE);

    URI_CODE_TABLE_MAP.put(CODE_ALL_MANUFACTURERS,
            DevicesOpenHelper.Tables.MANUFACTURER);

    URI_CODE_TABLE_MAP.put(CODE_MANUFACTURER_ID,
            DevicesOpenHelper.Tables.MANUFACTURER);

    URI_MATCHER.addURI(DevicesContract.AUTHORITY,
            DevicesContract.Device.PATH,
            CODE_ALL_DEVICES);

    URI_MATCHER.addURI(DevicesContract.AUTHORITY,
            DevicesContract.Device.PATH + "/#",
            CODE_DEVICE_ID);

    URI_MATCHER.addURI(DevicesContract.AUTHORITY,
            DevicesContract.Manufacturer.PATH,
            CODE_ALL_MANUFACTURERS);

    URI_MATCHER.addURI(DevicesContract.AUTHORITY,
            DevicesContract.Manufacturer.PATH + "/#",
            CODE_MANUFACTURER_ID);

    URI_MATCHER.addURI(DevicesContract.AUTHORITY,
            DevicesContract.DeviceManufacturer.PATH,
            CODE_DEVICE_MANUFACTURER);
}
```

```
private DevicesOpenHelper helper;

public DevicesProvider() {
    // no-op
}
```

As expected, DevicesProvider extends ContentProvider. The constant declarations in Listing 6.7 are used to process incoming URIs. Recall from previous sections that it is the job of the content provider to process the URIs it receives and map the URIs to the correct tables. The constant ints in the DevicesProvider are used to map URIs to tables. They are registered with the URI_MATCHER constant and used to match URIs later in the class implementation.

The URI_CODE_TABLE_MAP is used to map URIs to table names. This was added as a convenient way to look up table names given a URI. Some content provider methods, like insert(), differ only in the table that is operated on. The URI_CODE_TABLE_MAP constant allows the same code to vary only by the table name.

The same static block that initializes URI_CODE_TABLE_MAP is also used to initialize URI_MATCHER for use later in the class when performing operations on a table based on a URI.

The URI_MATCHER is constructed passing UriMatcher.NO_MATCH to its constructor. This is used as the base case for URI matching. URI_MATCHER maps a URI, or a URI pattern, to an integer value. Passing UriMatcher.NO_MATCH sets the return value when there is no URI_MATCHER mapping for a given URI. A value of UriMatcher.NO_MATCH indicates a URI that is not supported by the devices provider.

After the URI_MATCHER object is instantiated, it can be configured by mapping a URI to an int return value by calling the addUri() method. UriMatcher.addUri() can map either a URI or a URI pattern to an int value, and the static block does both. This is needed to support URIs that reference a table in the content provider (content://authority/path) and URIs that reference a single item in a table (content://authority/path/id). The static block matches both URI formats for each table in the database.

Listing 6.8 shows the code where the device table URIs are matched to a table.

Listing 6.8 Mapping UriMatcher

```
URI_MATCHER.addURI(DevicesContract.AUTHORITY,
        DevicesContract.Device.PATH,
        CODE_ALL_DEVICES);
```

```
URI_MATCHER.addURI(DevicesContract.AUTHORITY,

        DevicesContract.Device.PATH + "/#",

        CODE_DEVICE_ID);
```

The first call to `UriMatcher.addUri()` matches a URI that references the entire device table. This URI would be used, for example, to query over all devices by passing the authority, path, and mapped integer value to the method. The mapped integer value passed in the third parameter is what is returned by the `UriMatcher` object if a URI matches.

The second call to `UriMatcher.addUri()` matches a URI that references an individual row in the `device` table. This is done by passing a URI pattern in the form of

`content://authority/path/#`

The # at the end of the URI matches against any number. Since the primary key of the `device` table is a number (column `_id`), this URI pattern can be used to reference an individual device as long as the last part of the path is the ID of the device.

Note

UriMatcher.addUri() can also use a pattern of `content://authority/path/*` to match any text after the path. This pattern is not used in this app, however.

The `helper` member variable holds a reference to a `DevicesOpenHelper` object and is used to get `SQLiteDatabase` objects to perform database operations on.

Listing 6.9 shows the implementation of `DevicesProvider.onCreate()`.

Listing 6.9 Implementing `DevicesProvider.onCreate()`

```
@Override
public boolean onCreate() {
    helper = DevicesOpenHelper.getInstance(getContext());
    return true;
}
```

The `onCreate()` method should not perform long tasks since it will be called on the UI thread while the app is loading. The only operation being done in `DevicesProvider.onCreate()` is to assign `helper` to the `DevicesOpenHelper` singleton instance. This does not actually open the database, so it is safe to run on the UI thread because it has a short runtime.

Now that the code to create and initialize the `DevicesProvider` has been discussed, focus can be turned to the more interesting parts of the `DevicesProvider` where the insert, delete, update, and query operations are implemented.

insert()

Listing 6.10 shows the implementation of the insert() method.

Listing 6.10 Implementing insert()

```
@Override
public Uri insert(@NonNull Uri uri, ContentValues values) {
    long id;
    final int code = URI_MATCHER.match(uri);
    switch (code) {
        case CODE_ALL_DEVICES:
        case CODE_ALL_MANUFACTURERS:
            id = helper
                    .getWritableDatabase()
                    .insertOrThrow(URI_CODE_TABLE_MAP.get(code),
                            null,
                            values);
            break;
        default:
            throw new IllegalArgumentException("Invalid Uri: " + uri);
    }


    getContext().getContentResolver().notifyChange(uri, null);
    return ContentUris.withAppendedId(uri, id);
}
```

The first task of any of the methods that read/write to the database is to map the uri parameter to a table. This is where the URI_MATCHER that was initialized earlier is used. UriMatcher.match() returns the mapped integer that was set using the addUri() method calls. Thus resolving the table from the URI means making a single call to UriMatcher. match() instead of writing code to manually inspect and match the URI. This becomes really useful because all the methods that perform read/write operations on the database have to perform this check.

The insert() method gets the matcher value and uses that to determine which table is the target of the database operation. The only supported operation is to perform an insert on one of the two tables of the database, so any other URI is invalid. For the invalid case, the insert() method throws an exception to let the client know of the problem. If the URI does map to either the device or manufacturer table, the table name is looked up from the URI_CODE_TABLE_MAP, and SQLiteDatabase. insertOrThrow() is called to insert the values passed to the insert() method via the values parameter.

After the insert operation is completed, any content observers listening for database changes on the URI should be notified of the update to the database. This is done with a call to ContentResolver.notifyChange(), passing the uri of the updated table and a null for the observer parameter.

Recall from Chapter 5 that the SQLiteDatabase.insertOrThrow() method returns a long value that is the ID for the newly inserted row. The ID can be used to reference the new row as part of a URI. ContentProvider.insert() generates that URI by calling ContentUris.withAppendedId(), which is a convenience method that returns a URI when passed the base URI and a long value as the ID. The insert() method returns the generated URI and finishes execution.

delete()

The delete() method also needs to interrogate the UriMatcher to map a URI to an integer value that was initialized earlier in the class. However, it needs to support both the table-related URIs (content://authority/path) and URIs that reference a specific row (content://authority/path/id). The implementation of delete() is shown in Listing 6.11.

Listing 6.11 Implementing delete()

```
@Override
public int delete(@NonNull Uri uri,
                  String selection,
                  String[] selectionArgs) {
    int rowCount;

    final int code = URI_MATCHER.match(uri);
    switch (code) {
        case CODE_ALL_DEVICES:
        case CODE_ALL_MANUFACTURERS:
            rowCount = helper
                    .getWritableDatabase()
                    .delete(URI_CODE_TABLE_MAP.get(code),
                            selection,
                            selectionArgs);
            break;
```

```
        case CODE_DEVICE_ID:

        case CODE_MANUFACTURER_ID:

            if (selection == null && selectionArgs == null) {

                selection = BaseColumns._ID + " = ?";


                selectionArgs = new String[] {

                    uri.getLastPathSegment()

                };


                rowCount = helper

                        .getWritableDatabase()

                        .delete(URI_CODE_TABLE_MAP.get(code),

                            selection,

                            selectionArgs);

            } else {

                throw new IllegalArgumentException("Selection must be " +

                        "null when specifying ID as part of uri.");

            }

            break;

        default:

            throw new IllegalArgumentException("Invalid Uri: " + uri);

    }


    getContext().getContentResolver().notifyChange(uri, null);

    return rowCount;

}
```

The ContentProvider.delete() method follows a similar pattern to the ContentProvider.insert() method. It resolves the table from the URI using URI_MATCHER, then performs an action on the correct table. However, since individual rows can be deleted from a table, the ContentProvider.delete() method must support URIs that map to the entire table as well as URIs that reference individual rows in a table.

In Listing 6.11, both table-based URIs are handled by the same case in the switch statement. This is, once again, because the same operation is performed with only the table name changing. If the SQLiteDatabase.delete() method is called with no selection parameters, all rows are removed from the table specified by the URI. The values passed to SQLiteDatabase.delete() are set by the code that makes the delete call from the content provider.

When a specific row is referenced by the URI, the ContentProvider.delete()
method needs to perform some additional work and use the URI to determine the ID of
the row to delete. This is accomplished by making a call to Uri.getLastPathSegment(),
which returns the right-most part of the path. Since this code is run only when the
URI matches the pattern content://authority/path/id, the last path segment can be
assumed to be the ID.

Next, the ContentProvider.delete() method constructs a selection clause that
is passed to SQLiteDatabase.delete() using the ID that was part of the URI. The
return value of the SQLiteDatabase.delete() method call is stored in a variable and
returned by ContentProvider.delete() to indicate the number of rows that were
deleted by the operation.

The code in Listing 6.11 also makes a check to determine if the selection and
selectionArgs are null when processing a URI that references a specific row. This
is because having a URI that references a row in the table *and* a non-null selection
clause could result in an ambiguous method call if the ID in the URI and the selection
arguments do not reference the same row in the table. Instead of assuming the caller's
intent, the method throws an exception in order to preserve the data and prevent
accidental data deletion.

The last task the ContentProvider.delete() method performs before returning
is to make a call to ContentResolver.notifyChange(). This informs any registered
content observers that a change has happened to the database and they can respond
accordingly.

update()

Listing 6.12 includes the implementation of the ContentProvider.update() method.

Listing 6.12 Implementing update()

```
@Override
public int update(@NonNull Uri uri,
                  ContentValues values,
                  String selection,
                  String[] selectionArgs) {
    int rowCount;

    final int code = URI_MATCHER.match(uri);
    switch (code) {
        case CODE_ALL_DEVICES:
        case CODE_ALL_MANUFACTURERS:
```

```
            rowCount = helper
                    .getWritableDatabase()
                    .update(URI_CODE_TABLE_MAP.get(code),
                            values,
                            selection,
                            selectionArgs);
        break;
    case CODE_DEVICE_ID:
    case CODE_MANUFACTURER_ID:
        if (selection == null
                && selectionArgs == null) {
            selection = BaseColumns._ID + " = ?";

            selectionArgs = new String[] {
                    uri.getLastPathSegment()
            };
        } else {
            throw new IllegalArgumentException("Selection must be " +
                    "null when specifying ID as part of uri.");
        }
        rowCount = helper           ,
                    .getWritableDatabase()
                    .update(URI_CODE_TABLE_MAP.get(code),
                            values,
                            selection,
                            selectionArgs);
        break;
    default:
        throw new IllegalArgumentException("Invalid Uri: " + uri);
    }


getContext().getContentResolver().notifyChange(uri, null);
return rowCount;
}
```

The `ContentProvider.update()` method is similar to the `ContentProvider.delete()` method. Both methods select the table for the target of the operation by making calls to `UriMatcher.match()`, passing in the uri. Also, each method must process URIs for entire tables and individual rows since both the `delete` and `update` operations can work on multiple rows of a table.

The only difference between the `ContentProvider.delete()` and the `ContentProvider.update()` methods is that `SQLiteDatabase.update()` is called instead of `SQLDatabase.delete()`. As expected, the `ContentProvider.update()` method makes a call to `SQLiteDatabase.update()`.

After the call to `SQLiteDatabase.update()` is made, `ContentResolver.notifyChange()` is called and the number of rows affected by the `SQLiteDatabase.update()` call is returned to the caller.

query()

The next part of the `DevicesProvider` that will be discussed is the `query()` method which makes up Listing 6.13.

Listing 6.13 Implementing query()

```
@Override
public Cursor query(@NonNull Uri uri,
                    String[] projection,
                    String selection,
                    String[] selectionArgs,
                    String sortOrder) throws IllegalArgumentException {
    Cursor cursor;
    if (projection == null) {
        throw new IllegalArgumentException("Projection can't be null");
    }


    sortOrder = (sortOrder == null ? BaseColumns._ID : sortOrder);


    SQLiteDatabase database = helper.getReadableDatabase();


    final int code = URI_MATCHER.match(uri);
    switch (code) {
        case CODE_ALL_DEVICES:
        case CODE_ALL_MANUFACTURERS:
            cursor = database.query(URI_CODE_TABLE_MAP.get(code),
```

```
                projection,

                selection,

                selectionArgs,

                null,

                null,

                sortOrder);

        break;
case CODE_DEVICE_ID:
case CODE_MANUFACTURER_ID:

        if (selection == null) {

            selection = BaseColumns._ID

                    + " = "

                    + uri.getLastPathSegment();

        } else {

            throw new IllegalArgumentException("Selection must " +
                    "be null when specifying ID as part of uri.");

        }

        cursor = database.query(URI_CODE_TABLE_MAP.get(code),

                projection,

                selection,

                selectionArgs,

                null,

                null,

                sortOrder);

        break;
case CODE_DEVICE_MANUFACTURER:

        SQLiteQueryBuilder builder = new SQLiteQueryBuilder();


        builder.setTables(String

                .format("%s INNER JOIN %s ON (%s.%s=%s.%s)",

                DevicesOpenHelper.Tables.DEVICE,

                DevicesOpenHelper.Tables.MANUFACTURER,

                DevicesOpenHelper.Tables.DEVICE,

                DevicesContract.Device.MANUFACTURER_ID,
```

```
            DevicesOpenHelper.Tables.MANUFACTURER,
            DevicesContract.Manufacturer._ID));


    final Map<String, String> projectionMap = new HashMap<>();
    projectionMap.put(DevicesContract.DeviceManufacturer.MODEL,
            DevicesContract.DeviceManufacturer.MODEL);


    projectionMap
            .put(DevicesContract.DeviceManufacturer.SHORT_NAME,
            DevicesContract.DeviceManufacturer.SHORT_NAME);


    projectionMap
            .put(DevicesContract.DeviceManufacturer.DEVICE_ID,
            String.format("%s.%s AS %s",
                    DevicesOpenHelper.Tables.DEVICE,
                    DevicesContract.Device._ID,
                    DevicesContract.DeviceManufacturer.DEVICE_ID));


    projectionMap.put(DevicesContract
            .DeviceManufacturer.MANUFACTURER_ID,
            String.format("%s.%s AS %s",
                    DevicesOpenHelper.Tables.MANUFACTURER,
                    DevicesContract.Manufacturer._ID,
                    DevicesContract
                        .DeviceManufacturer.MANUFACTURER_ID));


    builder.setProjectionMap(projectionMap);


    cursor = builder.query(database,
            projection,
            selection,
            selectionArgs,
            null,
            null,
```

```
                    sortOrder);


            break;
        default:
            throw new IllegalArgumentException("Invalid Uri: " + uri);
    }
```

The `DevicesProvider.query()` method first checks for a null `sortOrder` parameter. Instead of relying on the default sort order of SQLite, the `query()` method sorts the result set by ID if the caller does not provide a `sortOrder` parameter.

Next, the `query()` method uses the `uri` and the `URI_MATCHER` member variable to determine which table should be queried. This is similar to the `insert()`, `update()`, and `delete()` methods that were previously discussed. If the URI references a table-based URI, the `SQLiteDatabase.query()` is called with the values that were passed to `DevicesProvider.query()`. If the `uri` matches a row in a table, the `selection` and `selectionArgs` parameters are checked for values of null.

Specifying the row ID in the URI and specifying selection parameters once again makes the `query()` method ambiguous and causes the query to throw an exception rather than trying to determine the intent of the call from its possibly conflicting parameters. This is similar to what occurs in the `update()` and `delete()` methods where an exception is thrown if a row URI is passed to the method while also passing non-null selection criteria.

The cursor returned from `SQLiteDatabase.query()` is returned to the caller after making a call to `Cursor.setNotificationUri()`. The call to `Cursor.setNotificationUri()` causes the cursor to "watch" for changes to the URI passed to it as a parameter. This call allows the caller of `DevicesProvider.query()` to process changes in the database when they occur without having to requery the database.

Thus far, the `DevicesProvider.query()` method has followed a similar algorithm to the `insert()`, `update()`, and `delete()` methods, using the `uri` parameter and the `URI_MATCHER` member variable to determine which table to run the operation against, then performing the operation. The `update()`, `insert()`, and `delete()` methods all used a `switch` statement to map destination tables with the integer constants that were used to initialize `URI_MATCHER`.

What makes the `query()` method different from the other methods is that it also needs to support the use of an `INNER JOIN` on the `device` and `manufacturer` tables so that a client can receive data from both tables in a single query operation. The `INNER JOIN` functionality happens in the `switch` statement when the URI matches the `CODE_DEVICE_MANUFACTURER` constant.

Recall from the contract class discussion that a contract class can specify URIs that can be used to map paths to table names. In the case of the `device` contract, it also specifies a URI that can be used to reference a join of multiple tables. This works because the contract class defines only *what* URIs the content provider will support. It does not define *how* the content provider will support them.

This level of abstraction allows the content provider to support complex queries that can span multiple tables if needed. The devices provider supports the `DevicesContract.DeviceManufacturer.CONTENT_URI` by performing a join on the device and manufacturer tables and returning a cursor object with columns from both tables. Listing 6.14 shows the `DevicesContract.DeviceManufacturer` inner class from the device contract.

Listing 6.14 Extending Contracts with `DevicesContract.DeviceManufacturer`

```java
public interface DeviceManufacturer extends Device, Manufacturer {

    /* default */ static final String PATH = "device-manufacturer";

    public static final String DEVICE_ID = "device_id";

    public static final String MANUFACTURER_ID = "manufacturer_id";


    public static final Uri CONTENT_URI =
            Uri.withAppendedPath(AUTHORITY_URI, PATH);

}
```

Notice in Listing 6.14 that `DeviceManufacturer` extends both the device and manufacturer contracts. This means that the client can choose to include columns from both tables in a query, and that there will be column name collisions that will need to be resolved because a column of the same name (ID) exists in both tables.

Something to note in the `query()` method is the use of `SQLiteQueryBuilder`. While the `SQLiteDatabase.query()` method is convenient for simple queries, it can be difficult to use for more advanced queries as it often requires large amounts of string concatenation to construct the queries. The goal of `SQLiteQueryBuilder` is to make complex queries easier to write in Java code.

In the case of `DevicesProvider.query()` an `SQLiteQueryBuilder` object is used to build a query with an `INNER JOIN`. The following snippet from Listing 6.14 shows an `SQLiteQueryBuilder` object being created and initialized:

```java
SQLiteQueryBuilder builder = new SQLiteQueryBuilder();


builder.setTables(String.format("%s INNER JOIN %s ON (%s.%s=%s.%s)",

        DevicesOpenHelper.Tables.DEVICE,

        DevicesOpenHelper.Tables.MANUFACTURER,

        DevicesOpenHelper.Tables.DEVICE,

        DevicesContract.Device.MANUFACTURER_ID,

        DevicesOpenHelper.Tables.MANUFACTURER,

        DevicesContract.Manufacturer._ID));
```

After instantiating an `SQLiteQueryBuilder` instance, a call to `setTables()` is made. For a simpler query, the `setTables()` method can be used to build a query with a single table by simply passing the name of the table. However, when building an `INNER JOIN` query, the `setTables()` is passed the `INNER JOIN` SQL statement. The result of `String.format()` is

```
device INNER JOIN manufacturer on (device._id=manufacturer._id)
```

This forms the base of the `SELECT` clause for the query.

After the call to `setTables()`, the `ContentProvider.query()` method needs to build the projection map and set it with a call to `SQLiteQueryBuilder.setProjectionMap()`. This call allows the `SQLiteQueryBuilder` to map from the column names passed into the content provider to the column names that will appear in the query. An important detail with building projection maps is that if a call to `SQLiteQueryBuilder.setProjectionMap()` is made, every column specified by the client must appear in the map even if the column name maps to itself. Following is the code that builds the projection map from Listing 6.13:

```
final Map<String, String> projectionMap = new HashMap<>();
projectionMap.put(DevicesContract.DeviceManufacturer.MODEL,
        DevicesContract.DeviceManufacturer.MODEL);


projectionMap.put(DevicesContract.DeviceManufacturer.SHORT_NAME,
        DevicesContract.DeviceManufacturer.SHORT_NAME);


projectionMap.put(DevicesContract.DeviceManufacturer.DEVICE_ID,
        String.format("%s.%s AS %s",
                DevicesOpenHelper.Tables.DEVICE,
                DevicesContract.Device._ID,
                DevicesContract.DeviceManufacturer.DEVICE_ID));


projectionMap.put(DevicesContract.DeviceManufacturer.MANUFACTURER_ID,
        String.format("%s.%s AS %s",
                DevicesOpenHelper.Tables.MANUFACTURER,
                DevicesContract.Manufacturer._ID,
                DevicesContract
                        .DeviceManufacturer.MANUFACTURER_ID));


builder.setProjectionMap(projectionMap);
```

Notice that the column `DevicesContract.DeviceManufacturer.MODEL` is mapped to itself in the map. Again, every column specified by the query must be in the projection map.

The more interesting projection map cases in this code snippet are shown in bold text. Because both the `device` and `manufacturer` tables contain an id column, the projection map must be used to clarify what otherwise would be ambiguous column names. For both the `device_id` and the `manufacturer_id`, the columns can be resolved by appending the table name to the front of the column name. This produces the following raw SQL:

```
SELECT device._id, manufacturer._id
```

Along with appending the table name to the id columns, the projection map maps the fully qualified string name to the column names that were defined in the device contract and used by the client in the call to `DevicesProvider.query()`.

Once the projection map is built, it is set on the `SQLiteQueryBuilder` object with a call to `SQLiteQueryBuilder.setProjectionMap()`.

Once the projection map is set, the query builder can be used to run the query against the database with a call to `SQLiteQueryBuilder.query()`. The method used to query a database is a little different from what has been discussed elsewhere in the chapter. Instead of making a call to `SQLiteData.query()`, the `SQLiteQueryBuilder.query()` method takes an `SQLiteDatabase` object as its first parameter, then makes the query. Here is the code snippet from Listing 6.13 where the `SQLiteQueryBuilder.query()` method is called:

```
cursor = builder.query(database,
        projection,
        selection,
        selectionArgs,
        null,
        null,
        sortOrder);
```

Other than the first parameter, `SQLiteQueryBuilder.query()` takes the same parameter list as `SQLiteDatabase.query()` and returns a cursor object. This object is then returned by the content provider back to its client.

getType()

The last method that needs to be implemented in the `DevicesProvider` is `getType()`. The `getType()` method is shown in Listing 6.15.

Listing 6.15 Implementing `getType()`

```java
@Override
public String getType(@NonNull Uri uri) {

    final int code = URI_MATCHER.match(uri);
    switch (code) {
        case CODE_ALL_DEVICES:
            return String.format("%s/vnd.%s.%s",
                    ContentResolver.CURSOR_DIR_BASE_TYPE,
                    DevicesContract.AUTHORITY,
                    DevicesContract.Device.PATH);
        case CODE_ALL_MANUFACTURERS:
            return String.format("%s/vnd.%s.%s",
                    ContentResolver.CURSOR_DIR_BASE_TYPE,
                    DevicesContract.AUTHORITY,
                    DevicesContract.Manufacturer.PATH);
        case CODE_DEVICE_ID:
            return String.format("%s/vnd.%s.%s",
                    ContentResolver.CURSOR_ITEM_BASE_TYPE,
                    DevicesContract.AUTHORITY,
                    DevicesContract.Device.PATH);
        case CODE_MANUFACTURER_ID:
            return String.format("%s/vnd.%s.%s",
                    ContentResolver.CURSOR_ITEM_BASE_TYPE,
                    DevicesContract.AUTHORITY,
                    DevicesContract.Manufacturer.PATH);
        default:
            return null;
    }
}
```

Like other methods discussed previously in this chapter, the `getType()` method first needs to determine which URI it was called with by interrogating the `URI_MATCHER`. Once the mapped `int` value has been returned from `UriMatcher.match()`, the `getType()` method can use a `switch` statement to process different URIs much like the other device provider methods do.

What makes `getType()` different is that it does not need to make a call to the database. Instead, it constructs a MIME type string based in the path of the `uri` parameter. Earlier in the chapter, the MIME type prefixes were discussed for both table- and item-based URIs. These values are stored in the constants `ContentResolver.CURSOR_ITEM_BASE_TYPE` for item URIs and `ContentResolver.CURSOR_DIR_BASE_TYPE` for table URIs.

Using the constants, the `getType()` method uses `String.format()` to construct the string MIME type and return it to the caller.

At this point, we now have a fully functioning content provider that can provide access to the device database for both the local app components as well as external apps. The next section of this chapter discusses some things to consider when deciding if a content provider is the correct choice for your app.

When Should a Content Provider Be Used?

The discussion as to whether to add a content provider to an app can be a bit of a heated one. While content providers do provide a level of abstraction between Android components that display data to the user, activities, and fragments, there is also a level of complexity involved with writing and using them. Ultimately, there is probably no right or wrong answer to this question as the decision to add a content provider to an app always depends on multiple factors surrounding the app. This section simply points out some strengths and weaknesses of content providers so you can make an informed decision about their use.

Content Provider Weaknesses

While using content providers can alleviate certain annoyances that go along with accessing a database, they are not without their faults. The following sections detail some of the weaknesses of content providers.

The Need for Extra Code

One of the major negatives that is often cited with using content providers is the additional amount of "boilerplate" code that needs to be written. When compared to using an `SQLiteOpenHelper` and `SQLiteDatabase` object directly, there is definitely more code that needs to be written to use a content provider. For starters, the content provider itself needs to be written and maintained. This means writing the code to determine which table will be accessed by which URI and delegating operation calls to a lower-level database access object. Often, as the number of tables that are supported by the content provider increases, so does the length of the content provider. At a minimum, `switch` statements may need to be extended to handle new tables as well as additional `INNER JOIN` queries.

Along with the content provider itself, contract classes need to be written and maintained as a database evolves. This becomes especially important if an app needs to expose its data to other apps. However, it is often a good idea to have contract classes even when the data will be used only by local app components.

What does make the amount of boilerplate code required to support content providers less of an issue is the number of projects released by the Android community to address this issue. A quick Google search will reveal projects that leverage tools such as code generation to aid in building a content provider.

Use of URIs and Cursors over Objects

When using a content provider, components need to make use of URIs and cursors instead of just using Java classes to represent an app's model data. This can be seen as a higher learning curve, especially for developers who are new to Android development as they are very likely to be familiar with POJOs (plain old Java objects) and less likely to be familiar with content providers.

Also, at least when this book was written, the Android data binding library does not support cursors. This means that in order to use a content provider to bind database information to a UI, an app has to make a query to a content provider and create Java objects out of the cursor that is returned by the content provider. This additional layer, converting cursors to objects, causes additional memory churn as the OS must allocate memory for the objects, then the garbage collector must reclaim the memory when the object is no longer used.

No Convenient Place to Close the Database

When performing database tasks, a connection to the database needs to be opened. Typically, it is beneficial to keep the same database connection open as long as additional database tasks might be needed to avoid the overhead of creating a new database connection multiple times to perform multiple tasks.

Since the database is opened by an app's code, it seems logical that the database needs to be closed by the same app's code. This is where things can get a little sticky when it comes to content providers. Usually, all database operations use the same SQLiteDatabase object and open it only once. Even if the SQLiteOpenHelper.getWritable() method is called multiple times, it internally caches the SQLiteDatabase instance it returns in an effort to eliminate the overhead of creating multiple connections. While there is a method that gets called at the beginning of a content provider's lifecycle (ContentProvider. onCreate()), there is no method that is guaranteed to be called when a content provider gets destroyed. This means that if a database connection is opened, there is no convenient place to close the connection other than in each insert()/update()/delete()/query() method (which would also require each method to reopen the database connection, injecting the overhead that was just discussed).

This issue seems to worry some people more than others. Some Android platform engineers have posted, publicly, that the database will be closed when Android cleans up the process, but there are still people who feel it is good practice for an app to clean up after itself and close the database connection.

Content Provider Strengths

While content providers have their weaknesses, they also have their strengths and can, at times, make things easier. The following sections detail why the use of content providers can be advantageous.

Abstraction Layer for Structured Data

Content providers are good at hiding the details of data storage and retrieval from apps. Because a content provider is actually an interface to structured data, the actual mechanism of data storage is irrelevant to other app components. For example, a content provider can expose data that is stored in a database, stored as files on disk, or even stored on a remote system and accessed via a Web service. Because those other components never know the details of how the data is stored, the storage mechanism can change without affecting any of a content provider's clients (assuming the contract classes don't change).

The content provider also allows all data store information to be accessed the same way whether the client accessing the data is the local component or an external app. Providing a single interface for all data access, whether local or remote, limits the complexity around data access.

Most apps that need to persist data to a database need a layer that handles interfacing between the database and the rest of the business logic. In Android, the content provider is a natural option for that layer that offers many benefits over other architectures.

Well Supported by Other Android Components

Content providers are well supported across the Android SDK (with the exception of the data binding API as discussed previously) when using other Android components. One of the most convenient uses of a content provider is with a cursor loader. The Android docs make a strong claim that a content provider should be used when using a cursor loader. While it is possible to use a cursor loader without a content provider, it can make the cursor loader implementation more complex.

Cursor loaders can be a great way for apps to eliminate the complexity of manually supporting configuration changes in activities and fragments. In addition, loaders handle the asynchronous nature of loading data from a database off the UI thread while providing the results of a database operation (usually a query) on the main thread allowing UI updates. Recall from the discussion of cursor loaders in Chapter 5 that neither the cursor loader nor the activity needs to explicitly make calls to a content resolver or content provider when using a cursor loader. This is because the cursor loader handles these tasks on its own.

Once a content provider is implemented, making use of a cursor loader to load data to the UI is pretty straightforward and does not require much code. Additionally, activity lifecycle events, as they relate to cursor objects, are handled by the Android system, freeing the developer from worrying about memory leaks from a cursor that was not closed.

In addition to cursor loaders, the sync adapter and the search API make use of content providers. In some cases, certain APIs mandate the use of a content provider.

Handles Interprocess Communication

One of the major strengths of content providers is that they allow apps to easily send data across process boundaries. This can foster communication between two different apps, or even within a single app that needs to run across two different processes. As discussed earlier in the chapter, the interaction between the content resolver and a content provider allows this interprocess communication to happen transparently in apps.

Android does provide other mechanisms to send data between components that are running in two different processes. One alternative approach is to use a bound service and define an Android Interface Definition Language (AIDL) interface for interprocess communication. While this allows communication to take place, it does not always fit the needs of an app.

Services are good at supporting long-running tasks that need to happen in the background with no UI. While they can be used to transfer data across a process boundary, services do not seem like a good fit if that long-running use case is not needed. In addition, a service still needs to make calls to the database to retrieve the data, then manually manipulate it so it can be sent to another process.

Summary

Content providers can be a convenient way to both expose internal data to external apps and provide an abstraction layer between an app's database and UI logic. When used with a content resolver, a developer does not need to worry about the details of getting data from one process to another.

By setting permissions, apps can also control the level of access an external app will have to the data they provide. This provides flexibility when deciding to allow external apps to have access to an internal database.

When coupled with the use of a cursor loader, a content provider can be a useful Android component for handling chores normally associated with data access in Android.

The next chapter dives deeper into the details of using cursor loaders to load data into views that are displayed to a user.

7
Databases and the UI

As apps increase in complexity, the need for data stored in a local database also increases. While previous chapters have discussed the details of storing data, they have not discussed how to take the data from a database and present it to a user. This topic is of significant importance since it is such a common usage pattern. This chapter presents some strategies for using the Android database APIs to show data to the user.

Getting Data from the Database to the UI

Before a UI can present data to the user, it must obtain the data from a database. This is an area where special attention needs to be paid to Android threads. Reading from a database requires reading from internal app storage and should not be done on the main thread. While database access is usually quick, reading from internal storage on the main thread is usually a bad idea as it can block the main thread. In addition, database connections can block the calling thread in order to support multithreaded database access.

While the database read operation should happen on a background thread, updating the UI always needs to happen on the main thread in Android. Attempting to update a view on a thread other than the main thread will result in a runtime exception being thrown.

As mentioned in Chapter 5, "Working with Databases in Android," a cursor loader can help solve the problem of accessing a database on a background thread while updating the UI on the main thread.

Using a Cursor Loader to Handle Threading

A cursor loader can be used to read data from a local database. An activity or fragment can use the loader framework to create a cursor loader with the desired projection and selection parameters. A nice feature of the loader framework is that it takes care of threading concerns on its own. For a cursor loader, this means reading from the database on a background thread and making the call to `LoaderManager.LoaderCallbacks.onLoadFinished()` on the main thread. The cursor that is passed to the `onLoadFinished()` method can then be used to update the UI with the data it contains.

One thing to remember when using cursor loaders is that the default implementation expects to use a content provider for data access. If an app does not implement a content provider, it needs to use an alternative to the cursor loader.

Binding Cursor Data to a UI

Once the cursor has been returned from the loader manager, it can be used to update the UI. Depending on the needs of the UI, there are different ways this can be done. Simple UIs may need to reference only a single row from the result set in the cursor. When this is the case, the cursor data can be read and views can be updated directly from the onLoadFinished() method. Listing 7.1 shows an example of using a single row in a cursor to update views.

Listing 7.1 Updating a View from a Single Row in a Cursor

```
@Override
public void onLoadFinished(Loader<Cursor> loader, Cursor data) {
    if (data != null && data.moveToFirst()) {
        String model =
                data.getString(data.getColumnIndexOrThrow(DevicesContract
                    .DeviceManufacturer.MODEL));

        modelView.setText(model);

        String nickname =
                data.getString(data.getColumnIndexOrThrow(DevicesContract
                                        .DeviceManufacturer
                                        .NICKNAME));
        nicknameView.setText(nickname);

        String manufacturerShortName =
                data.getString(data.getColumnIndexOrThrow(DevicesContract
                                        .DeviceManufacturer
                                        .LONG_NAME));
        manufacturerShortNameView.setText(manufacturerShortName);
    }
}
```

The code in Listing 7.1 is useful for a list/detail scenario where the user has selected a single item from a list and the details of that item need to be displayed.

Using a cursor to display a list of items from a database is a bit more involved. This is partly because it depends on how the list of items is represented in the activity or fragment. Android provides two views that can be used to efficiently present a list of items to the user: ListView and RecyclerView.

ListView

A ListView uses an adapter to bind a list of data to the UI. The Android SDK
provides classes that can be used to bind a cursor to a ListView. One such class is
SimpleCursorAdapter. The SimpleCursorAdapter class can be used to map column
names in a cursor to TextView in the list items of the ListView. Listing 7.2 shows the use
of a SimpleCursorAdapter to connect a cursor returned to a ListView in an activity.

Listing 7.2 Connecting a Cursor with SimpleCursorAdapter

```
private simpleCursorAdapter SimpleCursorAdapter;


@Override
protected void onCreate(Bundle savedInstanceState) {
    super.onCreate(savedInstanceState);


    String[] columnNames = {
            DevicesContract.Device.MODEL,
            DevicesContract.Device.NICKNAME
    };


    int[] viewNames = {
            R.id.modelView,
            R.id.nicknameView
    };


    simpleCursorAdapter = new SimpleCursorAdapter(this,
            R.layout.list_item,  // layout
            null,                // cursor
            columnNames,         // column names
            viewNames,           // view names
            0);


    listView.setAdapter(simpleCursorAdapter);


    getLoaderManager().initLoader(LOADER_ID_DEVICES, null, this);
}
```

```
@Override
public void onLoaderReset(Loader<Cursor> loader) {

    simpleCursorAdapter.changeCursor(null);

}


@Override
public void onLoadFinished(Loader<Cursor> loader, Cursor data) {

    simpleCursorAdapter.changeCursor(data);

}
```

The SimpleCursorAdapter used in Listing 7.2 is created in the activity's onCreate() method. It has a parameter list that includes the layout to use for each row in the cursor, the cursor containing the data, an array of column names available in the cursor, and an array of view IDs in the layout used to display the data in the cursor. The array of column names and the array of view IDs are parallel arrays that map view IDs to column names by using the same offset in the two arrays.

The array of column names contains values from the DevicesContract which maps to columns in the content provider that provides the cursor. The view IDs are all contained in the layout that is also passed to the constructor of the SimpleCursorAdapter.

Notice that instead of passing a cursor to the SimpleCursorAdapter constructor, a value of null is passed in Listing 7.2. This is because during onCreate() the cursor that will contain the data is not yet available. The SimpleCursorAdapter accepts a value of null during its creation, allowing the activity to update the adapter when the cursor becomes available.

The onCreate() method ends by setting the adapter on the ListView and making a call to have the loader manager read the data from the database.

When the query result set from the database is available, the loader manager calls onLoadFinished(). In Listing 7.2, the onLoadFinished() implementation only makes a call to simpleCursorAdapter.changeCursor(). This causes the adapter to use the new cursor as the source of input data and close the old one if it exists.

The final method implementation in Listing 7.2 is onLoaderReset(). This method is called by the loader manager to indicate that the loader has been reset and its data should no longer be used. Since the SimpleCursorAdapter has a reference to the cursor data provided by the loader, a call to changeCursor() is made, passing in a null value. This ensures that the adapter and the ListView don't use data that is possibly invalid.

While SimpleCursorAdapter can be easy to use, it sacrifices flexibility for ease of use. When SimpleCursorAdapter does not provide enough flexibility, CursorAdapter can be used instead.

CursorAdapter is a more general form of SimpleCursorAdapter. SimpleCursorAdapter actually extends CursorAdapter and implements the abstract methods. When using CursorAdapter, the abstract methods need to be implemented in the application code. Listing 7.3 shows an example of using `CursorAdapter` to bind a cursor to the view of an activity.

Listing 7.3 Binding a Cursor with `CursorAdapter`

```
public class DeviceAdapter extends CursorAdapter {
    public DeviceAdapter() {
        super(DeviceListActivity.this, null, 0);
    }


    @Override
    public View newView(Context context, Cursor cursor, ViewGroup parent) {
        View view
            = LayoutInflater.from(context).inflate(R.layout.list_item,
                                                        parent,
                                                        false);

        Holder holder = new Holder(view);
        view.setTag(holder);


        return view;
    }


    @Override
    public void bindView(View view, Context context, Cursor cursor) {
        String model =
            cursor.getString(cursor
            .getColumnIndexOrThrow(DevicesContract.Device.MODEL));
        String nickname =
            cursor.getString(cursor
                .getColumnIndexOrThrow(DevicesContract.Device.NICKNAME));

        Holder holder = (Holder) view.getTag();
        holder.modelView.setText(model);
        holder.nicknameView.setText(nickname);
}
```

> **Note**
>
> Listing 7.3 shows only the implementation details of `DeviceAdapter`, which extends `CursorAdapter` and implements the abstract methods. The use of `DeviceAdapter` is the same as the use of `SimpleCursorAdapter` in Listing 7.2 except for its instantiation in the activity's `onCreate()` method.

When creating a class that extends `CursorAdapter`, the abstract methods `newView()` and `bindView()` need to have concrete implementations. In Listing 7.3, `newView()` simply inflates a layout, adds it to a view holder to prevent superfluous calls to `findViewById()`, and returns the view. Binding the cursor to the list item view happens in the `bindView()` method.

The `bindView()` method takes the cursor that it is passed to the method in the parameter list, reads its data, and populates the view passed to it in the parameter list. Notice that there is no need to edit the cursor's internal pointer with method calls like `Cursor.moveToFirst()` or `Cursor.moveToPosition()`. This is because `CursorAdapter` handles the task of updating the cursor to point to the relevant row of the result set.

RecyclerView

A `RecyclerView` is a newer alternative to `ListView` that can also be used to display lists of items to the user. Like `ListView`, a `RecyclerView` needs an adapter that will be used to bind each row in the cursor to a view. However, unlike `ListView`, there are currently no predefined adapters available that support binding a `RecyclerView` to a cursor. This means that in order to use a `RecyclerView`, an adapter that supports a cursor must be written.

All `RecyclerView` adapters extend `RecyclerView.Adapter`. A full implementation of a `RecyclerView` adapter that supports cursors is provided later in the chapter.

> ### Object-Relational Mapping
>
> Object-relational mapping (ORM) is the process of mapping Java objects to a relational database. This mapping allows an application's model objects to be easily persisted into a relational database as the ORM software takes care of the details of reading and writing to the database. ORM is a popular paradigm when persisting objects to a relational database is needed.
>
> The Android SDK does not provide any support for ORM. However, a number of third-party libraries exist to provide ORM functionality. While these libraries may seem more convenient when writing an Android app than using components such as cursor loaders, their functionality does come at a cost.
>
> All Android data access happens with the cursor class when using the standard Android database tools. Cursors provide a layer of abstraction above the actual database and hold the result set in memory so it can be easily accessed by application code.
>
> When an ORM library is used, it provides another layer of abstraction on top of the Android cursor in order to map the cursor to a Java object. This means that additional objects are being created and will eventually need to be garbage collected.
>
> While this object creation and garbage collection may seem trivial, an argument can be made that it is also unnecessary because a cursor can be bound to the UI almost as easily as a Java object.

Cursors as Observers

One of the strengths of using cursors to access relational data in Android is that they can act as observers to the underlying database. When an Android component has access to a cursor, it can register an observer that will be notified when the cursor's underlying data changes. This can be useful for keeping a UI up-to-date when changes are made to the underlying database.

The cursor class provides the following methods to expose the observer pattern to a source of data:

- `Cursor.registerContentObserver()`
- `Cursor.registerDataSetObserver()`
- `Cursor.unregisterContentObserver()`
- `Cursor.unregisterDataSetObserver()`
- `Cursor.setNotificationUri()`

Using these methods, it is possible to respond to data changes using the observer pattern rather than polling the database for changes, which can be inefficient.

registerContentObserver(ContentObserver)

The `registerContentObserver()` method is used to register an observer that will receive a callback when the data backing the cursor is changed. Although the data source has been changed, the cursor may not have been updated to reflect the changes in the data source. In fact, a `ContentObserver` can be used to update the cursor in response to the underlying data being changed. The cursor can be refreshed with a call to `Cursor.requery()`, but it is generally more advisable to just obtain another cursor that represents the backing data from the data source on a background thread.

The single parameter passed to the `registerContentObserver()` method is the observer to be registered. The observer must extend `ContentObserver` and can override any or all of the following methods:

- `public boolean deliverSelfNotification()`: The `deliverSelfNotification()` is used to indicate whether the observer should receive change notifications for changes that the observer made to the backing data.

- `public void onChange(boolean selfChange, Uri uri)`: The `onChange()` method is called when a change to the backing data is made. The value passed as the `selfChange` parameter indicates if the change was caused by a self-change.

- `public void onChange(boolean selfChange)`: This overloaded version of the `onChange()` method was added in API 16. It has a similar functionality to the other overloaded form of `onChange()`. Both are called when a change to the backing data is made and passed a `boolean` flag to indicate if the change was a self-change. This form of the `onChange()` method is also passed a `Uri` parameter which is the URI of the changed data. To ensure compatibility with versions of Android older than API 16, it is good practice to chain a call between the two onChange() methods as shown in Listing 7.4.

Listing 7.4 Chaining onChange() Method Calls

```
public void onChange(boolean selfChange, Uri uri) {
    // React to change notification
}


public void onChange(boolean selfChange) {
    selfChange(selfChange, null);

}
```

ContentObserver has a single constructor which is passed a Handler object. This Handler instance is used to make the callbacks in response to data being changed.

registerDataSetObserver(DataSetObserver)

The registerDataSetObserver() method is used to register an observer that will be notified when the data inside the cursor has been changed. The difference between this method and registerContentObserver() is that registerContentObserver() is used to track the underlying data changes, whereas registerDataSetObserver() is used to track changes in the cursor that represent the underlying data.

The registerDataSetObserver() method takes a single parameter of type DataSetObserver that provides the callbacks that will be used when a change in the cursor data is detected. A DataSetObserver must be extended to override one or both of the following methods:

- public void onChange(): The onChange() method is called when the data set in the cursor changes. This is usually in response to a call to requery().
- public void onInvalidate(): This method is called when the data in the cursor becomes invalid and should no longer be used. A cursor being closed causes the onInvalidate() method to be called.

unregisterContentObserver(ContentObserver)

The unregisterContentObserver() method unregisters the ContentObserver so it no longer receives any callbacks. It is important to unregister any registered observer to prevent memory leaks.

unregisterDataSetObserver(DataSetObserver)

The unregisterDataSetObserver() method unregisters the DataSetObserver.

setNotificationUri(ContentResolver, Uri uri)

The setNotificationUri() method registers the URI that should be monitored for changes. The URI may be for either a single item in a ContentResolver or an entire table of items.

Accessing a Content Provider from an Activity

Now that the various ways to use a content provider to support an activity's UI have been discussed, let's take a look at an example. This example uses an extension of the example app that has been discussed in previous chapters which tracks mobile device data. The opening activity (DeviceListActivity) of the app shows a list of the devices that are stored in the database along with some manufacturer information.

Activity Layout

DeviceListActivity uses a RecyclerView to display the list of devices to the user. Let's take a look at the code that is responsible for retrieving the data from the database and presenting it to the user.

Listing 7.5 shows the XML layout for DeviceListActivity.

Listing 7.5 Layout Definition for `DeviceListActivity`

```
<android.support.design.widget.CoordinatorLayout
    xmlns:android="http://schemas.android.com/apk/res/android"
    xmlns:app="http://schemas.android.com/apk/res-auto"
    xmlns:tools="http://schemas.android.com/tools"
    android:layout_width="match_parent"
    android:layout_height="match_parent"
    android:fitsSystemWindows="true"
    tools:context=".device.DeviceListActivity">


    <include layout="@layout/appbar" />


    <android.support.v7.widget.RecyclerView
        android:id="@+id/recycler_view"
        android:layout_width="match_parent"
        android:layout_height="match_parent"
        app:layout_behavior="@string/appbar_scrolling_view_behavior"
        android:paddingTop="8dp"
        android:paddingBottom="8dp"/>
```

```
<TextView

    android:id="@+id/empty"

    android:layout_width="match_parent"

    android:layout_height="match_parent"

    android:text="@string/no_devices_message"

    android:gravity="center"/>


    <android.support.design.widget.FloatingActionButton

        android:id="@+id/fab"

        android:layout_width="wrap_content"

        android:layout_height="wrap_content"

        android:layout_margin="@dimen/fab_margin"

        android:src="@drawable/ic_add_white_24dp"

        android:layout_gravity="bottom|end" />

</android.support.design.widget.CoordinatorLayout>
```

The layout for `DeviceListActivity` includes both a `RecyclerView` to display the device information and a view that will be used when there are no devices in the database. Both view declarations are in bold in Listing 7.5.

In order to show the device in the `RecyclerView`, a layout must be defined which is used to show summary information for the device. This layout uses a `CardView` and contains a single `TextView` to show the device summary. Listing 7.6 shows the contents of `list_item_device.xml`, which is used to display the device summary information to the user.

Listing 7.6 `list_item_device.xml` Definition

```
<android.support.v7.widget.CardView

    xmlns:android="http://schemas.android.com/apk/res/android"

    xmlns:tools="http://schemas.android.com/tools"

    android:layout_width="match_parent"

    android:layout_height="wrap_content"

    android:layout_marginStart="16dp"

    android:layout_marginEnd="16dp"

    android:layout_marginTop="8dp"

    android:layout_marginBottom="8dp">

    <TextView

        android:id="@+id/name"
```

```
        android:layout_width="match_parent"

        android:layout_height="wrap_content"

        android:padding="16dp"

        tools:text="model"/>

</android.support.v7.widget.CardView>
```

Activity Class Definition

With the layout code listed, it is time to dive into the details of the `DeviceListActivity`
itself, starting with the class definition in Listing 7.7.

Listing 7.7 `DeviceListActivity` Class Definition

```
public class DeviceListActivity extends BaseActivity

        implements LoaderManager.LoaderCallbacks<Cursor> {
```

The `DeviceListActivity` class extends `BaseActivity` and implements the
`LoaderManager.LoaderCallback<Cursor>` interface. `BaseActivity` is just a common
base class that all activities in the project extend from and does not contain any useful
implementation code as it relates to database access.

Because `DeviceListActivity` implements `LoaderManager.`
`LoaderCallback<Cursor>`, it can be used as the callback object by the loader manager.
This allows the activity to interact with the database and respond to changes in the
underlying data.

The `DeviceListActivity.onCreate()` method is fairly unexciting. It is where the
views are initialized and where `LoaderManager.initLoader()` is called to start reading
the device information from the database. These parts of `onCreate()` are shown in
Listing 7.8.

Listing 7.8 `onCreate()` Method Implementation

```
@Override

protected void onCreate(Bundle savedInstanceState) {

    super.onCreate(savedInstanceState);

    setContentView(R.layout.activity_device_list);


    Toolbar toolbar = (Toolbar) findViewById(R.id.toolbar);

    toolbar.setTitle(getTitle());


    // Additional initialization...
```

```
recyclerView = (RecyclerView) findViewById(R.id.recycler_view);
empty = (TextView) findViewById(R.id.empty);


recyclerView.setLayoutManager(new LinearLayoutManager(this));
recyclerView.setAdapter(new DeviceCursorAdapter());


getLoaderManager().initLoader(LOADER_ID_DEVICES, null, this);
}
```

Creating the Cursor Loader

DeviceListActivity does not contain any additional Android lifecycle initialization methods (onStart(), onResume(), etc.). The call to LoaderManager.initLoader() moves execution of the activity to onCreateLoader() where a cursor loader is created and returned to the loader manager. The implementation of onCreateLoader() is shown in Listing 7.9.

Listing 7.9 Creating a Loader with `onCreateLoader()`

```
@Override
public Loader<Cursor> onCreateLoader(int id, Bundle args) {
    Loader<Cursor> loader = null;
    String[] projection = {
            DevicesContract.DeviceManufacturer.MODEL,
            DevicesContract.DeviceManufacturer.DEVICE_ID,
            DevicesContract.DeviceManufacturer.SHORT_NAME
    };


    switch (id) {
        case LOADER_ID_DEVICES:
            loader = new CursorLoader(this,
                    DevicesContract.DeviceManufacturer.CONTENT_URI,
                    projection,
                    null,
                    null,
                    DevicesContract.DeviceManufacturer.MODEL);
            break;
```

```
    }

        return loader;
}
```

The implementation of onCreateLoader() is similar to the example discussed in Chapter 6, "Content Providers," where cursor loaders were introduced. The DevicesContract.DeviceManufacturer contract class is used to specify the projection of the query. Since DeviceListActivity needs to display every device in the database, no selection criteria are passed to the cursor loader constructor. Other than the projection and the URI of the data to be returned by the content provider, the only other non-null parameter passed to the cursor loader constructor is the last parameter, which defines the sort order. Passing the DevicesContract.DeviceManufacturer.MODEL value causes the content provider to issue a query to the database which sorts the result set by the model name. This causes the list of devices to be displayed in alphabetical order by DeviceListActivity.

Handling Returned Data

Once the cursor loader has been created and returned from onCreateLoader(), DeviceListActivity needs to wait for the data to be returned from the content provider in a call to onLoadFinished(). Because the loader manager causes the database read operation to happen on a background thread, the main thread will not be blocked, so there is no fear of an application not responding (ANR) error while the activity waits for the data to be returned.

Listing 7.10 shows the onLoadFinished() implementation where DeviceListActivity starts to interact with the data returned from the content provider.

Listing 7.10 Processing a Cursor in `onLoadFinished()`

```
@Override
public void onLoadFinished(Loader<Cursor> loader, Cursor data) {
    if (data == null || data.getCount() == 0) {
        empty.setVisibility(View.VISIBLE);
        recyclerView.setVisibility(View.GONE);
    } else {
        empty.setVisibility(View.GONE);
        recyclerView.setVisibility(View.VISIBLE);
        ((DeviceCursorAdapter)recyclerView.getAdapter()).swapCursor(data);
    }
}
```

When `onLoadFinished()` is called, it firsts check to validate that it has received a cursor that has a result set. If the returned cursor is `null`, or has no rows in the result set, the `RecyclerView` is hidden and a view is shown to indicate that there is no data to be shown. Figure 7.1 shows the `DeviceListActivity` in this empty state.

The empty state of a list activity provides a good opportunity to instruct the user on how to add data to the app. `DeviceListActivity` instructs the user to click the "+" button in order to start populating the device list.

If the cursor returned from the content provider in `onLoadFinished()` contains data, the "empty state" view is hidden, and the `RecyclerView` is shown so the data can be presented to the user. In addition, the `RecyclerView`'s adapter (which was set in `onCreate()`) is retrieved from the `RecyclerView` and then updated with the cursor from the content provider by making a call to `swapCursor()`. Once the adapter is updated with the new data, it starts processing the cursor and displays the cursor contents to the user.

Before looking at the implementation of `DeviceCursorAdapter`, let's take a quick look at the `onLoaderReset()` method which also needs to be implemented because it is part of

Figure 7.1 Device list in an empty state

the LoaderManager.LoaderCallbacks<Cursor> interface. The onLoaderReset() method implementation is shown in Listing 7.11.

Listing 7.11 Loading a New Cursor with onLoaderReset()

```
@Override
public void onLoaderReset(Loader<Cursor> loader) {
    ((DeviceCursorAdapter) recyclerView.getAdapter()).swapCursor(null);
}
```

The implementation of the onLoaderReset() method is pretty simple. It retrieves the RecyclerView's adapter and sets its cursor value to null to prevent the RecyclerView from performing any additional processing on a cursor that could be invalid.

The first interaction with the DeviceCursorAdapter, other than the call to its constructor, is the call to DeviceCursorAdapter.swapCursor() on onLoadFinished(). The DeviceCursorAdapter.swapCursor() implementation is shown in Listing 7.12.

Listing 7.12 Implementing DeviceCursorAdapter.swapCursor()

```
private class DeviceCursorAdapter
        extends RecyclerView.Adapter<DeviceViewHolder> {
    public void swapCursor(Cursor newDeviceCursor) {
        if (deviceCursor != null) {
            deviceCursor.close();
        }


        deviceCursor = newDeviceCursor;


        notifyDataSetChanged();
    }
}
```

The DeviceCursorAdapter.swapCursor() method mimics the behavior found in the CursorAdapter class that can be used with ListView. It closes the previous cursor, if it was not null, updates its internal state to use the new cursor, then makes a call to DeviceCursorAdapter.notifyDataSetChanged(). The call to DeviceCursorAdapter.notifyDataSetChanged() causes the RecyclerView to update itself with the new data from the adapter.

While the RecyclerView is updating in response to the DeviceCursorAdapter.notifyDataSetChanged() method, it makes a call to DeviceCursorAdapter.getItemCount() to get the number of items in the data set. Because the adapter is backed by a cursor, the number of items in the adapter is the same as the number of rows in the cursor, or 0 if the cursor is null. See Listing 7.13 for the getItemCount() implementation.

Listing 7.13 Returning the Number of Items

```
@Override
public int getItemCount() {
    return (deviceCursor == null ? 0 : deviceCursor.getCount());
}
```

Once the number of items in the cursor has been returned, RecyclerView starts to make calls to DeviceCursorAdapter.onBindViewHolder() to populate its view with the data from the adapter. Listing 7.14 shows the implementation of onBindViewHolder().

Listing 7.14 Updating the UI in `onBindViewHolder()`

```
@Override
public void onBindViewHolder(DeviceViewHolder holder, int position) {
    if (deviceCursor != null && deviceCursor.moveToPosition(position)) {
        String model = deviceCursor
                .getString(deviceCursor
                        .getColumnIndexOrThrow(DevicesContract
                                .DeviceManufacturer
                                .MODEL));


        int deviceId = deviceCursor
                .getInt(deviceCursor
                        .getColumnIndexOrThrow(DevicesContract
                                .DeviceManufacturer
                                .DEVICE_ID));


        String shortName = deviceCursor
                .getString(deviceCursor
                        .getColumnIndexOrThrow(DevicesContract
                                .DeviceManufacturer
                                .SHORT_NAME));


        holder.name.setText(getString(R.string.device_name,
```

```
                        shortName,

                        model,

                        deviceId));

                holder.uri = ContentUris

                        .withAppendedId(DevicesContract.Device.CONTENT_URI,

                                deviceId);

        }

}
```

The onBindViewHolder() method is passed a DeviceViewHolder which contains the views for the list item in the RecyclerView and a position that is the offset of the current item in the RecyclerView. With this information, onBindViewHolder() first checks to make sure the deviceCursor is not currently null, and if it is not it checks to see if the cursor point can be moved to the required position. If both of these cases are true, onBindViewHolder() reads the cursor information and uses it to populate the views contained in the viewHolder.

For the DeviceListActivity, the ViewHolder contains views for the device model, device ID, and manufacturer's name. The holder also keeps track of the URI that can be used to retrieve the device from the DeviceContentProvider so that when the user clicks on a device, the URI can be passed to the DeviceDetailsActivity so it can read the device from the database and show the user more information about the device.

Listing 7.15 shows the complete implementation of both the DeviceCursorAdapter and the DeviceViewHolder classes.

Listing 7.15 Implementing DeviceCursorAdapter and DeviceViewHolder

```
private class DeviceCursorAdapter

        extends RecyclerView.Adapter<DeviceViewHolder> {

    private Cursor deviceCursor;


    @Override

    public DeviceViewHolder onCreateViewHolder(ViewGroup parent,

                                    int viewType) {

        View view = LayoutInflater.from(parent.getContext())

                .inflate(R.layout.list_item_device, parent, false);


        return new DeviceViewHolder(view);

    }
```

```
        @Override
        public void onBindViewHolder(DeviceViewHolder holder,
                                     int position) {
            if (deviceCursor != null
                    && deviceCursor.moveToPosition(position)) {
                String model = deviceCursor
                        .getString(deviceCursor
                                .getColumnIndexOrThrow(DevicesContract
                                    .DeviceManufacturer
                                    .MODEL));


                int deviceId = deviceCursor
                        .getInt(deviceCursor
                                .getColumnIndexOrThrow(DevicesContract
                                    .DeviceManufacturer
                                    .DEVICE_ID));


                String shortName = deviceCursor
                        .getString(deviceCursor
                                .getColumnIndexOrThrow(DevicesContract
                                    .DeviceManufacturer
                                    .SHORT_NAME));


                holder.name.setText(getString(R.string.device_name,
                        shortName,
                        model,
                        deviceId));
                holder.uri = ContentUris
                        .withAppendedId(DevicesContract.Device.CONTENT_URI,
                                deviceId);
            }
        }


        @Override
```

```
    public int getItemCount() {
        return (deviceCursor == null ? 0 : deviceCursor.getCount());
    }


    public void swapCursor(Cursor newDeviceCursor) {
        if (deviceCursor != null) {
            deviceCursor.close();
        }


        deviceCursor = newDeviceCursor;


        notifyDataSetChanged();
    }
}


private class DeviceViewHolder
        extends RecyclerView.ViewHolder
        implements View.OnClickListener {
    public TextView name;
    public Uri uri;

    public DeviceViewHolder(View itemView) {
        super(itemView);


        itemView.setOnClickListener(this);
        name = (TextView) itemView.findViewById(R.id.name);
    }


    @Override
    public void onClick(View view) {
        Intent detailIntent =
                new Intent(view.getContext(),
                        DeviceDetailActivity.class);
```

```
        detailIntent.putExtra(DeviceDetailActivity.EXTRA_DEVICE_URI, uri);

        startActivity(detailIntent);

    }

}
```

Reacting to Changes in Data

Because `DeviceListActivity` makes use of a cursor loader to read data from a database, `DeviceListActivity` has an implicit content observer that gets registered with a cursor on its behalf to monitor database changes. Internally, a cursor loader creates a content observer and registers it with a content provider so it can be notified when data is changed and, in turn, notify the loader manager. This means that when changes to the database are made, `DeviceListActivity` automatically reacts and updates itself using the same API that it used to initialize itself during creation. A change to the database causes the `onLoadFinished()` method to be called, which will update the adapter and cause the `RecyclerView` to be updated with fresh data.

This is one of the strengths of using a cursor loader instead of directly accessing the database (along with built-in main thread management). The cursor loader takes care of registering and unregistering a content observer that is used to react to changes in the underlying data.

While the cursor loader takes care of the register/unregister content observer operations, it does not perform some of the other tasks that are necessary to alert the content observer to changes in the database. Recall from a previous section that a call to `setNotificationUri()` is also needed to ensure that the content observer is notified of database changes. This happens in the `DevicesProvider` when a cursor is returned from the `query()` method.

Listing 7.16 shows the `DevicesProvider.query()` method.

Listing 7.16 Sending Updates from `DevicesProvider.query()`

```
@Override
public Cursor query(@NonNull Uri uri,
                    String[] projection,
                    String selection,
                    String[] selectionArgs,
                    String sortOrder) throws IllegalArgumentException {
    Cursor cursor;
    if (projection == null) {
        throw new IllegalArgumentException("Projection can't be null");
    }
```

```
sortOrder = (sortOrder == null ? BaseColumns._ID : sortOrder);

SQLiteDatabase database = helper.getReadableDatabase();

final int code = URI_MATCHER.match(uri);
switch (code) {
    case CODE_ALL_DEVICES:
    case CODE_ALL_MANUFACTURERS:
        cursor = database.query(URI_CODE_TABLE_MAP.get(code),
                projection,
                selection,
                selectionArgs,
                null,
                null,
                sortOrder);
        break;
    case CODE_DEVICE_ID:
    case CODE_MANUFACTURER_ID:
        if (selection == null) {
            selection = BaseColumns._ID
                    + " = "
                    + uri.getLastPathSegment();
        } else {
            throw new IllegalArgumentException("Selection must " +
                    "be null when specifying ID as part of uri.");
        }
        cursor = database.query(URI_CODE_TABLE_MAP.get(code),
                projection,
                selection,
                selectionArgs,
                null,
                null,
                sortOrder);
        break;
    case CODE_DEVICE_MANUFACTURER:
```

```
SQLiteQueryBuilder builder = new SQLiteQueryBuilder();

builder.setTables(String
        .format("%s INNER JOIN %s ON (%s.%s=%s.%s)",
        DevicesOpenHelper.Tables.DEVICE,
        DevicesOpenHelper.Tables.MANUFACTURER,
        DevicesOpenHelper.Tables.DEVICE,
        DevicesContract.Device.MANUFACTURER_ID,
        DevicesOpenHelper.Tables.MANUFACTURER,
        DevicesContract.Manufacturer._ID));

final Map<String, String> projectionMap = new HashMap<>();
projectionMap.put(DevicesContract.DeviceManufacturer.MODEL,
        DevicesContract.DeviceManufacturer.MODEL);

projectionMap
        .put(DevicesContract.DeviceManufacturer.SHORT_NAME,
        DevicesContract.DeviceManufacturer.SHORT_NAME);

projectionMap
        .put(DevicesContract.DeviceManufacturer.DEVICE_ID,
        String.format("%s.%s AS %s",
            DevicesOpenHelper.Tables.DEVICE,
            DevicesContract.Device._ID,
            DevicesContract.DeviceManufacturer.DEVICE_ID));

projectionMap.put(DevicesContract
        .DeviceManufacturer.MANUFACTURER_ID,
        String.format("%s.%s AS %s",
            DevicesOpenHelper.Tables.MANUFACTURER,
            DevicesContract.Manufacturer._ID,
            DevicesContract
                    .DeviceManufacturer.MANUFACTURER_ID));
```

```
        builder.setProjectionMap(projectionMap);

        cursor = builder.query(database,
                projection,
                selection,
                selectionArgs,
                null,
                null,
                sortOrder);

        break;
    default:
        throw new IllegalArgumentException("Invalid Uri: " + uri);
    }

    cursor.setNotificationUri(getContext().getContentResolver(), uri);
    return cursor;
}
```

The last operation the DevicesProvider.query() method performs after
it has retrieved the cursor from the database is to make the call to Cursor.
setNotificationUri(), passing in the URI that was specified by the caller. Placing the call
to setNotificationUri() in the content provider instead of the DeviceCursorAdapter
ensures that all cursors returned by the content provider receive updates if the database
changes.

In addition to making the call to setNotificationUri() for each query, the
DevicesProvider needs to makes a call to ContentResolver.notifyChange() whenever
any insert, update, or delete action is performed.

ContentResolver.notifyChange() is what notifies all the registered observers about a
change to a given URI. In order to make sure this notification is sent to all the observers,
DevicesProvider makes this call whenever a database write operation is performed.
Listing 7.17 shows snippets of the insert(), update(), and delete() methods.

Listing 7.17 Snippets of **insert()**, **update()**, and **delete()**

```
@Override
public Uri insert(@NonNull Uri uri, ContentValues values) {
    // insert operations
```

```
        notifyUris(uri);
        // return uri
}


@Override
public int delete(@NonNull Uri uri,
                  String selection,
                  String[] selectionArgs) {
    // delete operations
    notifyUris(uri);
    // return deleted row count
}


@Override
public int update(@NonNull Uri uri,
                  ContentValues values,
                  String selection,
                  String[] selectionArgs) {
    // delete operations
    notifyUris(uri);
    // return updated row count
}
```

The one complication with calling ContentResolver.notifyChange() directly is the JOIN between the device and manufacturer tables represented by the DevicesContract.DeviceManufacturer contract class. Since DevicesContract.DeviceManufacturer has a different URI from DevicesContract.Device and DevicesContract.Manufacturer, it must also be notified of changes to either table. Because this is common functionality needed in the insert(), update(), and delete() methods, it is implemented in a notifyUris() method which insert(), update(), and delete() all call. Listing 7.18 contains the implementation of notifyUris().

Listing 7.18 Implementing notifyUris()

```
private void notifyUris(Uri affectedUri) {
    final ContentResolver contentResolver =
            getContext().getContentResolver();
```

```
    if (contentResolver != null) {

        contentResolver.notifyChange(affectedUri, null);


        contentResolver.
                notifyChange(DevicesContract
                        .DeviceManufacturer.CONTENT_URI, null);
    }
}
```

The notifyUris() method has an affectedUri parameter which is the URI that was used by one of the insert(), update(), or delete() methods. In order to make sure all ContentObservers are notified of a change, notifyUris() sends an update notification to the original content URI as well as the URI of the joined tables.

Summary

Once data has been stored in a database, it frequently needs to be read and shown to the user. Android offers classes to help simplify this task. Using a cursor loader helps relieve application code from worrying about threading when either reading the database or updating the UI.

Through the use of content observers, a cursor loader and content provider can notify activities and fragments of changes to the underlying data source.

When using a RecyclerView, the application code must contain an adapter that binds the RecyclerView's adapter to the UI. This chapter provided an example of such an adapter that can be used in a similar way to how a CursorAdapter is used with a ListView.

8

Sharing Data with Intents

One of the strengths of Android is the ability to share data between multiple components of an app as well as with components of an external app. In previous chapters, the content provider was discussed as a mechanism to perform internal and external data sharing. While a content provider can be a useful mechanism to share data in Android, it is not the only method.

This chapter discusses an alternative method for sharing data in Android by using the Android intent API.

Sending Intents

Intents provide a convenient way to send data from one Android component to another. They are frequently used to pass data from one activity to another when starting a new activity or service.

Explicit Intents

Listing 8.1 shows a typical paradigm for starting an activity and passing that activity some information using an explicit intent.

Listing 8.1 Creating an Explicit Intent

```
Intent intent = new Intent(CurrentClass.this, TargetClass.class)
        .putExtra("NameOfExtra1", payload));
```

The intent created in Listing 8.1 is referred to as an **explicit intent** because it explicitly defines the target Android component that should receive the intent. In Listing 8.1, TargetClass is the target of the intent because it is passed to the intent's constructor. The intent also contains data that the target activity can access and process which is added to the intent with a call to Intent.putExtra().

While explicit intents are useful for sharing data between components that are internal to an app, they are not useful for sharing data with external components. To share data externally, an **implicit intent** needs to be created.

Implicit Intents

The only difference between implicit and explicit intents is the data they contain. Implicit intents are created using the same class as an explicit intent. Listing 8.2 shows the creation of an implicit intent.

Listing 8.2 Creating an Implicit Intent

```
Intent intent = new Intent(Intent.ACTION_SEND)
        .setType("text/plain")
        .putExtra(Intent.EXTRA_TEXT, payload));
```

Unlike the explicit intent created in Listing 8.1, the intent created in Listing 8.2 does not specify a target activity. Instead, it provides an *action* and a MIME type that allow Android to deliver the intent to the correct activity, which can be either part of the same app or part of a different app. The action is supplied to the intent constructor, and the MIME type is set with a call to `Intent.setType()`. In addition to helping Android find an activity that can process the intent, the intent's MIME type provides an indication of what kind of data the intent holds.

After the intent is created and its MIME type set, a call to `Intent.putExtra()` is made, which adds the actual data to the intent. Intent "extras" can be thought of as a key/value pair collection of data contained in the intent. In Listing 8.2, the data being sent in the intent (contained in the `payload` variable) is being added to the intent with the `Intent.EXTRA_TEXT` key.

Once the intent has been created, it can be used to start an activity to process the data.

Starting a Target Activity

One important difference between using implicit intents and explicit intents to start activities is that there might be multiple activities that are capable of handling the implicit intent. This is because implicit intent activity resolution is based on the intent's action and MIME type rather than an actual target component. When multiple activities are capable of handling an implicit intent, Android displays a dialog to users that allows them to pick which activity they would like to process the intent. Figure 8.1 shows this dialog.

To start an activity with an implicit intent, the intent either can be directly passed to the `Context.startActivity()`, or it can first be wrapped in another intent with a call to `Intent.createChooser()`, with the resulting intent being passed to `Context.startActivity()`. The first approach, passing directly to `Context.startActivity()`, shows the activity chooser from Figure 8.1 only if the user has told Android to ask every time. The user can override this functionality and decide not to have the chooser shown.

In addition, a runtime exception is thrown if no activity can process the given action and MIME type. To prevent the exception, it is good practice to make a call to `Intent.resolveActivity()` first. Listing 8.3 shows a protected call to `Context.startActivity()` without using `Intent.createChooser()`.

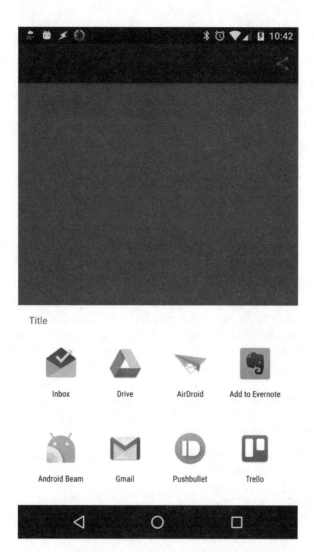

Figure 8.1   Activity chooser dialog

Listing 8.3 Protected Call to `Context.startActivity()`

```
if (intent.resolveActivity(this.getPackageManager()) == null) {
    // Show user something
} else {
    startActivity(intent);
}
```

Wrapping the intent with a call to `Intent.createChooser()` ensures that the activity chooser is always shown. In addition, it allows an app to have control over the title of the chooser dialog to present users with some text to guide them through the selection process. It also prevents the runtime exception should Android not be able to find an activity to handle the intent. For actions like `ACTION_SEND`, which have numerous apps that can implement them, apps will want to force the display of the picker. Actions that are implemented by one or two apps should allow a default to be set. Listing 8.4 shows the use of the `Intent.createChooser()` method.

Listing 8.4 Calling `Intent.createChooser()`

```
startActivity(intent.createChooser(intent, "Custom Title"));
```

Once the user selects an activity from the chooser, that activity starts and receives the intent to process. The next section discusses how to receive external data from an implicit intent.

Receiving Implicit Intents

Because implicit intents do not specify an Android component to start, Android must keep a list of which components can handle the various intents. Indicating which activities can process which intents is done on app installation by adding an intent filter to the `AndroidManifest.xml` file for an activity. The intent filter indicates which actions and MIME types an activity can process so Android can include the activity in the activity chooser dialog that is shown to the user when an implicit intent is used. Listing 8.5 shows a snippet of an Android manifest file that declares an activity and defines an intent filter for the activity.

Listing 8.5 Activity with an Intent Filter

```
<activity
    android:name=".MyActivity">
    <intent-filter>
        <action android:name="android.intent.action.SEND"/>
    </intent-filter>
</activity>
```

In Listing 8.5, the `MyActivity` class is registered to support the `android.intent.action.SEND` action. This means that if another activity calls `startActivity()` and passes an intent with the `android.intent.action.SEND` action, Android adds `MyActivity` to the list of activities that can process that intent.

> **Note**
>
> `android.intent.action.SEND` and `Intent.ACTION_SEND` are the same action. `Intent.ACTION_SEND` is the constant used in Java code and has the value of `android.intent.action.SEND` which is used in XML.

In addition to filtering based on actions, an intent filter can filter based on MIME types so that only certain types of data are passed to an activity through an implicit intent. For example, an activity can be configured to handle only intents with image data by adding a MIME type of image/png to the intent filter.

When the target activity is started by an implicit intent, the implicit intent can be retrieved with a call to Activity.getIntent(). Once the intent has been retrieved, the activity can access the action and MIME type as well as retrieve data from the intent.

Even though the intent filter from the manifest ensures that only matching intents are routed to an activity, the action and MIME type might still need to be inspected by the activity because an intent filter can specify multiple actions and MIME types for an activity. When this happens, the activity likely needs to process the data differently depending on the action and MIME type of data. For example, an activity that supports both textual URL data and binary image data would need to have different functionality for different intent MIME types.

Listing 8.6 shows a snippet from an Activity.onCreate() method where the intent is retrieved and verified and the data is retrieved.

Listing 8.6 Handling an Implicit Intent

```
Intent intent = getIntent();

if (intent != null) {

    if (Intent.ACTION_SEND.equals(intent.getAction())
        && "text/plain".equals(intent.getType())) {

        String htmlPayload = intent.getStringExtra(Intent.EXTRA_TEXT);


        //.... process htmlPayload

    }

}
```

So far, the mechanics of sending and receiving data with an implicit intent have been discussed. While these are important details, the actual data being sent is also very important. The next sections go into the details of the various actions, MIME types, and types of data that can be sent with an implicit intent.

Building an Intent

Before sending an implicit intent, the action, MIME type, and data must all be added to the intent. In previous examples, the ACTION_SEND action was used along with the text/plain MIME type to send textual data. The intent API allows for additional actions to be used and supports sending binary data to an activity.

Actions

When working with intents, multiple actions can be used. By convention, the actions
`Intent.ACTION_SEND` and `Intent.ACTION_SEND_MULTIPLE` are typically used to send data
from one activity to another through an implicit intent.

Intent.ACTION_SEND

`ACTION_SEND` is used to send a single piece of text or binary data to another Android
component. The type of data can be either textual or binary, but there should be only one
piece of data.

With only a single piece of data being sent, one of the overloaded `Intent.getExtra()`
methods that take non-collection data should be used to store the data in the intent.

All of the examples thus far have used `Intent.ACTION_SEND`.

Intent.ACTION_SEND_MULTIPLE

`ACTION_SEND_MULTIPLE` is used to send multiple pieces of data in an intent. In addition
to setting the action, the intent should use an `Intent.setExtra()` overloaded method
that takes an array or collection of data as a parameter. Listing 8.7 shows the
`ACTION_SEND_MULTIPLE` action.

Listing 8.7 Using the `ACTION_SEND_MULTIPLE` Action

```
String[] urls = {
        "URL1",
        "URL2",
        "URL3"
};


new Intent(Intent.ACTION_SEND_MULTIPLE)
        .setType("text/plain")
        .putExtra(Intent.EXTRA_TEXT, urls);
```

When the intent in Listing 8.7 is received by the target activity, the extra data can be
read as an array of strings and handled accordingly.

Setting the action can let a target activity know how many pieces of data are included
in an implicit intent. Setting the MIME type indicates the type of data in the intent.
Thus far, all the examples have covered only text data. It is also possible to send binary
data in an implicit intent.

Extras

Extras are used in an intent to hold the actual data for the intent. As mentioned previously,
the intent extra data can be thought of as a collection of key/value pairs. By convention,

an implicit intent should use two different keys when sending text and binary data: `Intent.EXTRA_TEXT` should be used when sending text data, and `Intent.EXTRA_STREAM` should be used when sending binary data.

Because the data is stored using different keys, the target activity needs to know which key to use in order to read the data. The MIME type is a good indicator of which type of data the intent contains. For example, an intent with a MIME type of `text/*` should have its data populated in the `Intent.EXTRA_TEXT` key, whereas an intent with a MIME type of `image/*` should use the `Intent.EXTRA_STREAM` key to read the data.

EXTRA_TEXT

`EXTRA_TEXT` is used to store textual data in an implicit intent. In most cases, the type of data in the intent is either `text/plain`, or `text/html` if the text contains HTML. Creating an intent to send text data was presented in Listing 8.2. The payload to the `Intent.putExtra()` method call contains the textual data that is sent to an activity.

EXTRA_STREAM

`EXTRA_STREAM` is used to store binary data in an intent. This could be an image, sound file, or anything else that can be represented as binary content. When using `EXTRA_STREAM`, the MIME type set on the intent becomes even more important as it indicates how the receiving activity should handle the binary data. For example, to send a JPEG in an intent, Listing 8.8 might be used.

Listing 8.8 Sending a JPEG Extra

```
Intent intent = new Intent(Intent.ACTION_SEND)
        .setType("image/jpeg")
        .putExtra(Intent.EXTRA_STREAM, payload));
```

The intent in Listing 8.8 allows the receiving activity to access the actual image data from the intent.

Extra Data Types

Intents can hold many different types of data as "extra" fields. To support the different types, the `Intent` class has multiple overloaded `putExtra()` methods, all taking a string as the name of the extra and a second parameter as the data itself. Among the overloaded `putExtra()` methods are variants that accept each of the Java primitive data types (`byte`, `short`, `int`, `long`, `float`, `double`, `boolean`, and `char`) as well as arrays of all the Java primitives. The `Intent` class also contains overloaded methods to add an extra of type `String` and `String[]`.

Intent extras can get a little more complicated when other objects need to be added to an intent. While the `Intent` class does have methods to accept a class implementing `Serializable`, this tends to be inefficient as it relies on Java serialization and deserialization. Instead, Android includes a `Parcelable` interface that should be used to add objects to intents.

Implementing Parcelable

The Parcelable interface allows a class to determine how it should serialize and deserialize itself for use in an intent. Listing 8.9 shows the implementation of a class that implements the Parcelable interface.

Listing 8.9 Parcelable Implementation

```java
public class ParcelableClass implements Parcelable {
    private String stringField;
    private int intField;
    private float floatField;
    private boolean booleanField;

    public String getStringField() {
        return stringField;
    }

    public void setStringField(String stringField) {
        this.stringField = stringField;
    }

    public int getIntField() {
        return intField;
    }

    public void setIntField(int intField) {
        this.intField = intField;
    }

    public float getFloatField() {
        return floatField;
    }

    public void setFloatField(float floatField) {
        this.floatField = floatField;
    }
```

```java
    protected ParcelableClass(Parcel in) {
        this.stringField = in.readString();
        this.intField = in.readInt();
        this.floatField = in.readFloat();
        this.booleanField = in.readInt() == 1;
    }


    @Override
    public int describeContents() {
        return 0;
    }


    @Override
    public void writeToParcel(@NonNull Parcel dest, int flags) {
        dest.writeString(stringField);
        dest.writeInt(intField);
        dest.writeFloat(floatField);
        dest.writeInt(booleanField ? 1 : 0);
    }

    public static final Creator<ParcelableClass> CREATOR =
            new Creator<ParcelableClass>() {
        @Override
        public ParcelableClass createFromParcel(Parcel in) {
            return new ParcelableClass(in);
        }

        @Override
        public ParcelableClass[] newArray(int size) {
            return new ParcelableClass[size];
        }
    };
}
```

The class in Listing 8.9 is a bean-style class containing member data and methods to both access and set the member data ("getters" and "setters"). The `Parcelable` support is shown in bold text in Listing 8.9, including a non-public constructor, concrete method implementations `describeContents()` and `writeToParcel()`, and the `CREATOR` member variable.

Writing a Parcel

The `Parcelable.writeToParcel()` method is responsible for deconstructing a class into a parcel object which is used by the Android SDK. The parcel object that is created is used to eventually reconstruct the class.

In Listing 8.9, the `writeToParcel()` method uses overloaded `write` methods to add the member data from `ParcelableClass` to the parcel object. The `Parcel` class has methods for different data types which add an element of type safety to the parceling operation. Notice in Listing 8.9 that there is no method to write a `boolean` value to the parcel. Instead, an `int` value is used to record the value of a `boolean` field.

CREATOR

The `CREATOR` member variable is required for any class that implements `Parcelable`. The Android SDK mandates that to use the parcelable API, a class must contain a field named "CREATOR" and that field must be a non-null `static` value that implements the `Parcelable.Creator` interface. The `Parcelable.Creator` interface contains methods to create a new array of the class type, in this case `ParcelableClass`, and to create a `ParcelableClass` instance from a parcel object. The parcel object contains all the data to reconstruct an instance of `ParcelableClass`. The parcel object that is passed to the `CREATOR.createFromParcel()` method will contain the same values as the parcel object that was returned from the call to `ParcelableClass.writeToParcel()`.

Reading a Parcel

The `protected ParcelableClass()` constructor is used to reconstruct a `ParcelableClass` object from a parcel object. Notice in Listing 8.9 that the constructor reads the parcel object and sets the member variables of a `ParcelableClass` instance.

Notice that there are no field names associated with reading the values inside a parcel object. This is because the `Parcel` class uses the order in which data was added to internally store values. This means that values *must* be read from a parcel in the same order in which they were written.

What Not to Add to an Intent

With the use of `Parcelable`, it is possible to add almost any type of data to an intent and have it sent to other Android components, potentially across process boundaries. However, it is important to keep in mind that not every class should be added to an intent for transmission to other Android components.

The `Cursor` class was introduced in earlier chapters of this book when discussing reading data from a database. While it might be tempting to add a cursor to an intent, by using either standard Java serialization or `Parcelable`, it can be problematic. The cursor class contains low-level connections to the SQLite database which allow Android to update the cursor when data in the database changes. Attempting to deconstruct a cursor, add it to an intent, and reconstruct it in a different component breaks these connections, possibly causing the cursor to no longer respond to database updates. In addition, there is a limit to the amount of memory that an intent can use when moving from one Android component to another. Using a large cursor in an intent may cause a runtime exception should the cursor contain too much data.

ShareActionProvider

The ShareActionProvider allows an activity to make use of the app bar to aid in the sharing of data using an intent. In previous examples, the code to create an implicit intent to start an activity could be activated with a button click. If action and MIME types are included in the filters used by multiple activities, users would then be presented with the activity chooser dialog where they can tell Android how they want to handle the intent.

The ShareActionProvider removes some of the code needed to send implicit intents and handles the cases where multiple activities can respond to it. Recall Figure 8.1, which displayed the activity chooser dialog. The dialog is displayed when the user clicks the

Figure 8.2   Share action provider

"share" button on the app bar. Contrast that to Figure 8.2, which shows the share action being displayed after the user clicks the "share" button on the app bar.

Notice in Figure 8.2 that the list of activities that can process the intent now appears as a spinner on the app bar. Also, the user's last selection appears to the right of the spinner. This allows the user to reuse the last selection without having to perform an additional click.

Implementing the `ShareActionProvider` involves adding a menu to an activity, setting the intent that the `ShareActionProvider` should use to start an activity, and responding to click events from the app bar icon.

Share Action Menu

Before a `ShareActionProvider` can be used, it must be included in a menu that will be inflated by an activity. Listing 8.10 shows a menu resource definition that includes a button that is attached to a `ShareActionProvider`.

Listing 8.10 Share Action Provider Menu Item

```
<menu xmlns:android="http://schemas.android.com/apk/res/android"

  xmlns:app="http://schemas.android.com/apk/res-auto">

    <item android:id="@+id/action_share"

          android:title="@string/action_share"

          app:showAsAction="always"

          app:actionProviderClass="android.support.v7.widget.ShareAction
          ➥Provider"/>

</menu>
```

> **Note**
>
> Because the `ShareActionProvider` was not introduced until API 14, the support library version is used to backport functionality to older versions.

The `ShareActionProvider` is a specialization of the more general `Action Provider` class. To use a `ShareActionProvider` in a menu, it must be declared as the `ShareProvider` for a menu item. In Listing 8.10, this is done with the following:

```
app:actionProviderClass="android.support.v7.widget.ShareActionProvider"
```

Once the `ActionProvider` is declared in the menu resource file, the activity needs to configure the `ShareActionProvider` to send the appropriate implicit intent when it is clicked. Listing 8.11 shows an implementation of `Activity.onCreateOptionsMenu()` that configures the `ShareActionProvider`.

Listing 8.11 Configuring the Provider with `onCreateOptionsMenu`

```
@Override
public boolean onCreateOptionsMenu(Menu menu) {
    MenuInflater inflater = getMenuInflater();
    inflater.inflate(R.menu.activity_details, menu);

    MenuItem menuItem = menu.findItem(R.id.action_share);
    shareIntent = new Intent(Intent.ACTION_SEND)
                        .setType("text/plain")
                        .putExtra(Intent.EXTRA_TEXT, payload);
    ShareActionProvider provider =
            (ShareActionProvider)
                MenuItemCompat.getActionProvider(menuItem);
    provider.setShareIntent(shareIntent);

    return true;
}
```

The code in Listing 8.11 first finds the `MenuItem` that is associated with the `ShareActionProvider`. This is the `MenuItem` that was declared in the menu resource from Listing 8.10. After finding the correct `MenuItem`, the `MenuItem`'s `ActionProvider` can be retrieved. The `ShareActionProvider` is provided with the implicit intent it will use to start an activity when the app bar action item is clicked.

The intent that is created and passed to the `ShareActionProvider` follows the same form as the intents discussed previously in this chapter. This is because the `ShareActionProvider` does not manipulate or interfere with how the intent shares information. Instead, it only provides a simple way to add a UI around sharing data.

Summary

Previous chapters discussed how to use a `ContentProvider` to share data across activities in different apps. This can also be done using implicit intents in Android.

Implicit intents do not specify an Android component that will be started but instead specify an action and MIME type which are used to find activities that can receive the data.

Implicit intents can contain either text or binary data, and the different types of data should be set using different keys in the intent. Using the MIME type, an implicit intent can define which type of data it contains.

Using a `ShareActionProvider` can be a convenient way to add share functionality to an activity. The `ShareActionProvider` still uses an implicit intent to share data but limits the amount of code that is necessary to send the intent while using a common UX pattern to allow the user to share data.

9

Communicating with Web APIs

As both the complexity of mobile applications and the capabilities of mobile devices increase, app developers frequently find themselves in a situation where their app needs to communicate with a Web API. While this communication vastly increases the capability of an app, it also injects significant complexity from both the user experience and technical standpoints. This chapter discusses some of the problems that commonly occur with app-to-server communication, and it presents some tools and guidance for making app-to-server communication easier for the developer and transparent to the user.

REST and Web Services

A common architecture for creating a system that allows a mobile device to communicate with a back-end server is a Web service that is based on the Representational State Transfer (REST) architecture with which mobile devices communicate. With a REST-based approach, the server allows the mobile app to read data as well as add and update its data. A REST architecture is a common solution for this problem and is well supported across multiple platforms and languages used for the back-end implementation.

REST Overview

REST is a software architecture that was introduced by Roy Thomas Fielding in 2000. While REST is not a formal specification, it does provide a list of constraints that a true RESTful Web service needs to follow. While many Web services claim to be RESTful, few actually follow all those constraints. The formal list of REST constraints is as follows:

- **Client-server:** The client(s) and the server have different roles in the system. This provides separation of concerns to the REST system. The client does not need to worry about details such as data storage, and the server can ignore the details of displaying the data to the user. The REST API is the interface between the clients and the server.

- **Stateless:** The server does not store any client information between requests. Each request is entirely self-contained and provides all the data needed for the server to perform the desired operation.

- **Cacheable:** Responses from the server are labeled as either cacheable or non-cacheable so a component in the system may save the response for reuse.

- **Layered system:** All layers in the system should be self-contained such that they do not know the implementation details of other layers in the systems. This allows layers to be seamlessly added to or removed from the system when needed.

- **Code on demand:** Client functionality can be altered, when appropriate, by the server without changing the server functionality.

- **Uniform interface:** The REST interface is the same for all servers and clients in the system.

Even though a Web service may not follow *all* the REST constraints, many do follow at least some of them, giving them similar architecture and the ability to be accessed in a similar manner. It can be more appropriate to refer to these kinds of Web resources as Web APIs rather than Web services as their intent is to provide an API that is accessible by remote machines.

REST-like Web API Structure

Many modern Web APIs follow an architecture that is similar to REST. While the Web APIs may not implement *all* of the formal REST constraints, many implement at least a few. The reason for the divergence is usually convenience. For many systems it does not make sense to incur the additional engineering effort to implement every formal REST constraint.

For the purposes of this chapter, it is assumed that accessing a Web API means communicating with a remote API that uses the HTTP protocol with JSON as the data interchange format. This is becoming more common as remote services look to provide a lightweight interface for remote clients.

What makes these APIs REST-like is the way they are accessed. Typically, accessing the API means using one of the standard HTTP methods and sending the request to a specific URL. The path segment of the URL often defines an operation or piece of data that should be either accessed or manipulated.

For example, Twitter uses a RESTful API that allows remote clients to access pieces of data, such as the contents of a user's Twitter feed, and perform operations such as posting a tweet. For the Twitter RESTful API, the list of tweets that shows up on a user's feed can be accessed by sending the HTTP GET method to https://api.twitter.com/1.1/statuses/home_timeline.json. Assuming the request also includes the correct credentials, the Twitter API returns a JSON response that represents the user's Twitter feed.

This API architecture supports writing to the Web API. In the case of the Twitter Web API, a client can submit a tweet for a user by sending the HTTP POST method to https://api.twitter.com/1.1/statuses/update.json. The HTTP POST request often carries a payload, in this case the contents of the tweet, along with any other parameters that are needed to satisfy the request. The payload for a POST request is also in JSON, and the Web API can respond with a response.

While REST and REST-like APIs are not the only ways to support data access by remote clients, they are becoming more widely used because of their simplicity. Publishing an API entails setting up an HTTP server to handle the requests and making sure the documentation that describes the API is publicly available.

The remainder of this chapter uses the terms *Web API* and *Web service* interchangeably to mean a remote Web resource that follows this REST-like pattern.

Accessing Remote Web APIs

As stated in the beginning of the chapter, accessing a Web service from Android can be complicated. While the standard Android SDK does contain the tools to successfully access a Web service, it leaves many implementation details to the developer. The Android SDK contains multiple HTTP clients as well as classes to help with the reading and writing of JSON. This section describes the APIs that can be used to access an HTTP/JSON Web service as well as some of the problems that need to be solved to use them.

Accessing Web Services with Standard Android APIs

In order to communicate with a Web service that uses HTTP as the protocol and JSON as the interchange format, an app must use an HTTP client to send requests to and receive responses from the Web service. Historically, Android has had multiple HTTP clients. However, as of Gingerbread (2.3), HttpURLConnection is the preferred HTTP client to use, and the other Web clients are considered deprecated.

Communicating with the Web Service

Before an HTTP request can be sent to the Web service, a connection to an HTTP server must be established. Listing 9.1 shows code that opens a connection to an HTTP server and sends the HTTP GET method.

Listing 9.1 Opening an **HttpURLConnection** Connection

```
HttpURLConnection connection = null;
StringBuffer buffer = new StringBuffer();
BufferedReader reader = null;


try {
    connection = (HttpURLConnection) new URL(params[0]).openConnection();
    InputStream input =
        new BufferedInputStream(connection.getInputStream());


    reader = new BufferedReader(new InputStreamReader(input));
    String line;
```

```
    while ((line = reader.readLine()) != null) {
        buffer.append(line);
    }


    // Process data
} catch (IOException | JSONException e) {
    // Log error
} finally {
    if (connection != null) {
        connection.disconnect();
    }


    if (reader != null) {
        try {
            reader.close();
        } catch (IOException e) {
            // do something meaningless
        }
    }
}
```

In addition to making the request to the Web service, the code in Listing 9.1 reads the response and makes use of the JSON API that is included with Android to parse the response for further processing.

While Listing 9.1 is not overly complicated, it does present some complexities that will only increase as the number of requests that an app needs to make increases. For example, the code should also handle any error cases that may arise. These can be issues such as the device not currently being connected to a network, a slow network connection resulting in a timeout, or any of the error responses that the Web service may return. It is the job of the developer to handle all these cases in a way that presents a good user experience.

Something else to consider is that Listing 9.1 must not be run on the main thread because it accesses the network. On devices running Honeycomb and above, accessing a network resource on the main thread results in a NetworkOnMainThreadException being thrown. Older versions of Android just cause the main thread to pause, which could result in ANR issues. In addition to making the request off the main thread, the app must make sure to update the UI on the main thread. Failure to update a view on the main thread causes Android to throw runtime exceptions that could crash an app.

To handle the threading complexities, a common approach is to use some of the Android threading APIs such as `AsyncTask`. Listing 9.2 shows the code updated to run with an `AsyncTask`.

Listing 9.2 Using `AsyncTask` to Make the Request

```
public class NetworkCallAsyncTask
    extends AsyncTask<String, Void, JSONObject> {
    @Override
    protected JSONObject doInBackground(String... params) {
        HttpURLConnection connection = null;
        StringBuffer buffer = new StringBuffer();
        BufferedReader reader = null;
        JSONObject response = null;

        try {
            connection =
                    (HttpURLConnection) new URL(params[0])
                            .openConnection();

            InputStream input =
                    new BufferedInputStream(connection.getInputStream());

            reader = new BufferedReader(new InputStreamReader(input));
            String line;

            while ((line = reader.readLine()) != null) {
                buffer.append(line);
            }

            response = new JSONObject(buffer.toString());

        } catch (IOException | JSONException e) {
            // Log error
        } finally {
            if (connection != null) {
```

```
                    connection.disconnect();
                }


            if (reader != null) {
                try {
                    reader.close();
                } catch (IOException e) {
                    // do something meaningless
                }
            }
        }


        return response;
    }


    @Override
    protected void onPostExecute(JSONObject response) {
        super.onPostExecute(response);


        // update display
    }
}


// Activity that will use the NetworkCallAsyncTask
public class NetworkActivity extends Activity {
    @Override
    protected void onStart() {
        super.onStart();
        new NetworkCallAsyncTask().execute("http://remote-web-server");

    }
}
```

With the updates in Listing 9.2, the request is now sent on a background thread, and the JSON response can be handled on the UI thread, allowing the UI to be updated in onPostExecute(). The Web service request starts with the call to NetworkCallAsyncTask.execute() in the activity's onStart() method.

While the code in Listing 9.2 does address the threading issues, it can still be problematic. When making network calls, it is important to remember that many factors contribute to the overall time it takes the request/response pair to make a round trip from the device to the Web service and back. Network speed, server load, request size, response size, and the time it takes to parse the response can all lead to a request/ response pair taking multiple seconds to transmit. While the asynchronous HTTP call is running on a background thread (preventing a janky UI, or ANRs), the user can navigate away from the activity after the request has been sent but before the response has been received by the device. When this happens, Android may destroy the activity. If the activity gets destroyed, attempting to update the activity's views causes another runtime exception to be thrown.

To handle this case, the activity that starts the `AsyncTask` must cancel the task before it becomes detached from its view. In addition, the `AsyncTask` needs to check if the task has been canceled. Listing 9.3 shows the updated code to handle the lifecycle changes and canceling of the `AsyncTask`.

Listing 9.3 Adding Cancel Support to `AsyncTask`

```
public class NetworkCallAsyncTask

        extends AsyncTask<String, Void, JSONObject> {

    @Override

    protected JSONObject doInBackground(String... params) {

        HttpURLConnection connection = null;

        StringBuffer buffer = new StringBuffer();

        BufferedReader reader = null;

        JSONObject response = null;


        try {

            connection =

                    (HttpURLConnection) new URL(params[0])

                            .openConnection();


            InputStream input =

                    new BufferedInputStream(connection.getInputStream());


            reader = new BufferedReader(new InputStreamReader(input));
            String line;


            while ((line = reader.readLine()) != null) {
```

```
                buffer.append(line);
        }


        if (!isCancelled()) {
            response = new JSONObject(buffer.toString());
        }
    } catch (IOException | JSONException e) {
        // Log error
    } finally {
        if (connection != null) {
            connection.disconnect();
        }

        if (reader != null) {
            try {
                reader.close();
            } catch (IOException e) {
                // do something meaningless
            }
        }
    }


    return response;
}


@Override
protected void onPostExecute(JSONObject response) {
    super.onPostExecute(response);

    if (!isCancelled()) {
        // update display
    }
}
}
```

```
// Activity that will use the NetworkCallAsyncTask
public class NetworkActivity extends Activity {
    private NetworkCallAsyncTask networkCallAsyncTask;

    @Override
    protected void onStart() {
        super.onStart();
        networkCallAsyncTask =
            new NetworkCallAsyncTask().execute("http://remote-web-server");
    }

    @Override
    protected void onStop() {
        super.onStop();
        networkCallAsyncTask.cancel(true);
    }
}
```

With the code in Listing 9.3, both the threading and the lifecycle issues have been addressed.

While use of an AsyncTask is *one* solution for dealing with the threading and lifecycle complexities of communicating with a Web service, it is not the only one. Other popular solutions involve using an IntentService, or manually starting and managing threads. Rather than building a complex threading solution from scratch, many developers use frameworks like RxJava. However, RxJava is not part of the Android SDK and would need to be added as a third-party dependency.

Once an app is able to communicate with a Web service, it must process the response it receives from the Web service into a format that can be used by the rest of the app's code. When using a Web service that uses JSON as an interchange format, this usually means either converting the returned JSON into a Java object that is used by the app or saving the values in a database. The raw JSON can be used as a representation of the app's state, but this tends to be tedious.

Working with JSON

As shown in Listings 9.1 through 9.3, the Android SDK contains an API for working with JSON. Listing 9.4 shows the NetworkCallAsyncTask with code to convert the JSON response that was received from the Web service to Java objects using the default Android JSON API.

Listing 9.4 Converting JSON to a Data Model

```java
public class NetworkCallAsyncTask
        extends AsyncTask<String, Void, List<Manufacturer>> {
    @Override
    protected List<Manufacturer> doInBackground(String... params) {
        HttpURLConnection connection = null;
        StringBuffer buffer = new StringBuffer();
        BufferedReader reader = null;
        List<Manufacturer> manufacturers = new ArrayList<>();

        try {
            connection =
                    (HttpURLConnection) new URL(params[0])
                            .openConnection();

            InputStream input =
                    new BufferedInputStream(connection.getInputStream());

            reader = new BufferedReader(new InputStreamReader(input));
            String line;

            while ((line = reader.readLine()) != null) {
                buffer.append(line);
            }

            if (!isCancelled()) {
                JSONObject response = new JSONObject(buffer.toString());

                JSONArray jsonManufacturers =
                        response.getJSONArray("manufacturers");

                for (int i = 0; i < jsonManufacturers.length(); i++) {
                    JSONObject jsonManufacturer =
                            jsonManufacturers.getJSONObject(i);
```

```
Manufacturer manufacturer = new Manufacturer();

manufacturer
      .setShortName(jsonManufacturer
            .getString("short_name"));

manufacturer
      .setLongName(jsonManufacturer
            .getString("long_name"));

JSONArray jsonDevices =
      jsonManufacturer.getJSONArray("devices");

List<Device> devices = new ArrayList<>();

for (int j = 0; j < jsonDevices.length(); j++) {
   JSONObject jsonDevice =
            jsonDevices.getJSONObject(j);

   Device device = new Device();

   device.setDisplaySizeInches((float) jsonDevice
         .getDouble("display_size_inches"));

   device.setNickname(jsonDevice
         .getString("nickname"));

   device.setModel(jsonDevice.getString("model"));

   devices.add(device);
}
```

```java
                    manufacturer.setDevices(devices);
                    manufacturers.add(manufacturer);
                }
            }
        } catch (IOException | JSONException e) {
            // Log error
        } finally {
            if (connection != null) {
                connection.disconnect();
            }

            if (reader != null) {
                try {
                    reader.close();
                } catch (IOException e) {
                    // do something meaningless
                }
            }
        }


        return manufacturers;
    }


    @Override
    protected void onPostExecute(List<Manufacturer> manufacturers) {
        super.onPostExecute(manufacturers);

        if (!isCancelled()) {
            // update display
        }
    }
}
```

```
// Activity that will use the NetworkCallAsyncTask
public class NetworkActivity extends Activity {
    private NetworkCallAsyncTask networkCallAsyncTask;

    @Override
    protected void onStart() {
        super.onStart();
        networkCallAsyncTask =
            new NetworkCallAsyncTask().execute("http://remote-web-server");
    }

    @Override
    protected void onStop() {
        super.onStop();
        networkCallAsyncTask.cancel(true);
    }
}
```

In Listing 9.4, the JSON response from the Web service is converted to Java POJOs using the JSON API that comes with the Android SDK. The conversion is a manual process with the app developer mapping all the JSON data to the Java objects.

At this point, we have a reasonable implementation of an architecture that can support sending and receiving data from a remote Web service. However, the solution presented in Listing 9.4 is a very manual one and needs to be changed and updated as new API calls are added. In addition, as the JSON returned from the Web service grows, the NetworkCallAsyncTask will need to be updated to map the JSON to model objects. While this approach works, there are other tools and libraries that simplify the code by addressing some of these issues (threading, activity lifecycle, JSON parsing) out of the box. The next sections discuss two of these solutions: Retrofit and Volley.

Accessing Web Services with Retrofit

Retrofit (https://square.github.io/retrofit/) is a popular open-source solution for communicating with a Web service that supports HTTP. Retrofit can ease the pain of communicating with a remote Web service by handling the communication and threading details. Instead of needing to worry about making a request off the main thread, and handling the response on the main thread, an app only needs to let Retrofit know which request it needs to make, and Retrofit does the rest.

Along with handling the low-level communication details, Retrofit supports using other third-party libraries to handle the serialization/deserialization of requests and responses. Because Retrofit allows these converters to be specified by the app, it can support multiple interchange formats, such as JSON, XML, protocol buffers, and so on.

In addition to handling the communication and serialization support, Retrofit has support for canceling a request that has been sent but has not received a response. This allows developers to work around the issues that are caused by an activity attempting to update a view when it is no longer alive.

Adding Retrofit to an Android Project

Because Retrofit is a third-party library, it must be added to a project as a dependency. For Gradle-backed Android projects, this is as easy as adding the Retrofit entries to the project's `build.gradle` file. Listing 9.5 shows the typical Retrofit declarations in a `build.gradle` file.

Listing 9.5 Adding Retrofit to `build.gradle`

```
final RETROFIT_VERSION = '2.0.0'

compile "com.squareup.retrofit2:retrofit:${RETROFIT_VERSION}"

compile "com.squareup.retrofit2:converter-gson:${RETROFIT_VERSION}"

compile "com.squareup.okhttp3:logging-interceptor:3.2.0"
```

Listing 9.5 has two dependencies for Retrofit: the core Retrofit library (`com.squareup.retrofit2:retrofit`) and the GSON converter (`com.squareup.retrofit2:converter-gson`).

The core Retrofit library is what adds the base Retrofit support to the project. This includes the ability to communicate asynchronously with a Web service off the main thread and receive the response on the main thread. The ability to cancel a request is also included in the core library.

The Retrofit GSON converter allows Retrofit to use GSON to transform a JSON response into Java POJOs for use in the app. GSON is a popular JSON library written by Google. It can be used to bind JSON objects to Java objects by using either matching property names or annotations. A library like GSON can replace the standard Android JSON API and eliminate the need to manually map JSON objects to Java objects.

The third dependency (`compile "com.squareup.okhttp3:logging-interceptor:3.2.0"`) in Listing 9.5 adds a library that provides HTTP request and response logging. This will be discussed in more detail in the next section.

Once the `build.gradle` file has been updated with the code from Listing 9.5, Gradle automatically downloads the required files and adds them to the project.

Using Retrofit

Once Retrofit has been added to a project, it can be used to ease the pain of communicating with a remote Web service. In order to use Retrofit, an interface must first be declared that represents the calls that are supported by the Web service. This interface allows the rest of the app to use the Web service as if it were a class containing methods for each of the calls the Web service supports. This adds an object-oriented feel to Web service communication as the code using the interface simply makes method calls on an implementation of the interface, passing Java objects as parameters and receiving Java objects as the result. The actual implementation of the interface is defined by Retrofit. Listing 9.6 shows the interface for a Web service that contains a single call to support the device database app. It returns the list of devices and manufacturers.

Listing 9.6 Defining the Web Service Interface

```
public interface DeviceService {

    @GET("v2/570bbaf6110000b003d17e3a")

    Call<ManufacturersAndDevicesResponse> getManufacturersAndDevices();

}
```

In Listing 9.6, the DeviceService interface is declared containing the method getManufacturersAndDevices(). Notice that there is a @GET annotation attached to the getManufacturersAndDevices() method. The @GET annotation tells Retrofit that the HTTP request should be made using the HTTP GET method. In addition, the @GET annotation contains the path for the Web service call. The rest of the URL, protocol and host, is defined when retrieving an implementation of the DeviceService interface from Retrofit.

The getManufacturersAndDevices() method returns an implementation of the Call interface. The returned Call implementation can be used to make either a synchronous or an asynchronous call to the Web service. A synchronous Web service request is made on the current thread, and an asynchronous request is made on a background thread.

Listing 9.7 shows how to use Retrofit to get an implementation of the DeviceService interface defined in Listing 9.6. Since the configuration of Retrofit often needs to be the same for the entire app, it can be convenient to wrap the configuration in a singleton. The initialization of Retrofit can also be expensive from a performance perspective, giving added motivation to wrap the Retrofit.Builder method calls in a singleton.

Listing 9.7 Configuring Retrofit

```
public class WebServiceClient {

    private static final String TAG =
            WebServiceClient.class.getSimpleName();


    private static WebServiceClient instance = new WebServiceClient();


    private final DeviceService service;
```

```java
public static WebServiceClient getInstance() {
    return instance;
}


private WebServiceClient() {
    final Gson gson = new GsonBuilder()
            .setFieldNamingPolicy(FieldNamingPolicy
                    .LOWER_CASE_WITH_UNDERSCORES)
            .create();


    Retrofit.Builder retrofitBuilder = new Retrofit.Builder()
            .baseUrl("http://www.mocky.io")
            .addConverterFactory(GsonConverterFactory.create(gson));


    if (BuildConfig.DEBUG) {
        final HttpLoggingInterceptor loggingInterceptor =
                new HttpLoggingInterceptor(new HttpLoggingInterceptor
                        .Logger() {
            @Override
            public void log(String message) {
                Log.d(TAG, message);
            }
        });


        retrofitBuilder.callFactory(new OkHttpClient
                .Builder()
                .addNetworkInterceptor(loggingInterceptor)
                .build());


        loggingInterceptor.setLevel(HttpLoggingInterceptor.Level.BODY);
    }


    service = retrofitBuilder.build().create(DeviceService.class);
}
```

```
    public DeviceService getService() {

        return service;

    }

}
```

In order to use GSON with Retrofit, the `GsonBuilder` must be used to create and configure a GSON instance which then needs to be passed to `Retrofit.Builder`. In Listing 9.7, the `GsonBuilder` builds the GSON instance and configures it with the `LOWER_CASE_WITH_UNDERSCORES` naming policy. This constant is used to control how GSON maps JSON field names into Java POJO field names. More specifically, it maps underscores in the JSON properties to camel-case property names when creating Java POJOs from the JSON response.

Once the GSON instance has been created, it can be passed to the `Retrofit.Builder`, which generates the Retrofit-backed service that implements the `DeviceService` interface and is used by the rest of the app to access the Web service. Notice that the `Retrofit.Builder` is also used to define the base URL for the Web service. Remember from Listing 9.6 that the methods on the `DeviceService` interface contain annotations that specify the path of the Web service call. The base URL passed to the `Retrofit.Builder` is prepended to each of the paths to define the full URL of the Web service call. For example, the full URL of the `getManufacturersAndDevices` call is http://www.mocky.io/v2/570bbaf6110000b003d17e3a.

Once the Retrofit service has been configured with the `Retrofit.Builder`, the code in Listing 9.7 adds request/response logging to the Retrofit service for debug builds.

Retrofit uses another library, OkHttp, as its actual HTTP client. OkHttp can be thought of as a replacement for `HttpURLConnection` from earlier in the chapter. OkHttp has a powerful feature known as interceptors which allow developers to define code that can be run while processing a Web service request or response. In the case of Listing 9.7, an `OkHttpLoggingInterceptor` is added to the `OkHttpClient` used by Retrofit for DEBUG builds. The `OkHttpLoggingInterceptor` implementation simply prints out information about each request or response that is processed by the `OkHttpClient`. This information can be really useful when debugging integration issues between the app and the Web service. Listing 9.8 shows the information that is sent to LogCat for a request/response pair.

Listing 9.8 `OkHttpLoggingInterceptor` Output

```
D/WebServiceClient: --> GET http://www.mocky.io/v2/570bbaf6110000b003d17e3a
➡ http/1.1

D/WebServiceClient: Host: www.mocky.io

D/WebServiceClient: Connection: Keep-Alive

D/WebServiceClient: Accept-Encoding: gzip

D/WebServiceClient: User-Agent: okhttp/3.2.0
```

```
D/WebServiceClient: --> END GET
D/WebServiceClient: <-- 200 OK http://www.mocky.io/v2/570bbaf6110000b003d17
➥e3a(116ms)
D/WebServiceClient: Server: Cowboy
D/WebServiceClient: Connection: close
D/WebServiceClient: Content-Type: application/json; charset=utf-8
D/WebServiceClient: Date: Wed, 13 Apr 2016 03:34:25 GMT
D/WebServiceClient: Via: 1.1 vegur
D/WebServiceClient: OkHttp-Sent-Millis: 1460508929836
D/WebServiceClient: OkHttp-Received-Millis: 1460508929950
D/WebServiceClient: {
                     "manufacturers": [
                       {
                         "short_name": "Samsung",
                         "long_name": "Samsung Electronics",
                         "devices": [
                           {
                             "model": "Nexus S",
                             "nickname": "Crespo",
                             "display_size_inches": 4.0,
                             "memory_mb": 512
                           },
                           {
                             "model": "Galaxy Nexus",
                             "nickname": "Toro",
                             "display_size_inches": 4.65,
                             "memory_mb": 1024
                           }
                         ]
                       },
                       {
                         "short_name": "LG",
                         "long_name": "LG Electronics",
                         "devices": [
```

```
                            {

                              "model": "Nexus 4",

                              "nickname": "Mako",

                              "display_size_inches": 4.7,

                              "memory_mb": 2048

                            }

                          ]

                        },

                        {

                          "short_name": "HTC",

                          "long_name": "HTC Corporation",

                          "devices": [

                            {

                              "model": "Nexus One",

                              "nickname": "Passion",

                              "display_size_inches": 3.7,

                              "memory_mb": 512

                            }

                          ]

                        }

                      ]

                    }
D/WebServiceClient: <-- END HTTP (944-byte body)
D/DeviceListActivity: Got response -> 9
```

In Listing 9.8, you can see that the OkHttpLoggingInterceptor can be configured to print out all the HTTP headers for both the request and the response as well as the JSON that was received in the response.

Notice that in the request, the Accept-Encoding: gzip header is set. Setting the Accept-Encoding header to a value of gzip tells the HTTP server that the client can accept responses compressed with GZip. This header is set because OkHttp takes care of unzipping any GZipped requests that it receives automatically. If the HTTP server hosting the Web service is configured to compress responses with GZip, this is transparent to the application developer.

Because the OkHttpLoggingInterceptor has the capability to log *all* information about an HTTP request and response, it is important to make sure that production builds have this logging disabled. In addition to a possible performance loss caused by logging potentially frequent and large HTTP requests/responses, this could also cause sensitive data to be logged to the central Android logging system, which can be accessed by multiple apps. It is common for Web services to require some sort of authorization information when making a request, and this is generally information that should be kept private and out of the Android logs. In the case of Listing 9.7, the OkHttpLoggingInterceptor is enabled for debug builds only by interrogating the BuildConfig.DEBUG flag.

Once the OkHttpClient has been set, the Retrofit.Builder can be used to generate a concrete implementation of the DeviceService interface. This service is used by the app to make Web service calls.

Now that the Retrofit-backed service has been created, other parts of the app can use it to make Web services calls. Listing 9.9 shows how this can be done.

Listing 9.9 Making a Retrofit Call

```
Call<ManufacturersAndDevicesResponse> call = WebServiceClient

        .getInstance()

        .getService()

        .getManufacturersAndDevices();


call.enqueue(new Callback<ManufacturersAndDevicesResponse>() {

    @Override

    public

    void onResponse(Response<ManufacturersAndDevicesResponse> response) {

        List<Manufacturer> manufacturerList =

        response.body().getManufacturers();

        // process response

    }


    @Override

    public void onFailure(Throwable t) {

        // handle error case

    }

});
```

As mentioned previously, there are two ways to make the Web service call with Retrofit: synchronously and asynchronously. The code in Listing 9.9 makes an asynchronous call by using the WebServiceClient singleton to get a reference to the Retrofit-based service created in Listing 9.7. The code then uses the service to get an object that implements the Call interface by calling getManufacturersAndDevices(). A concrete implementation of the `Call` interface is what is used to make both the synchronous and asynchronous calls. Listing 9.9 makes the asynchronous call so it is safe to perform on the main thread. The asynchronous call is made by calling `Call.enqueue()`. The `Call.enqueue()` methods take an object that implements the `Callback` interface as a parameter and uses the `Callback` instance to either deliver the result of the Web service call or return an error.

The `Callback` interface defines two methods that need to be implemented: `onResponse()` and `onFailure()`. `onResponse()` is where the response from a successful Web service call is returned, and `onFailure()` is called when there is an error.

The parameter passed to `onResponse()` is an instance of the Retrofit `Response` object. This object contains details of the HTTP response such as the headers, the HTTP response code, and the raw body of this response. In addition, it contains the deserialized Java POJO containing the response data. The POJO is what is usually important to the app, and Retrofit allows the app to work with Java objects instead of working with a JSON response.

Because the Web service call in Listing 9.9 is asynchronous, there may be a need to cancel a request that has not yet had a response returned. The `Call` interface declares the `Call.cancel()` method that may be used to cancel a request that is still pending. This is useful to ensure that an activity does not receive a response after it has been stopped or destroyed.

That was a quick overview of Retrofit. It is worth mentioning that the code presented in the previous listings is based on Retrofit2. The API for Retrofit1 is similar, but there are some differences. The ability to cancel a call with `Call.cancel()` was introduced in Retrofit2 and is not part of Retrofit1.

Accessing Web Services with Volley

Volley started as an internal Google project for accessing remote services. Like Retrofit, Volley makes it easy to construct remote Web service requests by taking care of the threading concerns. It does this by making HTTP requests on a background thread and providing the response on the UI thread. In addition, Volley allows requests to be canceled to ensure that responses are not delivered to a stopped or destroyed activity.

Adding Volley to an Android Project

Volley is part of the Android Open Source Project (AOSP) and does not have an official release from Google. Instead, to get Volley, you need to retrieve it from the AOSP Git repository. Once the source code has been retrieved, the Volley project can either be added to an Android project as a library project or built into a JAR file and added to the project.

In addition to the official Volley library from Google, there are unofficial Volley mirrors that pull changes from the official repository, package a JAR, and push that JAR to a Maven-compatible repository. These mirrors allow Volley to be added as a Gradle dependency like other third-party libraries. However, these unofficial mirrors may also make changes to the Volley library. This is not necessarily a bad thing as some of the mirrors also address issues that have not yet been addressed in the upstream AOSP Volley repository. This section focuses on the AOSP version of Volley and its API.

The source code for AOSP Volley can be retrieved from the AOSP Git repository. To download the source using Git, first install Git, then use the following command to download the repository:

```
git clone https://android.googlesource.com/platform/frameworks/volley
```

Once downloaded, the `volley` directory can be added to a Gradle project as a third-party library. If a project uses Git as its source control tool, the `volley/.git` directory can also be removed to prevent any issues.

Adding Volley as a library project involves copying the `volley` directory into the project and configuring Gradle to use it. The device database app project keeps all third-party projects in a directory named `thirdParty` in the root of the project. This allows any third-party source code to be kept out of the main app source code. Figure 9.1 shows the Project view in Android Studio.

Once the Volley folder has been copied to the project structure, Gradle must be configured to add the Volley source code to the project. For most Gradle-powered Android projects, this is accomplished by editing two `.gradle` files: `settings.gradle` and `build.gradle`.

`settings.gradle` is typically found in the root folder of the main Gradle project. Listing 9.10 shows how to update the `settings.gradle` file to add Volley. It makes the assumption that Volley is located in `thirdParty/volley` as is depicted in Figure 9.1.

Listing 9.10 Adding Volley to `settings.gradle`

```
include ':app', ':thirdParty:volley'
```

Once Volley has been added to the project, it needs to be added to the list of dependencies for all project modules that require it. Like other dependencies, adding Volley is done in the `build.gradle` for a module. Listing 9.11 shows the Gradle entry for adding the Volley project that is located in the `thirdParty/volley` directory.

Listing 9.11 Adding the Volley Dependency

```
dependencies {
    compile fileTree(dir: 'libs', include: ['*.jar'])
    compile project(':thirdParty:volley')
```

With Volley added to the project, it can now be used in the app's source code.

Using Volley

Volley's architecture is different from Retrofit's. Recall from the previous section that to use Retrofit, an interface is defined that includes methods that map to remote Web service calls. Volley maps individual Web service calls to requests that are passed to a `RequestQueue` for processing. Once the response to a request has been received, Volley provides the response to a callback.

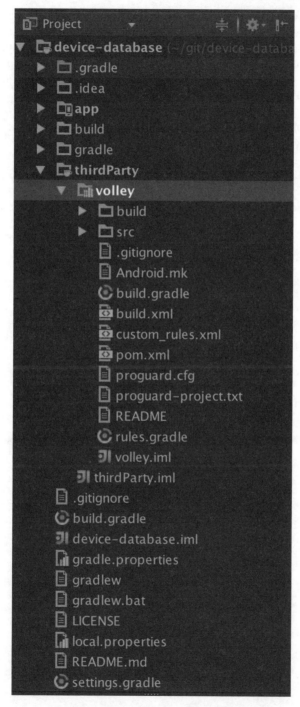

Figure 9.1   Volley in Android Studio

When setting up the Volley `RequestQueue`, a best practice is to wrap the `RequestQueue` in a singleton to ensure that every part of an app is using the same `RequestQueue`. The device database sample app has a singleton called `VolleyApiClient` that handles the details of setting up a Volley `RequestQueue` for use by other parts of the app. The implementation of `VolleyApiClient`, which is the singleton that wraps the Volley `RequestQueue`, is shown in Listing 9.12.

Listing 9.12 Implementing `VolleyApiClient`

```java
public class VolleyApiClient {
    private static VolleyApiClient instance;

    private RequestQueue requestQueue;

    public static synchronized VolleyApiClient getInstance(Context ctx) {
        if (instance == null) {
            instance = new VolleyApiClient(ctx);
        }

        return instance;
    }

    private VolleyApiClient(Context context) {
        requestQueue =
                Volley.newRequestQueue(context.getApplicationContext());
    }

    public <T> Request<T> add(Request<T> request) {
        return requestQueue.add(request);
    }

    public void cancelAll(Object tag) {
        requestQueue.cancelAll(tag);
    }

}
```

VolleyApiClient creates a new RequestQueue by making a call to Volley.new RequestQueue() and passing an application context as the parameter. As with most Android development, it is important to not leak contexts as they can be activities that hold references to their views and can be cleaned up by Android when memory is needed. The application context will be around for the lifecycle of the app, however.

In addition to creating the RequestQueue needed to use Volley, VolleyApiClient has two delegate methods for the RequestQueue: add() and cancelAll().

The VolleyApiClient.add() method is used to add a request to the RequestQueue. Adding a request to the RequestQueue allows Volley to send the request to a remote Web service and handle the response.

The VolleyApiClient.cancelAll() method is used to cancel all requests that have been given a specific tag. This is useful for when an activity has added multiple requests to the RequestQueue and needs to cancel them as the activity is stopped. It can assign the same tag to each request that it adds to the RequestQueue and call VolleyApiClient. cancelAll() when it is being stopped to cancel all its requests. Canceling a request ensures that Volley does not deliver the response to the request callbacks.

Once the Volley RequestQueue has been set up, it can start accepting requests to process. The Volley Request class handles request-specific functionality such as setting a priority, setting a retry count, and serializing/deserializing requests and responses.

Volley comes with multiple subclasses of Request for handling different types of data, including JsonObjectRequest and JsonArrayRequest. Unfortunately, both JsonObjectRequest and JsonArrayRequest use the standard JSON parsing API that comes with Android. As was discussed earlier, this API can be cumbersome to use, especially when there are alternatives that directly map JSON to Java POJOs.

In the device database app, there is a Volley request that uses the Jackson JSON parser. Like GSON, Jackson can map JSON to Java objects. Listing 9.13 shows the implementation of JacksonRequest which uses Jackson to parse the JSON body of a Volley response.

Listing 9.13 Parsing JSON with JacksonRequest

```
public class JacksonRequest<T> extends Request<T> {
    private static final ObjectMapper objectMapper = new ObjectMapper()
            .setPropertyNamingStrategy(PropertyNamingStrategy.SNAKE_CASE)
            .setSerializationInclusion(JsonInclude.Include.NON_NULL);


    private final Response.Listener<T> listener;
    private final Class<T> clazz;


    public JacksonRequest(int method,
                    String url,
```

```
                        Class<T> clazz,

                        Response.Listener<T> listener,

                        Response.ErrorListener errorListener) {
        super(method, url, errorListener);

        this.listener = listener;
        this.clazz = clazz;
    }


    @Override
    protected Response<T> parseNetworkResponse(NetworkResponse response) {
        T responsePayload;

        try {
            responsePayload = objectMapper.readValue(response.data,
                    clazz);

            return Response.success(responsePayload,
                    HttpHeaderParser.parseCacheHeaders(response));
        } catch (IOException e) {
            return Response.error(new ParseError(e));
        }
    }


    @Override
    protected void deliverResponse(T response) {
        listener.onResponse(response);
    }
}
```

The first thing to notice in Listing 9.13 is the static final ObjectMapper constant. ObjectMapper is part of the Jackson databind API and is used to bind JSON data to Java objects (Jackson has other methods to process JSON as well). The ObjectMapper is static to ensure that every JacksonRequest uses the same ObjectMapper. This is considered a Jackson best practice since the `ObjectMapper` can be expensive to create and caches serializers and deserializers as they are created.

Before the `ObjectMapper` can be used in the project, the `build.gradle` file must be updated to include the Jackson data binding library. Listing 9.14 shows the updated `build.gradle` file with the databind entry in bold.

Listing 9.14 Adding a Data Binding Library to `build.gradle`

```
final RETROFIT_VERSION = '2.0.0'

compile "com.squareup.retrofit2:retrofit:${RETROFIT_VERSION}"

compile "com.squareup.retrofit2:converter-gson:${RETROFIT_VERSION}"

compile "com.squareup.okhttp3:logging-interceptor:3.2.0"

compile 'com.fasterxml.jackson.core:jackson-databind:2.7.0'
```

To create a new `JacksonRequest`, the single constructor is used. This constructor takes the following parameters:

- `int method`: Defines the HTTP method that should be used to make the request. The `int` constants for this parameter are defined in the Volley `Method` class.
- `String url`: Contains the URL of the Web service endpoint to which the request should be sent. Unlike Retrofit, this should be the entire URL including the protocol, host, and path.
- `Class<T> clazz`: Defines the type of class that should be used to map the JSON response to a POJO. The type of class is needed by Jackson for deserializing, so it is required by the `JacksonRequest`.
- `Response.Listener<T> listener`: The listener that is called to process the response of the `JacksonRequest`. Because Volley supports only asynchronous HTTP requests/responses, a callback listener is always needed to process the results of the request.
- `Response.ErrorListener<T> errorListener`: Called when there is an error making the request.

The `JacksonRequest` constructor passes a subset of the parameters to its parent class constructor and saves the listener and `clazz` information to be used by its other two methods: `parseNetworkResponse()` and `deliverResult()`.

The `parseNetworkReponse()` method converts the `byte[]` data that is returned by Volley into a Java POJO using Jackson. This is done by using the `ObjectMapper` and `clazz` member variables to map the JSON to the Java POJO. If there are no errors deserializing the JSON response, a success status is returned with the Java POJO. If an exception is thrown converting the JSON to a Java object, an error response is returned that carries the exception.

With the `VolleyApiClient` in place, the app can use Volley to make asynchronous Web service requests. In the device database app, this is done to retrieve the list of manufacturers and devices from a Web service. Listing 9.15 shows a snippet of the `DeviceListActivity` that uses the `VolleyApiClient` to load the device list.

Listing 9.15 Using `VolleyApiClient` to Load Devices

```
public class DeviceListActivity extends AppCompatActivity {
    private static final String TAG =
            DeviceListActivity.class.getSimpleName();

    private static final String VOLLEY_TAG =
            DeviceListActivity.class.getCanonicalName();

    private void loadDataUsingVolley() {
        GetManufacturersAndDevicesRequest request =
                new GetManufacturersAndDevicesRequest(VOLLEY_TAG,
                new Response.Listener<GetManufacturersAndDevicesRequest
                    .Response>() {
                    @Override
                    public
                    void onResponse(GetManufacturersAndDevicesRequest
                                                .Response response) {
                        List<Manufacturer> manufacturersList =
                                response.getManufacturers();

                        updateDisplay(manufacturersList);
                    }
                }, new Response.ErrorListener() {
            @Override
            public void onErrorResponse(VolleyError error) {
                Log.e(TAG, "Received web API error", error);
            }
        });
```

```
VolleyApiClient
        .getInstance(DeviceListActivity.this)
        .add(request);
}


@Override
protected void onStop() {
    super.onStop();
    VolleyApiClient.getInstance(this).cancelAll(VOLLEY_TAG);
}
}
```

DeviceListActivity defines the constant VOLLEY_TAG that is used to set the tag for each request it submits to the RequestQueue. The request is also passed two anonymous classes: one that implements Response.Listener to handle successful responses and one that implements Response.ErrorListener to handle error responses.

The Response.Listener class declares the onResponse() method which the anonymous class implements. The onResponse() method is passed a Response object which contains the deserialized JSON response from the Web service as a Java POJO. Because the request handles the deserialization, it is easy for the client code to handle the response because it can work with model objects that are defined in the app.

The last part of the Volley implementation is the GetManufacturersAndDevices Request class which is shown in Listing 9.16.

Listing 9.16 Implementing GetManufacturersAndDevicesRequest

```
public class GetManufacturersAndDevicesRequest
        extends JacksonRequest<GetManufacturersAndDevicesRequest.Response> {
    public GetManufacturersAndDevicesRequest(Object tag,
                                        Listener<Response> listener,
                                        ErrorListener errorListener) {
        super(Method.GET,
            "http://www.mocky.io/v2/570bbaf6110000b003d17e3a",
            Response.class,
            listener,
            errorListener);

        this.setTag(tag);
    }
```

```
public static class Response {
    private List<Manufacturer> manufacturers;

    public List<Manufacturer> getManufacturers() {
        return manufacturers;
    }

    public void setManufacturers(List<Manufacturer> manufacturers) {
        this.manufacturers = manufacturers;
    }
}
}
```

The GetManufacturersAndDevices class contains an inner class representing the response to the request. While Volley does not strictly mandate this, it does make an association between the request and the response that is expected from the response.

Also notice that the GetManufacturersAndDevices constructor passes Method.GET and the URL to the parent class. This means that the request will use the HTTP GET method for the specified URL.

While Retrofit and Volley make communicating with a remote Web service easier, there are times when apps need additional functionality to provide a good user experience for Web service communication.

Persisting Data to Enhance User Experience

While using activities and fragments can be a convenient way to access remote Web services, it can also lead to a poor user experience. Activities typically display a single type of data, and each activity in an app may use only a subset of Web service calls that are used across the entire app. If each activity makes its own set of Web service calls, it can lead to a sluggish app and increased battery drain.

Data Transfer and Battery Consumption

To understand how multiple Web service calls can adversely affect battery life, consider how radios in mobile devices work. In order to send and receive data, a mobile device needs to power up its wireless radio, which can consume a considerable amount of power. However, the wireless radio does not power down immediately after the data transfer is complete. Instead, it remains in full power for a period of time. If there is no need to transfer or receive any additional data during that time, the radio enters a reduced-power mode where it is not fully powered up but also not completely powered down. If there is no need to transfer or receive data during this reduced-power time, the radio then powers all the way down. Wireless radios cycle through these states in an effort to minimize the latency that occurs while moving the wireless radio from the powered-down state to the high-power state where it can send and receive data.

The reason that sending frequent Web service requests can have adverse effects on battery life is that multiple requests can keep the wireless radio in a high-powered state instead of letting it power down after enough time has gone by.

Data Transfer and User Experience

While battery life is a concern for frequent remote Web service calls, the poor user experience that can accompany frequent remote Web service calls can be an even bigger problem. HTTP requests are asynchronous and not immediate. This means that an app needs to let the user know that "something" is happening while the device waits for a request/response pair to make a round trip. Too often, this results in some type of indeterminate progress bar being shown to the user on Android. While this is better than not showing anything, it is not the ideal situation for the user. This may be acceptable at certain points in the user experience, but it is certainly a bad idea to have every screen display a progress bar while the app receives data from a remote call.

Instead of making frequent Web service calls, a better approach is to batch the calls together. This allows the radio to power up, get data, and then power down. It also limits the number of remote Web service calls that are needed as well as the amount of time a user is waiting for the data. In an ideal scenario, all the data needed to present the UI to the user would be retrieved before it is needed so the user never has to wait for data to be transferred.

Storing Web Service Response Data

A solution to both of these problems is to use a local database to store the data retrieved by remote Web service calls and have UI functionality (activities and fragments) read the data from the database instead of directly accessing the Web service. This provides flexibility for when the data needs to be retrieved as well as an additional level of abstraction between UI functionality and the details of the Web service. The Web service can completely change its response format, and the UI functionality will be unaffected as long as the database schema remains the same.

Android SyncAdapter Framework

One way to allow an app to centralize the functionality needed to both retrieve data from a Web service and persist it into a database is to use a SyncAdapter. A SyncAdapter allows code to be run in the background at different times based on different conditions. For example, in an effort to limit the amount of time that a user waits for data to be retrieved from a remote server, it is sometimes useful to have the data be transferred before the app even starts. The `SyncAdapter` framework allows an app to retrieve data based on the time since the last sync, the time of day, or changes to the data. In addition, an app can trigger a `SyncAdapter` to run in response to a user's actions (like triggering swipe-to-refresh). This allows all the synchronization-related code to exist in one spot and be triggered by several different events.

In addition to allowing code to be run in response to different triggers, the `SyncAdapter` framework takes network connectivity into consideration. It prevents a sync task from running when the network is not connected. Also, the `SyncAdapter` framework attempts to batch an app's sync tasks with other apps across the system. This allows the wireless radio to power up, run several tasks that all need network connectivity, and then power back down. This can save battery life for a user as it allows network calls to be batched across apps.

In order to use a `SyncAdapter`, an app must contain three components: a `ContentProvider`, a `SyncAdapter`, and an `AccountManager`. The device database app already contains a `ContentProvider` which has been discussed in previous chapters. This means that only the `AccountAuthenticator` and `SyncAdapter` need to be implemented in order to use the Android `SyncAdapter` framework.

AccountAuthenticator

An `AccountAuthenticator` can be used to help manage account credentials for an app. Most Web services require some kind of authentication, and the `AccountAuthenticator` can be used to get credentials from the user and insecurely store those credentials.

For the device database app, no credentials are required to use the Web service. Even though the app does not otherwise need an `AccountAuthenticator`, one is still required for use with the `SyncManager` framework. Because of this requirement, the device database sample app creates a stub `AccountAuthenticator`.

To create an `AccountAuthenticator`, an app needs to include a class that extends `AbstractAccountAuthenticator`. Because the device database app needs only a stub `AccountAuthenticator`, it can create an `AccountAuthenticator` that extends the `AbstractAccountAuthenticator` with stub implementations for all the abstract methods. Listing 9.17 shows the implementation of the stub `AccountAuthenticator`.

Listing 9.17 Implementing a Stub `AccountAuthenticator`

```
public class Authenticator extends AbstractAccountAuthenticator {
    public Authenticator(Context context) {
        super(context);
    }


    @Override
    public Bundle editProperties(AccountAuthenticatorResponse response,
```

```
                                String accountType) {
        throw new UnsupportedOperationException("Not yet implemented");
    }


    @Override
    public Bundle addAccount(AccountAuthenticatorResponse response,
                             String accountType,
                             String authTokenType,
                             String[] requiredFeatures,
                             Bundle options) throws NetworkErrorException {
        throw new UnsupportedOperationException("Not yet implemented");
    }


    @Override
    public Bundle confirmCredentials(AccountAuthenticatorResponse response,
                                     Account account,
                                     Bundle options)
        throws NetworkErrorException {
        throw new UnsupportedOperationException("Not yet implemented");
    }


    @Override
    public Bundle getAuthToken(AccountAuthenticatorResponse response,
                               Account account,
                               String authTokenType,
                               Bundle options)
        throws NetworkErrorException {
        throw new UnsupportedOperationException("Not yet implemented");
    }


    @Override
    public String getAuthTokenLabel(String authTokenType) {
        throw new UnsupportedOperationException("Not yet implemented");
    }
```

```
    @Override
    public Bundle updateCredentials(AccountAuthenticatorResponse response,
                                    Account account,
                                    String authTokenType,
                                    Bundle options)
            throws NetworkErrorException {
        throw new UnsupportedOperationException("Not yet implemented");
    }


    @Override
    public Bundle hasFeatures(AccountAuthenticatorResponse response,
                              Account account,
                              String[] features)
            throws NetworkErrorException {
        throw new UnsupportedOperationException("Not yet implemented");
    }
}
```

The `SyncAdapter` framework uses a service to access the `AccountAuthenticator`.
This service needs to be created in order to provide the `AccountAuthenticator` to the
`SyncAdapter` framework. Listing 9.18 shows the `AuthenticatorService` that is used
in the device database app to bind the `AccountAuthenticator` to the `SyncAdapter`
framework.

Listing 9.18 Binding to the Framework with `AuthenticatorService`

```
public class AuthenticatorService extends Service {
    private Authenticator authenticator;

    public AuthenticatorService() {
    }

    @Override
    public void onCreate() {
        super.onCreate();
        authenticator = new Authenticator(this);
    }
```

```
    try {
        // Perform synchronous Web service call
        Response<ManufacturersAndDevicesResponse> wrappedResponse =
                call.execute();

        ArrayList<ContentProviderOperation> operations =
                generateDatabaseOperations(wrappedResponse.body());

        provider.applyBatch(operations);

    } catch (IOException
            | OperationApplicationException
            | RemoteException e) {
        Log.e(TAG, "Could not perform sync", e);
    }
}

private
ArrayList<ContentProviderOperation>
generateDatabaseOperations(ManufacturersAndDevicesResponse response) {
    final ArrayList<ContentProviderOperation> operations =
            new ArrayList<>();

    operations.add(ContentProviderOperation
            .newDelete(DevicesContract.Device.CONTENT_URI).build());

    operations.add(ContentProviderOperation
            .newDelete(DevicesContract.Manufacturer.CONTENT_URI)
            .build());

    for (Manufacturer manufacturer : response.getManufacturers()) {
        final ContentProviderOperation manufacturerOperation =
                ContentProviderOperation
```

```
                           .newInsert(DevicesContract.Manufacturer
                                   .CONTENT_URI)

                       .withValue(DevicesContract.Manufacturer
                               .SHORT_NAME,

                                   manufacturer.getShortName())
                       .withValue(DevicesContract.Manufacturer
                               .LONG_NAME,
                                   manufacturer.getLongName())
                       .build();

        operations.add(manufacturerOperation);

        int manufacturerInsertOperationIndex =
                operations.size() - 1;

        for (Device device : manufacturer.getDevices()) {
            final ContentProviderOperation deviceOperation =
                    ContentProviderOperation
                           .newInsert(DevicesContract.Device
                                   .CONTENT_URI)
                           .withValueBackReference(DevicesContract
                                   .Device.MANUFACTURER_ID,
                                   manufacturerInsertOperationIndex)
                           .withValue(DevicesContract.Device.MODEL,
                                   device.getModel())
                           .withValue(DevicesContract
                                   .Device
                                   .DISPLAY_SIZE_INCHES,
                                   device.getDisplaySizeInches())
                           .withValue(DevicesContract
                                   .Device
                                   .MEMORY_MB,
```

```
                                            device.getMemoryMb())
                            .withValue(DevicesContract
                                    .Device
                                    .NICKNAME, device.getNickname())
                        .build();


                operations.add(deviceOperation);
            }
        }


        return operations;
    }
}
```

The onPerformSync() method is an abstract method declared in AbstractThreadedSyncAdapter. It is the main entry point for the sync operation. The SyncAdapter implementation uses a Retrofit synchronous call to perform the Web service remote call and then persists the response in the database.

An important point about the onPerformSync() method is that the SyncAdapter framework takes care of calling onPerformSync() off the main thread. This means that any implementation of onPerformSync() does not need to worry about starting a new thread to handle potential long-running tasks. This makes the onPerformSync() method fairly convenient because, in the case of the device database sync task, both making the call to the remote Web service and saving the response to the data can take a long time depending on the size of the response.

Once the Retrofit Web service call returns with the response, SyncAdapter makes a call to generateDatabaseOperations(). This method takes the response and creates a list of ContentProviderOperations that can be used to update the internal database with the data. Once the list of database operations has been created, onPerformSync() uses a ContentProviderClient to apply the list of operations to the database. The ContentProviderClient is an interface to a content provider and can be used the same way as a ContentResolver.

Once the SyncAdapter implementation is in place, it needs to be wired into the Android SyncAdapter framework. This is done with another bound service and metadata file. The bound service that attaches the SyncAdapter is shown in Listing 9.22.

Listing 9.22 Attaching SyncAdapter with SyncService

```
public class SyncService extends Service {
    private static SyncAdapter syncAdapter = null;
```

```
@Override
public void onCreate() {
    super.onCreate();

    synchronized (SyncService.class) {
        syncAdapter = new SyncAdapter(getApplicationContext(), true);
    }
}


@Nullable
@Override
public IBinder onBind(Intent intent) {
    return syncAdapter.getSyncAdapterBinder();
}
}
```

`SyncService` creates a new `SyncAdapter` and returns it in the `onBind()` method. The `static synchronized` block in `onCreate()` is used to ensure that only one instance of the `SyncAdapter` exists. This essentially makes `SyncAdapter` a singleton to any code that is starting the `SyncService`.

In order for `SyncService` to be started, it needs to be declared in the manifest. Listing 9.23 shows the manifest declaration for `SyncService`.

Listing 9.23 `SyncService` Manifest Declaration

```xml
<service
    android:name=".sync.SyncService"
    android:exported="true"
    android:process=":sync">
    <intent-filter>
        <action android:name="android.content.SyncAdapter"/>
    </intent-filter>
    <meta-data android:name="android.content.SyncAdapter"
        android:resource="@xml/syncadapter" />
</service>
```

The SyncService manifest declaration indicates that it can be started with the android.content.SyncAdapter action. Like the action used to start the account authentication service from the previous section, the android.content.SyncAdapter action is used by Android to start the SyncService.

The manifest declaration for the SyncService also defines the location of the metadata file as res/xml/syncadapter.xml. Listing 9.24 shows the contents of that file.

Listing 9.24 Contents of `res/xml/syncadapter.xml`

```xml
<?xml version="1.0" encoding="utf-8"?>
<sync-adapter xmlns:android="http://schemas.android.com/apk/res/android"
    android:contentAuthority="me.adamstroud.devicedatabase.provider"
    android:accountType="stubAuthenticator"
    android:userVisible="false"
    android:supportsUploading="false"
    android:allowParallelSyncs="false"
    android:isAlwaysSyncable="true"/>
```

The SyncAdapter metadata file declares some of the properties of the sync adapter. In the case of the device database SyncAdapter, the metadata file defines the contentAuthority for the app's ContentProvider. The accountType attribute should contain the same value that was defined in the AccountAuthenticator discussed in the previous section.

Now that the SyncAdapter has been implemented and bound to the Android SyncAdapter framework, it can be invoked to update the internal database. As mentioned previously, a SyncAdapter can be triggered by many different events. In the case of the device database app, the only event that should trigger the SyncAdapter to run is a gesture from the user. This means that the SyncAdapter needs to run "on demand" instead of being triggered automatically by some external event.

The DeviceListActivity contains an action in its overflow menu that the user can use to trigger the SyncAdapter. The overflow action's handler is shown in Listing 9.25.

Listing 9.25 Manually Triggering the `SyncAdapter`

```java
Bundle bundle = new Bundle();
bundle.putBoolean(ContentResolver.SYNC_EXTRAS_MANUAL, true);
bundle.putBoolean(ContentResolver.SYNC_EXTRAS_EXPEDITED, true);
ContentResolver.requestSync(new Account("SyncAccount",
                                         "stubAuthenticator"),
        "me.adamstroud.devicedatabase.provider",
        bundle);
```

To trigger the `SyncAdapter`, a call to `ContentResolver.requestSync()` is made. For its parameters, it is passed the account information as well as a `Bundle` that contains flags to control how the `SyncAdapter` will run. Since the device database is using a stub account authenticator, the account credentials are unimportant. However, the flags passed to the `ContentResolver.requestSync()` method are important. The `Bundle` that is passed to `ContentResolver.requestSync()` contains the `ContentResolver.SYNC_EXTRAS_MANUAL` and `ContentResolver.SYNC_EXTRAS_EXPEDITED` flags. These flags tell the `SyncAdapter` framework to start a manual sync immediately, which is what is needed when running the sync in response to a user action.

The device database app now has a `SyncAdapter` that can be used to update the internal database with remote Web service information at any time. While `SyncAdapters` can be useful, they do contain a fair amount of boilerplate code and don't always fit the need of an app. The next section discusses another approach to persisting remote Web service data in an internal database.

Manually Synchronizing Remote Data

When a `SyncAdapter` does not fit an app's use case, the app can always include its own functionality to synchronize and persist the response to a remote Web service call to the database. The solution that an app uses needs to handle the asynchronous nature of HTTP communication as well as the threading concerns discussed earlier in the chapter. In order to address the asynchronous and threading concerns, the device database app makes use of Retrofit's RxJava support to make a remote Web service request where the response is saved in the database when it is received. The code for performing the manual sync without the `SyncAdapter` is located in the `SyncManager` class in the device database project.

A Short Introduction to RxJava

RxJava has been a hot topic in the world of Android development recently. The idea behind RxJava, and the reactive paradigm in general, is to support an asynchronous stream of events by using observables. These observables can be composed together using RxJava operators to form a chain of operators with each operator manipulating the data in the events that are being received.

In the case of Retrofit, each event can be thought of as the response to a Web service request. By using the RxJava operators, the `SyncManager` can transform each response into a list of database operations, then commit the entire list of operations to the database in a single transaction. This allows the entire sync process to be atomic to protect the integrity of the database. It is really important to guard against committing only a partial sync task because only a subset of the database operations are committed successfully to the database.

In addition to handling the asynchronous Web service calls, RxJava allows operations to be performed on different threads. This feature allows the sync operation to be performed on a background thread and, optionally, allows a routine to be run on the main thread when the sync operation is complete.

Adding RxJava Support to Retrofit

While Retrofit does have good support for RxJava, it is not included in the base library that was added to the device database earlier in the chapter. Because RxJava is not part of the standard Android SDK, it must be added to the project through the `build.gradle` file. The RxJava Retrofit adapter must also be added to the project to bring the libraries needed to add RxJava support to Retrofit. Listing 9.26 shows the `build.gradle` file that has been updated to include the required RxJava libraries. The RxJava entries are in bold.

Listing 9.26 Adding RxJava Support to `build.gradle`

```
final RETROFIT_VERSION = '2.0.0'

compile "com.squareup.retrofit2:retrofit:${RETROFIT_VERSION}"

compile "com.squareup.retrofit2:converter-gson:${RETROFIT_VERSION}"

compile "com.squareup.okhttp3:logging-interceptor:3.2.0"

compile 'com.fasterxml.jackson.core:jackson-databind:2.7.0'

compile "com.squareup.retrofit2:adapter-rxjava:${RETROFIT_VERSION}"


compile 'io.reactivex:rxandroid:1.1.0'

// Because RxAndroid releases are few and far between, it is

// recommended you also explicitly depend on RxJava's latest version

// for bug fixes and new features.

compile 'io.reactivex:rxjava:1.1.3'
```

In addition to adding the RxJava libraries to the project, the Retrofit client needs to be updated to use the RxJava adapter that was added to the `build.gradle` file. This adapter allows Retrofit to return Web service responses in the form of an RxJava observable in addition to the `Call` interface implementation that has previously been used in the device database app. Adding the RxJava adapter to Retrofit can be done using the `Retrofit.Builder` that was used to create the Retrofit client in the `WebServiceClient` class. Listing 9.27 shows how the `WebServiceClient` was updated to add the RxJava adapter to Retrofit.

Listing 9.27 Adding the RxJava Adapter to Retrofit

```
public class WebServiceClient {

    private static final String TAG =
            WebServiceClient.class.getSimpleName();


    private static WebServiceClient instance = new WebServiceClient();
```

```java
private final DeviceService service;

public static WebServiceClient getInstance() {
    return instance;
}

private WebServiceClient() {
    final Gson gson = new GsonBuilder()
            .setFieldNamingPolicy(FieldNamingPolicy
                    .LOWER_CASE_WITH_UNDERSCORES)
            .create();

    Retrofit.Builder retrofitBuilder = new Retrofit.Builder()
            .baseUrl("http://www.mocky.io")
            .addCallAdapterFactory(RxJavaCallAdapterFactory.create())
            .addConverterFactory(GsonConverterFactory.create(gson));

    if (BuildConfig.DEBUG) {
        final HttpLoggingInterceptor loggingInterceptor =
                new HttpLoggingInterceptor(new HttpLoggingInterceptor
                        .Logger() {
            @Override
            public void log(String message) {
                Log.d(TAG, message);
            }
        });

        retrofitBuilder.callFactory(new OkHttpClient
                .Builder()
                .addNetworkInterceptor(loggingInterceptor)
                .build());

        loggingInterceptor.setLevel(HttpLoggingInterceptor.Level.BODY);
    }
```

```
    service = retrofitBuilder.build().create(DeviceService.class);
}


public DeviceService getService() {
    return service;
}
```

The last step that needs to be performed before the RxJava observable can be used with Retrofit is to update the `DeviceService` interface that defines the Web service calls that can be made. Remember from earlier in the chapter that the `DeviceService` interface contains a method for each Web service call that can be made. Previously, there was a single method defined in the `DeviceService` interface because only one Web service call was made. This method call, `DeviceService.getManufacturersAnd Devices()`, returned an object that implemented the `Call` interface that could be used to perform either a synchronous or an asynchronous Web service call.

To add RxJava support to the `DeviceService` interface, an additional method needs to be added that returns an RxJava observable instead of a `Call` implementation. The addition of this method can be seen in Listing 9.28.

Listing 9.28 Observable Web Service Call to `DeviceService`

```
public interface DeviceService {
    @GET("v2/570bbaf6110000b003d17e3a")
    Call<ManufacturersAndDevicesResponse> getManufacturersAndDevices();


    @GET("v2/570bbaf6110000b003d17e3a")
    Observable<ManufacturersAndDevicesResponse>
    rxGetManufacturersAndDevices();
}
```

In Listing 9.28, the `rxGetManufacturersAndDevices()` method was added to the `DeviceService` interface. This method uses the same Web service path as the original `getManufacturersAndDevices()` method and still uses the HTTP GET method to retrieve the data. The only difference between the two methods is the return type. The original method returns the `Call` implementation, whereas the Rx version of the method returns an observable.

Using RxJava to Perform the Sync

Now that RxJava support for Retrofit has been added to the project, the implementation details of `SyncManager` can be described. `SyncManager` is implemented as a singleton that contains a single method, `syncManufacturersAndDevices()`, which performs the sync. The `syncManufactureresAndDevices()` method is presented in Listing 9.29.

Listing 9.29 Implementing `SyncManager.getManufacturersAndDevices()`

```
public void syncManufacturersAndDevices() {
    WebServiceClient
            .getInstance()
            .getService()
            .rxGetManufacturersAndDevices()
            .flatMap(this)
            .toList()
            .subscribeOn(Schedulers.io())
            .subscribe(this);
}
```

The `SyncManager.getManufacturersAndDevices()` implementation may look short, but there is actually a lot going on. It starts off by getting a reference to the Retrofit-backed Web service client in the same way as was done earlier in the chapter. Using this reference, it then makes a call to `rxGetManufacturersAndDevices()`, which returns the RxJava observable. At this point, the code has moved away from purely Retrofit functionality and has entered the world of RxJava by making calls to `flatMap()`, `toList()`, `subscribeOn()`, and `subscribe()`.

The first RxJava method to be called is `flatMap()`. This is an RxJava operator that transforms a collection of objects and returns an observable that emits the transformed objects. In the case of `SyncManager`, the `flatMap()` operator transforms the response from the Web service into a list of `ContentProviderOperations` that can be applied to the database through a `ContentResolver`.

To perform the transformation, the `flatMap()` method takes an implementation of the RxJava `Func1` interface. The `Func1` interface contains a single `Func1.call()` method that contains the functionality for the transformation. Because `SyncManager` implements the `Func1` interface, the singleton instance can be passed to `flatMap()` to perform the transformation. The implementation of the `SyncManager.call()` method is contained in Listing 9.30.

Listing 9.30 Implementing `SyncManager.getManufacturersAndDevices()`

```
@Override
public Observable<ContentProviderResult>
call(ManufacturersAndDevicesResponse response) {
    final ContentResolver contentResolver =
            context.getContentResolver();

    final ArrayList<ContentProviderOperation> operations =
            new ArrayList<>();

    final ContentProviderResult[] results;

    operations.add(ContentProviderOperation
            .newDelete(DevicesContract.Device.CONTENT_URI)
            .build());

    operations.add(ContentProviderOperation
            .newDelete(DevicesContract.Manufacturer.CONTENT_URI)
            .build());

    for (Manufacturer manufacturer : response.getManufacturers()) {
        final ContentProviderOperation manufacturerOperation =
                ContentProviderOperation
                .newInsert(DevicesContract.Manufacturer.CONTENT_URI)
                .withValue(DevicesContract.Manufacturer.SHORT_NAME,
                        manufacturer.getShortName())
                .withValue(DevicesContract.Manufacturer.LONG_NAME,
                        manufacturer.getLongName())
                .build();

        operations.add(manufacturerOperation);
```

```java
        int manufacturerInsertOperationIndex = operations.size() - 1;

        for (Device device : manufacturer.getDevices()) {
            final ContentProviderOperation deviceOperation =
                    ContentProviderOperation
                    .newInsert(DevicesContract.Device.CONTENT_URI)
                    .withValueBackReference(DevicesContract
                                .Device.MANUFACTURER_ID,
                        manufacturerInsertOperationIndex)
                    .withValue(DevicesContract.Device.MODEL,
                        device.getModel())
                    .withValue(DevicesContract
                                .Device.DISPLAY_SIZE_INCHES,
                        device.getDisplaySizeInches())
                    .withValue(DevicesContract.Device.MEMORY_MB,
                        device.getMemoryMb())
                    .withValue(DevicesContract.Device.NICKNAME,
                        device.getNickname())
                    .build();

            operations.add(deviceOperation);
        }
    }

    try {
        results =
                contentResolver.applyBatch(DevicesContract.AUTHORITY,
                        operations);
    } catch (RemoteException | OperationApplicationException e) {
        throw new RuntimeException(e);
    }

    return Observable.from(results);
}
```

The implementation of `call()` is similar to code that has been discussed in previous chapters. The list of manufacturers is iterated over and a `ContentProviderOperation` is added to the list of operations for each manufacturer. The same process is then followed for the list of devices for each manufacturer.

What makes the `call()` method different is that it does not simply return the list of operations that it has accumulated. Instead, it creates another observable from that list and returns it. This allows the RxJava operator chain to continue and potentially apply additional operators to the observable that is now emitting `ContentProviderOperations`.

The next operator to be applied in the operator chain is the `toList()` operator. The `toList()` method takes all the `ContentProviderOperations` that are emitted by the observable returned from `flatMap()` and puts them in a list.

The last operator in the operator chain is `subscribeOn()`. This operator defines on which thread the work will be done. By default, RxJava performs its work on the same thread on which `subscribe()` is called. In the case of `SyncManager`, this can be dangerous since communicating with the Web service and writing the response to the database need to happen on a background thread. The `subscribeOn()` operator can be used to specify the thread that will be used.

RxJava has a set of predefined threads that can be used to perform various operations. These are defined by RxJava schedulers. In the case of `SyncManager`, the I/O scheduler is used by passing `Schedulers.io()` to the `subscribeOn()` operator. This ensures that the network and database operations happen on a thread that is meant to be used for I/O.

After all the operators have been applied, the observable that has been manipulated with the operators can be subscribed to. In `SyncManager`, this is an important step because none of the work happens until the call to `subscribe()` is made. The `subscribe()` method is passed an instance of a `Subscriber`. Because `SyncManager` extends `Subscriber`, the singleton instance can be passed to `subscribe()`.

The `Subscribe` class defines three abstract methods that need to be implemented by any concrete class that extends it: `onCompleted()`, `onError()`, and `onNext()`. In RxJava, these methods are used to observe events and error cases that are emitted by an observable. `onCompleted()` is called when there are no longer any items for an observable to emit. `onError()` is called when an error is encountered when processing observable data. The `onNext()` method is called for each item that is emitted by the observable.

For `SyncManager`, there is only one item emitted from the observable, and that is the list of `ContentProviderResults` that is returned from the call to `ContentResolver`. `applyBatch()`. `SyncManager` simply makes a log statement about the results. However, if additional functionality is needed to alert other components that the sync has completed, `onNext()` would be the place to add such functionality.

Because `SyncManager` uses the `ContentResolver` to commit changes to the database, no further operation is needed to alert other app components that the sync is done. This is because the `ContentProvider` that is used in the device database app causes every cursor that it returns to watch the database for changes and react to those changes as was discussed in Chapter 6, "Content Providers."

Listing 9.31 shows the complete implementation of SyncManager.

Listing 9.31 Complete Implementation of SyncManager

```
public class SyncManager extends Subscriber<List<ContentProviderResult>>
    implements Func1<ManufacturersAndDevicesResponse,
➥Observable<ContentProviderResult>> {
    private static final String TAG = SyncAdapter.class.getSimpleName();

    private static SyncManager instance;

    private final Context context;

    public static synchronized SyncManager getInstance(Context context) {
        if (instance == null) {
            instance = new SyncManager(context);
        }

        return instance;
    }

    private SyncManager(Context context) {
        this.context = context.getApplicationContext();
    }

    public void syncManufacturersAndDevices() {
        WebServiceClient
                .getInstance()
                .getService()
                .rxGetManufacturersAndDevices()
                .flatMap(this)
                .toList()
                .subscribeOn(Schedulers.io())
                .subscribe(this);
    }
```

```java
@Override
public void onCompleted() {
    // no-op
}


@Override
public void onError(Throwable e) {
    Log.e(TAG, "Received web API error", e);
}


@Override
public void onNext(List<ContentProviderResult> contentProviderResults){
    Log.d(TAG, "Got response -> " + contentProviderResults.size());
}


@Override
public
Observable<ContentProviderResult>
call(ManufacturersAndDevicesResponse response) {
    final ContentResolver contentResolver =
            context.getContentResolver();

    final ArrayList<ContentProviderOperation> operations =
            new ArrayList<>();

    final ContentProviderResult[] results;

    operations.add(ContentProviderOperation
            .newDelete(DevicesContract.Device.CONTENT_URI)
            .build());

    operations.add(ContentProviderOperation
            .newDelete(DevicesContract.Manufacturer.CONTENT_URI)
            .build());
```

```
for (Manufacturer manufacturer : response.getManufacturers()) {
    final ContentProviderOperation manufacturerOperation =
            ContentProviderOperation
            .newInsert(DevicesContract.Manufacturer.CONTENT_URI)
            .withValue(DevicesContract.Manufacturer.SHORT_NAME,
                    manufacturer.getShortName())
            .withValue(DevicesContract.Manufacturer.LONG_NAME,
                    manufacturer.getLongName())
            .build();

    operations.add(manufacturerOperation);

    int manufacturerInsertOperationIndex = operations.size() - 1;

    for (Device device : manufacturer.getDevices()) {
        final ContentProviderOperation deviceOperation =
                ContentProviderOperation
                .newInsert(DevicesContract.Device.CONTENT_URI)
                .withValueBackReference(DevicesContract
                            .Device.MANUFACTURER_ID,
                        manufacturerInsertOperationIndex)
                .withValue(DevicesContract.Device.MODEL,
                        device.getModel())
                .withValue(DevicesContract
                            .Device.DISPLAY_SIZE_INCHES,
                        device.getDisplaySizeInches())
                .withValue(DevicesContract.Device.MEMORY_MB,
                        device.getMemoryMb())
                .withValue(DevicesContract.Device.NICKNAME,
                        device.getNickname())
                .build();

        operations.add(deviceOperation);
    }
}
```

```
    try {

        results =

                contentResolver.applyBatch(DevicesContract.AUTHORITY,

                        operations);

    } catch (RemoteException | OperationApplicationException e) {

        throw new RuntimeException(e);

    }


    return Observable.from(results);

}

}
```

Summary

There are multiple ways that a mobile client can access a Web service or Web API. While accessing remote data can provide a richer experience for the user, it also adds complexity. Issues such as battery drain and responsive UI are things that should be considered when designing how a mobile client will access a remote Web service.

While the standard Android SDK does provide the tools needed to effectively add support for remote Web service access, they may not be the most efficient way to access the Web service. Libraries such as Retrofit and Volley make it easy to access a remote service by handling the threading details of making remote calls, and libraries like GSON and Jackson make transforming JSON to Java objects painless.

Once a method for accessing a remote Web service has been established, determining when to access the remote data must be taken into consideration. For certain use cases, it is acceptable to access the remote service only in response to a user's action, but in others the remote Web service access needs to happen more automatically. The Android SyncAdapter framework provides a central place to perform sync operations while allowing the sync operation to have multiple different triggers.

If the remote data is retrieved before it needs to be displayed to a user, it needs to be stored until then. A local database can make a good place to store the data until it is needed by the app.

10

Data Binding

Data binding was announced at Google I/O 2015 as a way to bind an app's data to the views that display that data in the app. In addition to allowing Android developers to write less boilerplate code, it can speed up code performance. This chapter provides an overview of the data binding library and how it can use used.

The data binding library analyzes view layouts at compile time and generates code that can be used at runtime. This code generation can make some of the view-related tasks that are part of Android development (like calls to `findViewById()`) obsolete.

Adding Data Binding to an Android Project

Before the data binding API can be used in a project, it must be added to the project. For a Gradle-based Android project, adding data binding support is as easy as updating the `build.gradle` file for the module that needs data binding support, as shown in Listing 10.1.

In addition to updating `build.gradle`, the data binding API requires at least version 1.5.0-alpha1 of the Android plugin for Gradle as well as Android Studio 1.3 or later.

Listing 10.1 Adding Data Binding Support to `build.gradle`

```
android {

    // other gradle configuration

    dataBinding {

        enabled = true

    }

}
```

Once the data binding library has been added to the project, it can be used to simplify binding data to views and view access in general.

Data Binding Layouts

To use the data binding library, view layouts must be converted to data binding layouts. To convert a non–data binding layout to a data binding layout, the <layout> element must be the root element in a layout file. A data binding layout contains a view hierarchy as well as an optional <data> section that can be used to declare variables to be used in the layout file. Listing 10.2 provides an example of using the <layout> element.

Listing 10.2 Using the <layout> Element

```
<layout xmlns:android="http://schemas.android.com/apk/res/android"
    xmlns:tools="http://schemas.android.com/tools">
    <data>
        <variable name="device"
            type="me.adamstroud.devicedatabase.device.DeviceDetailActivity
.ObservableDevice"/>
    </data>
    <android.support.design.widget.CoordinatorLayout
        android:id="@+id/coordinator_layout"
        android:layout_width="match_parent"
        android:layout_height="match_parent"
        android:fitsSystemWindows="true"
        tools:context=".device.DeviceDetailActivity"
        tools:ignore="MergeRootFrame">
        <LinearLayout
            android:layout_width="match_parent"
            android:layout_height="match_parent"
            android:orientation="vertical">
            <include layout="@layout/appbar" />

            <TextView
                android:layout_width="wrap_content"
                android:layout_height="wrap_content"
                android:text="@{@string/model(device.model), default=
model}" />
```

```
    <TextView

        android:layout_width="wrap_content"

        android:layout_height="wrap_content"

        android:text="@{@string/nickname(device.nickname), default=
nickname}" />


    <TextView

        android:layout_width="wrap_content"

        android:layout_height="wrap_content"

        android:text="@{@string/memory_in_mb(device.memoryInMb),
default=memoryInMb}" />


    <TextView

        android:layout_width="wrap_content"

        android:layout_height="wrap_content"
android:text="@{@string/display_in_inches(device.displaySizeInInches),
default=displaySizeInInches}" />


    </LinearLayout>

  </android.support.design.widget.CoordinatorLayout>

</layout>
```

The variables declared under the <data> element can be used elsewhere in the layout by using the data binding expression language. In Listing 10.2, the two text fields that show the model and nickname are set to the values of Device.getModel() and Device. getNickname() respectively by the following code:

```
<TextView

    android:layout_width="wrap_content"

    android:layout_height="wrap_content"

    android:text="@{@string/model(device.model), default=model}" />


<TextView

    android:layout_width="wrap_content"

    android:layout_height="wrap_content"

    android:text="@{@string/nickname(device.nickname), default=nickname}"/>
```

Binding an Activity to a Layout

With the data binding layout in place, the activity that uses the layout can retrieve a reference to the data binding object and use it to both access the view from the layout as well as set the variables that were declared in the layout.

To get a reference to the data binding object, the `DataBindingUtil.setContentView()` method can be called. Listing 10.3 shows a call to the `DataBindingUtil.setContentView()` method in an activity. It can be used to replace the `Activity.setContentView()` method that would normally be called to associate an activity with a view hierarchy.

Listing 10.3 Binding a Layout to an Activity

```
public class DeviceDetailActivity extends BaseActivity
        implements LoaderManager.LoaderCallbacks<Cursor> {
    public static final String EXTRA_DEVICE_URI = "deviceUri";

    private static final int ID_DEVICE = 1;

    private Uri deviceUri;
    private CoordinatorLayout coordinatorLayout;
    private ActivityDeviceDetailBinding binding;

    @Override
    protected void onCreate(Bundle savedInstanceState) {
        super.onCreate(savedInstanceState);
        binding =
                DataBindingUtil.setContentView(this,
                        R.layout.activity_device_detail);
        // more initialization code

    }
}
```

In Listing 10.3, the call to `DataBindingUtil.setContentView()` takes the current activity and the resource ID from the layout in Listing 10.2 as parameters. The first parameter defines the activity that should have the content view updated, and the second parameter defines the layout to use for the content view of the activity. Like the call to `Activity.setContentView()` that was replaced, `DataBindingUtil.setContentView()` inflates the layout and uses the layout for the activity's content view. However, in addition, it performs the data binding for the layout.

The return type of `DataBindingUtil.setContentView()` is an
`ActivityDeviceDetailBinding` object. The `ActivityDeviceDetailBinding` class is
generated by the data binding library at compile time and contains methods for setting
variables defined in the layout XML file as well as views that are in the layout file.

Figure 10.1 shows the location of the generated code.

Using a Binding to Update a View

Once the data binding object is retrieved, it can be used to update the view data by
calling the setter methods of the variables that were declared in the layout file. Since the
device data is read from the database using a `CursorLoader`, the call to `DataBindingUtil`.

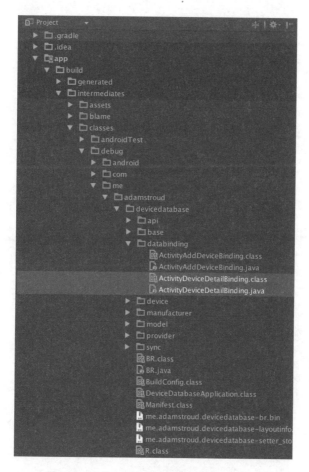

Figure 10.1   Data binding generated code

setDevice() is not made until the CursorLoader has returned the data in onLoadFinished(). Listing 10.4 contains the implementation of onLoadFinished().

Listing 10.4 Updating the Bound Views

```
@Override
public void onLoadFinished(Loader<Cursor> loader, Cursor data) {
    if (data != null && data.moveToFirst()) {
        ObservableDevice observableDevice = binding.getDevice();

        observableDevice
                .model
                .set(data.getString(data
                        .getColumnIndexOrThrow(DevicesContract
                        .Device
                        .MODEL)));

        observableDevice
                .nickname
                .set(data.getString(data
                        .getColumnIndexOrThrow(DevicesContract
                        .Device
                        .NICKNAME)));

        observableDevice
                .memoryInMb
                .set(data.getFloat(data
                        .getColumnIndexOrThrow(DevicesContract
                        .Device
                        .MEMORY_MB)));

        observableDevice
                .displaySizeInInches
                .set(data.getFloat(data
                        .getColumnIndexOrThrow(DevicesContract
                        .Device
                        .DISPLAY_SIZE_INCHES)));
    }
}
```

Once the `CursorLoader` finishes loading, the views are updated through the view binding and the display is updated.

The data binding implementation in Listings 10.2 through 10.4 shows the details of the device on the UI when the cursor is loaded. However, there is something wrong with the current implementation. If the database is updated, the UI will not be updated to reflect the changes in the database. The issue is not with the `CursorLoader`; `onLoadFinished()` will be called again and attempt to update the device details. The problem lies with the way the `DeviceDetailActivity` is using the data binding API.

Recall from Listing 10.2 that the data binding layout uses a variable from the model package:

```
<data>

    <variable name="device"

        type="me.adamstroud.devicedatabase.model.Device "/>

</data>
```

This use of the POJO from the model package allows the UI to show the original values of the POJO; however, it does not cause the UI to be updated when the values of the `Device` class are changed. In order to update the UI when the data of a bound data object is updated, the data object must contain **observable** fields.

> **Note**
>
> The observable field that is used with data binding is unrelated to the `Observable` class from RxJava discussed in the preceding chapter.

Because the `Device` class does not contain observable fields, it cannot be used to update the UI as the database changes. Instead, another class can be created that contains the observable fields that are needed to have the UI reflect changes in the data. Listing 10.5 shows the implementation of `ObservableDevice` which contains these observable fields. `ObservableDevice` is implemented as an inner class to `DeviceDetailActivity` because it is used only by `DeviceDetailActivity`.

Listing 10.5 Implementing `ObservableDevice`

```
public static class ObservableDevice extends BaseObservable {

    private String model;

    private String nickname;


    @Bindable

    public String getModel() {

        return model;

    }
```

```
public void setModel(String model) {

    this.model = model;

    notifyPropertyChanged(BR.model);

}


@Bindable

public String getNickname() {

    return nickname;

}


public void setNickname(String nickname) {

    this.nickname = nickname;

    notifyPropertyChanged(BR.nickname);

}

}
```

In order to have the UI views updated, ObservableDevice extends BaseObservable and makes calls to notifyPropertyChanged() in the setter that updated its state. In addition, the @Bindable annotation has been applied to each of the getter methods for values that require a UI update when they are modified.

Notice the parameter that is passed to notifyPropertyChange(). It is a public constant that represents the property that was changed. The BR class is a generated class that is used like the R class that identifies resources in Android. Both are generated by the Android toolchain and belong to the base package of the app as shown in Listing 10.6.

Listing 10.6 BR and R Class Imports

```
import me.adamstroud.devicedatabase.BR;

import me.adamstroud.devicedatabase.R;
```

The BR class can be thought of as a data-binding-specific version of the R class.

Reacting to Data Changes

With the ObservableDevice implemented, the last task in order to have a data binding implementation that reacts to database changes is to update the data binding layout to use the ObservableDevice instead of the Device class. The changes that are needed to make the update are displayed in Listing 10.7.

Listing 10.7 Updating the Layout to Use `ObservableDevice`

```xml
<layout xmlns:android="http://schemas.android.com/apk/res/android"
    xmlns:tools="http://schemas.android.com/tools">
    <data>
        <variable name="device"
            type="me.adamstroud.devicedatabase.device.DeviceDetailActivity
➥.ObservableDevice"/>
    </data>
    <android.support.design.widget.CoordinatorLayout
        android:id="@+id/coordinator_layout"
        android:layout_width="match_parent"
        android:layout_height="match_parent"
        android:fitsSystemWindows="true"
        tools:context=".device.DeviceDetailActivity"
        tools:ignore="MergeRootFrame">
        <LinearLayout
            android:layout_width="match_parent"
            android:layout_height="match_parent"
            android:orientation="vertical">
            <include layout="@layout/appbar" />

            <TextView
                android:layout_width="wrap_content"
                android:layout_height="wrap_content"
                android:text="@{@string/model(device.model), default=
➥model}" />


            <TextView
                android:layout_width="wrap_content"
                android:layout_height="wrap_content"
                android:text="@{@string/nickname(device.nickname), default=
➥nickname}" />
```

```
        <TextView

            android:layout_width="wrap_content"

            android:layout_height="wrap_content"

            android:text="@{@string/memory_in_mb(device.memoryInMb),
➥default=memoryInMb}" />


        <TextView

            android:layout_width="wrap_content"

            android:layout_height="wrap_content"

android:text="@{@string/display_in_inches(device.displaySizeInInches),
➥default=displaySizeInInches}" />


        </LinearLayout>

    </android.support.design.widget.CoordinatorLayout>

</layout>
```

While extending the `BaseObservable` class can get updated member data to the UI, it does contain some boilerplate code. A terser solution that can produce the same effect is to make the individual member variables observable instead of the entire class.

The data binding library contains `ObservableFields` that make individual fields observable without some of the boilerplate code that is needed to extend `BaseObservable`. To make an individual field observable, the field can be one of the following types:

- `ObservableField`
- `ObservableBoolean`
- `ObservableByte`
- `ObservableChar`
- `ObservableShort`
- `ObservableInt`
- `ObservableLong`
- `ObservableFloat`
- `ObservableDouble`
- `ObservableParcelable`

Because the `DeviceDetailActivity` will be updating its UI with `String` data, the `ObservableDevice` needs to have two `ObservableField<String>` members. Listing 10.8 shows the updated `ObservableDevice` implementation.

Listing 10.8 Updated `ObservableDevice` with `ObservableField`

```
public static class ObservableDevice {
    public final ObservableField<String> nickname =
            new ObservableField<>();

    public final ObservableField<String> model =
            new ObservableField<>();

    public final ObservableFloat memoryInMb =
            new ObservableFloat();

    public final ObservableFloat displaySizeInInches =
            new ObservableFloat();
}
```

Using the `ObservableField` type makes the code for `ObservableDevice` really simple. There is no need to use the `@Bind` annotation, and the fields automatically update the views they are bound to without a call to `notifyPropertyChange()`.

The last piece of code to change after migrating the `ObservableField` implementation is `onLoadFinished()`. It needs to be updated to set the values of the `ObservableFields`, which requires an additional method call as can be seen in Listing 10.9.

Listing 10.9 Setting `ObservableField` Values

```
@Override
public void onLoadFinished(Loader<Cursor> loader, Cursor data) {
    if (data != null && data.moveToFirst()) {
        ObservableDevice observableDevice = binding.getDevice();

        observableDevice
                .model
                .set(data.getString(data
                        .getColumnIndex(DevicesContract
                                .Device.MODEL)));

        observableDevice
                .nickname
```

```
                    .set(data.getString(data
                        .getColumnIndex(DevicesContract
                            .Device.NICKNAME)));

    }

}
```

Instead of directly setting the values on `ObservableDevice`, `ObservableField.set()` must be used to update the value. This takes care of all the details of making sure the UI gets updated.

In addition to automatically binding Java objects to the UI, the data binding library can be used to replace other boilerplate code often found in Android apps.

Using Data Binding to Replace Boilerplate Code

In order to access a view in its view hierarchy, an activity/fragment first needs to find the view. This is often done with a call to `findViewById()`. The `findViewById()` traverses the view hierarchy until it finds a view that matches the ID that it was passed. For complex views that have deep view hierarchies, this can be an expensive operation as the whole view hierarchy may need to be processed in order to find the view. In addition, *each* call to `findViewById()` incurs this performance hit. If an activity needs to update ten views, it has to make ten calls to `findViewById()` and have ten view hierarchy traversals. The performance hit of superfluous calls to `findViewById()` was the motivation behind the `ViewHolder` pattern that is often used with `ListView`.

The data binding library helps address these issues by removing the need to make calls to `findViewById()`. This both replaces the boilerplate code for finding views and makes the code faster by eliminating the need to have multiple view hierarchy traversals to get a reference to multiple views. Because the code generation functionality of the data binding library happens at compile time, data binding can provide a handle to all necessary views by making only a single pass over the view hierarchy.

To have the data binding library insert references to views in its data binding object, views only need to be given an ID in the layout file. All views that have an ID will be accessible from the activity's data binding object.

To see how the feature works, the device details layout is updated to add a view that contains an ID. Listing 10.10 shows the updated layout file.

Listing 10.10 Adding a View with an ID

```
<layout xmlns:android="http://schemas.android.com/apk/res/android"

    xmlns:tools="http://schemas.android.com/tools">

    <data>

        <variable name="device"

            type="me.adamstroud.devicedatabase.device.DeviceDetailActivity

➥.ObservableDevice"/>
```

```
    </data>
    <android.support.design.widget.CoordinatorLayout
        android:id="@+id/coordinator_layout"
        android:layout_width="match_parent"
        android:layout_height="match_parent"
        android:fitsSystemWindows="true"
        tools:context=".device.DeviceDetailActivity"
        tools:ignore="MergeRootFrame">
        <LinearLayout
            android:layout_width="match_parent"
            android:layout_height="match_parent"
            android:orientation="vertical">
            <include layout="@layout/appbar" />

            <TextView
                android:layout_width="wrap_content"
                android:layout_height="wrap_content"
                android:text="@{@string/model(device.model), default=
➥model}" />


            <TextView
                android:layout_width="wrap_content"
                android:layout_height="wrap_content"
                android:text="@{@string/nickname(device.nickname), default=
➥nickname}" />


            <TextView
                android:layout_width="wrap_content"
                android:layout_height="wrap_content"
                android:text="@{@string/memory_in_mb(device.memoryInMb),
➥default=memoryInMb}" />


            <TextView
                android:layout_width="wrap_content"
                android:layout_height="wrap_content"
```

```
                  android:text="@{@string/display_in_inches(device.display
➥SizeInInches), default=displaySizeInInches}" />


          <TextView
              android:id="@+id/id"
              android:layout_width="wrap_content"
              android:layout_height="wrap_content" />

       </LinearLayout>
    </android.support.design.widget.CoordinatorLayout>
</layout>
```

Once the ID has been added to one of the TextViews, it can be directly accessed from the binding class that is returned from DataBindingUtil.setContentView(). The only change to DeviceDetailActivity is to update the ID when the cursor is returned to onLoadFinished() to access the id view and update its content. This is shown in Listing 10.11.

Listing 10.11 Updating the ID

```
@Override
public void onLoadFinished(Loader<Cursor> loader, Cursor data) {
    if (data != null && data.moveToFirst()) {
        ObservableDevice observableDevice = binding.getDevice();


        observableDevice
                .model
                .set(data.getString(data
                        .getColumnIndexOrThrow(DevicesContract
                        .Device
                        .MODEL)));


        observableDevice
                .nickname
                .set(data.getString(data
                        .getColumnIndexOrThrow(DevicesContract
```

```
                    .Device

                    .NICKNAME)));


        observableDevice

                .memoryInMb

                .set(data.getFloat(data

                        .getColumnIndexOrThrow(DevicesContract

                        .Device

                        .MEMORY_MB)));


        observableDevice

                .displaySizeInInches

                .set(data.getFloat(data

                        .getColumnIndexOrThrow(DevicesContract

                        .Device

                        .DISPLAY_SIZE_INCHES)));


        binding

                .id

                .setText(getString(R.string.id,

                        data.getLong(data

                                .getColumnIndex(DevicesContract

                .Device

                ._ID))));
    }
}
```

Recall from Listing 10.2 that the binding member variable is of type `ActivityDevice DetailBinding`. With the ID added to the layout file, the `id` `TextView` can be accessed without a call to `findViewById()`. Because the data binding code generation happens at compile time, the type of `id` is also known, so there is no need to cast `id` to the correct type. The data binding library generates a binding class that uses a `TextView`.

In addition to binding data to views, the data binding library has an expression language that allows layout files to manipulate views. The next section introduces the data binding expression language.

Data Binding Expression Language

The data binding expression language allows for view manipulation directly in the XML layout file. Recall from Listing 10.2 that the values of both the device model and the device nickname are set in the data binding layout file. Listing 10.12 shows the portion of the data binding layout, in bold, that uses the expression language.

Listing 10.12 Using the Data Binding Expression Language

```
<TextView

    android:layout_width="wrap_content"

    android:layout_height="wrap_content"

    android:text="@{@string/model(device.model), default=model}" />


<TextView

    android:layout_width="wrap_content"

    android:layout_height="wrap_content"

    android:text="@{@string/nickname(device.nickname), default=
➥nickname}" />
```

Listing 10.12 references the model and nickname of the device variable that was declared in the data section of the layout.

The default keyword is used to show a placeholder in the Android Studio layout preview windows. It is useful for displaying text at design time for values that are not available until runtime.

In addition to accessing the actual data from the device object, the code in Listing 10.12 accesses string resources. This can be useful when string resources are needed to provide formatting and/or localization support to an app.

Use of the expression language is fairly simplistic. In addition to populating view values, expression language operators are available to give a layout a more dynamic nature. The operators supported by the data binding expression language are mostly the same as the standard Java operators. For example, the expression language supports the following operators:

- Mathematical operators
- String concatenation
- Unary operators
- Binary operators
- The ternary operator

- instanceof
- Shift operators
- Logical operators

In addition to the operators listed, the data binding expression language supports accessing individual array items, accessing object data members, making method calls, and typecasting.

On top of the familiar Java operators, the expression language adds support for the null coalescing operator. This operator is represented by two question marks ("??") and can be thought of as a shorthand notation for the ternary operator when checking for `null`. Listing 10.13 shows an example of the null coalescing operator.

Listing 10.13 Null Coalescing Operator

```
<TextView
    android:layout_width="wrap_content"
    android:layout_height="wrap_content"
    android:text="@{object.left ?? object.right}" />
```

In Listing 10.13, the null coalescing operator assigns the `object.left` if `object.left` is not `null`, and `object.right` if `object.left` is `null`. Conceptually, the statement is equivalent to

```
<TextView
    android:layout_width="wrap_content"
    android:layout_height="wrap_content"
    android:text="@{object.left == null? object.right : object.left}" />
```

Something important to remember when using the data binding expression language is that just because it supports complicated expressions, that does not mean these expressions should be used. A good rule of thumb would be not to use any expression that is more complicated than the ternary operator. For complex view expressions, Java may be a better alternative, especially since the overhead from making calls to `findViewById()` has been removed by the data binding library.

Summary

The data binding library can be a powerful addition to an Android project. Its ability to remove boilerplate code by working with views and performance gains caused by leveraging compile-time code generation make it an important tool in the Android toolkit.

Index